On the Arab Revolts and the
Iranian Revolution

Suspensions: Contemporary Middle Eastern and Islamicate Thought
Series editors: Jason Mohaghegh and Lucian Stone

This series interrupts standardized discourses involving the Islamicate world by introducing creative and emerging ideas. The incisive works included in this series provide a counterpoint to the reigning canons of theory, theology, philosophy, literature, and criticism through investigations of vast experiential typologies – such as violence, mourning, vulnerability, tension, and humour – in light of contemporary Islamicate thought.

On the Arab Revolts and the Iranian Revolution, Arshin Adib-Moghaddam
The Politics of Writing Islam, Mahmut Mutman
The Writing of Violence in the Middle East, Jason Bahbak Mohaghegh

On the Arab Revolts and the Iranian Revolution

Power and Resistance Today

Arshin Adib-Moghaddam

Suspensions: Contemporary Middle Eastern and
Islamicate Thought

B L O O M S B U R Y
LONDON • NEW DELHI • NEW YORK • SYDNEY

Bloomsbury Academic

An imprint of Bloomsbury Publishing Plc

50 Bedford Square	1385 Broadway
London	New York
WC1B 3DP	NY 10018
UK	USA

www.bloomsbury.com

Bloomsbury is a registered trade mark of Bloomsbury Publishing Plc

Hardback edition published 2013
The paperback edition published 2014

British Library Cataloguing-in-Publication Data
A catalogue record for this book is available from the British Library.

ISBN: HB:	978-1-4725-1189-8
PB:	978-1-4725-8904-0
ePDF:	978-1-4725-1240-6
ePub:	978-1-4725-0614-6

Library of Congress Cataloging-in-Publication Data
A catalog record for this book is available from the Library of Congress.

Typeset by Newgen Knowledge Works (P) Ltd., Chennai, India
Printed and bound in Great Britain

Contents

Series Foreword

Poets, artists, theologians, philosophers and mystics in the Middle East and Islamicate world have been interrogating notions of desire, madness, sensuality, solitude, death, time, space, etc. for centuries, thus constituting an expansive and ever-mutating intellectual landscape. Like all theory and creative outpouring, then, theirs is its own vital constellation – a construction cobbled together from singular visceral experiences, intellectual ruins, novel aesthetic techniques, social-political-ideological detours and premonitions of a future – built and torn down (partially or in toto), and rebuilt again with slight and severe variations. The horizons shift, and frequently leave those who dare traverse these lands bewildered and vulnerable.

Consequently, these thinkers and their visionary ideas largely remain unknown, or worse, mispronounced and misrepresented in the so-called western world. In the hands of imperialistic frameworks, a select few are deemed worthy of notice and are spoken on behalf of, or rather about. Their ideas are simplified into mere social formulae and empirical scholarly categories. Whereas so-called western philosophers and writers are given full leniency to contemplate the most incisive or abstract ideas, non-western thinkers, especially those located in the imagined realms of the Middle East and Islamicate world, are reduced to speaking of purely political histories or monolithic cultural narratives. In other words, they are distorted and contorted to fit within hegemonic paradigms that steal away their more captivating potential.

Contributors to this series provide a counterpoint to the reigning canons of theory, theology, philosophy, literature, and criticism through investigations of the vast experiential typologies of such regions. Each volume in the series acts as a 'suspension' in the sense that the authors will position contemporary thought in an enigmatic new terrain of inquiry, where it will be compelled to confront unforeseen works of critical and creative imagination. These analyses will not only highlight the full range of current intellectual and artistic trends and their benefits for the citizens of these phantom spheres, but also argue that the ideas themselves are borderless, and thus of great relevance to all citizens of the world.

Jason Bahbak Mohaghegh
and Lucian Stone

Acknowledgements

First and foremost I would to thank Jason Bahbak Mohaghegh and Lucian Stone for their invitation to contribute to their revolutionary book series. It has given me great strength and hope to know that there are such talented and dedicated comrades out there whose intellectuality represents the possibilities of a bright future and reveal the absurdity of past and present efforts to think and live in terms of one-dimensionalities. This generation is stating a case against monoliths, against seemingly primordial structures, against notions of east versus west, black against white, clashing civilizations. Our current era is creating spaces that are rewardingly hybrid and it is about time that the close dialectics between us and them are more centrally represented in scholarship and public discourse. To that end, Jason and Lucian's initiative is indispensable.

The scholarly sections of the present book benefitted from talks/conferences (among others) at Birkbeck College, London, Casa Arabe in Madrid and Cordoba, the Danish Institute of International Studies (DIIS) in Copenhagen, Georgetown's School of Foreign Service in Doha, the British Academy, the German Institute of Global and Area Studies (GIGA) in Hamburg, Medico International's annual meeting in Frankfurt, the British Museum, the Contemporary Art Museum in Nottingham, the London School of Economics and Political Science, the Metropolitan University and Institute of International Relations in Prague, and the universities of Aberystwyth, Amman, Brussels, Cambridge, Copenhagen, Durham, Illinois (Urbana-Champaign), Oxford, Southern Denmark and Strasbourg. The last chapter benefitted in particular from exchanges with colleagues and students during the eighth annual conference of the SOAS Palestine Society.

In addition, I have had the chance to interact with several diplomats and decision makers during lectures at the thirteenth Asian Security Conference in New Delhi, which was convened and inaugurated by the defence minister of India A.K. Antony, Chatham House, the German Foreign Office in Berlin as a part of an event organized by the Agha Khan Foundation, the Gulf

Research Meeting at the University of Cambridge, the Royal Air Force base at Molesworth, Cambridgeshire, the Royal United Service Institute (RUSI) in London and the NATO Parliamentary Assembly's Mediterranean and Middle East Special Group, which met in Catania and which brought together high ranking officials of the new Tunisia and Egypt and established politicians such as the former secretary of the Arab League Amr Moussa and the former prime minister of Italy, Lamberto Dini. I had another opportunity to make the case against war, in this case against Iran, with a lecture at Whitehall organized by the Global Strategy Forum and Michael Ancram (Lord Lothian) who chaired a panel that included Jonathan Fryer, Jeremy Greenstock and Malcolm Rifkind.

Interregnum 4 is based on 'Can the (Sub)altern Resist? A Dialogue between Foucault and Said', in Ian Netton (ed.), *Orientalism Revisited: Art, Land, Voyage* (Abingdon: Routledge, 2012), 33–54. Interregnum 5 is based on 'What Is Radicalism? Power and Resistance in Iran', *Middle East Critique*, Vol. 21, No. 3, (2012), 271–290 and the fourth interregnum is based on 'Discourse and Violence: The Friend–Enemy Conjunction in Contemporary Iranian–American Relations', *Critical Studies on Terrorism*, Vol. 2, No. 3 (2009), 512–526. Parts of the first interregnum have appeared in short commentaries for *opendemocracy.net* and I would like to thank the editor David Hayes for his helpful comments.

Introduction

This book should be read as an epilogue to the ongoing events in West Asia and North Africa (WANA) and the global changes to forms of power and resistance that the revolts have informed. In order to appreciate the fluidity of the current events, the sections comprising this study are termed 'interregnums'. An interregnum denotes a space in between, a period of discontinuity provoked by a 'fold' in history. My goal throughout this study is exactly to delineate the broad contours of this fold, to bring to the reader's attention a series of events that will change the way politics is enacted in the heartland of the Arab and Muslim world. To that end, I will analyse continuities in the politics of power and resistance and shifts within particular fields, from politics and art to socio-economics and religion, that go beyond experiences of the western world. In order to refine the analysis and give it comparative depth, I put particular emphasis on both the Arab revolts that started in Tunisia in 2010 and the Iranian revolution of 1979 and the politics of the country since then. These rapturous events have shifted the rules of knowledge in the way politics is made, power is exercised and resistance is organized. Throughout I will make clear that the shifts are not merely regional. This is not a book confined to a disciplinary ghetto or a confined cultural habitat. Rather, the Iranian revolution and the Arab revolts have provoked broader mutations in world politics that influence changes in perspectives and truth conditions throughout the world. We are entering a form of borderless politics that is spread out on a vast canvas. The present study attempts to function as a point of orientation in this bedazzling new space.

It is always perilous to 'summarize' the argument of a study along a few conceptual markers and most of the time it is not advisable to straight-jacket the flow of the analysis from the outset. But if I were to distil a few common themes that bind the book together I would start with the obvious emphasis:

my focus on the praxis and theory of power and resistance. In the Iranian revolution of 1979 that led to the demise of the Pahlavi dynasty and in the Arab revolts – in particular in Tunisia and Egypt – decisive political shifts from the past were achieved. And yet the forms of power and resistance that constituted those battles differ: The Iranian revolution was typically modernist, it followed a pattern typical for the revolutions of modernity, whether in the east or west: In Khomeini there was a revolutionary leader quite comparable to the role that Lenin, Mao or Castro played in Russia, China and Cuba respectively. And the Iranian revolution was engendered by all-encompassing ideologies (e.g. Islamism and to a lesser extent, Marxism and Maoism) with a utopian claim that promised to engineer a new, ideal human being. Yet the Arab revolts encompassing the urban centres in Tunisia and Egypt occurred in a rather more 'post-modern' context, there was no charismatic point of fixation for the masses, no utopian ideological framework that would promise a total break from the past, no revolutionary avant-garde coordinating the demonstrations. Islamism in Iran was deterministic, theocratically charged and apostolic. In Tunisia and Egypt political Islam is more technocratic, promiscuous and pragmatic. In Khomeini, the revolution in Iran produced a charismatic figurehead, a point of fixation for the masses. The Arab revolts did not engender a revolutionary leader. The Iranian revolutionaries were utopian, even romantic in their imagination of a new order. The Arab radicals are more realistic, and apprehensive of the Iranian experience. Iran in 1979 produced an anti-imperial narrative directed primarily against US foreign policies, the Soviet Union, Israel and Apartheid South Africa. None of the states that have emerged from the Arab revolts have called for an immediate rupture with the international system, despite the pronounced emphasis on independence that the protesters articulated from Amman, Cairo and Tunis to Rabat, Manama and Riyadh. The Islamic Republic of Iran immediately embraced the Palestinian cause. The new leaders of Tunisia, Egypt and Libya have treaded very carefully on Palestine. As indicated, Iran's revolution was informed by typically modern ideologies with a totalitarian agenda: Islamism, Marxism, Maoism. The Arab revolts are post-ideological. The mass communication strategy of the Khomeinist forces in the build-up to the revolution was partially dependent on tape recordings that were smuggled into the country and disseminated by the revolutionaries. The Arab revolts in Cairo and Tunis were partially organized on the world-wide-web, via networking sites such as Facebook and Twitter. The Iranian revolution created a new form of government and sovereignty and a political syntax that continues to be steeped in the authoritarian language that modernist revolutions provoked whether in Moscow, Havana, Peking *or* Tehran. The Arab revolts have produced more decentralized, democratic sovereignties and forms of governance that have transformed, rather than substituted, previous political systems. The Iranian revolution was permeated by metaphysical narratives that imagined a spirituality of politics that could negotiate with God. The Arab revolts are less hubristic. Iran in 1979 represented the apotheosis of 'Islamutopia'.[1] The Arab revolts have produced a post-modernized Islam that is more concerned with immediate 'bread and butter' issues. The Iranian revolution imagined *homo Islamicus*, the ultimate Islamic man. The Arab revolts pave the way for *homo pictor*, a transgendered subject that is not devoid of choice.

In the following interregnums, I will analyse those introductory signposts and unravel some of the changes and continuities in the way forms of power and resistance are practised today. Precisely because locality no longer appears to be an easily delineated notion, the historical deformations that occur in the Arab and Muslim world cannot be captured along iron-clad patterns and cannot be neatly dated. Perhaps, the current landscape is comparable to the borderland that opened up with the anti-colonial battles, which triggered a long fight for transition from formal western imperialism and the emergence of nominally independent states in the beginning and middle of the twentieth century. The iconoclasm of the Arab revolts seems to suggest this linkage. In Cairo and other urban centres in Egypt, many protesters carried posters of former Egyptian president Gamal Abdel Nasser and the Palestinian leader Yassir Arafat, two figures with pan-Arab appeal who continue to be revered in collective memory and popular culture for their stance against Israeli and western hegemony. There were no posters and pictures of Anwar Sadat, who signed the Egyptian–Israeli peace treaty in 1979, and none of Mahmoud Abbas (Abu Mazen), the current leader of the Palestine Liberation Organisation (PLO).[2] The mainstream media, especially in the United States, but also in western Europe, underemphasized the international messages of many protesters, choosing to focus on domestic grievances instead. And yet, the Arab revolts, like the Iranian revolution, were also about independence and national dignity. In Cairo, a quick spatial sketch of the demonstrations reveals that the protesters congregated not only on Tahrir Square, but also in front of the embassies of Israel and Saudi Arabia in order to protest foreign interference in Egyptian affairs. The most prominent acts of sabotage during the revolts in 2011 repeatedly targeted the compressor station near El-Arish, which supplies gas pipelines to Israel and Jordan. As a result of these attacks and the changing political climate after the ouster of Hosni Mubarak, the gas agreement had to be cancelled in April 2012.[3]

But the single most important aspect about the Arab revolts is their emphasis on democracy and social justice, on norms that used to be seen as particularly western but which have been cultivated in different historical periods around the world.[4] As a consequence, the conventional study books about the region have to be rewritten. If, as it is argued in one of the most prominent textbooks in the field of 'Middle Eastern' studies, authoritarian, one-party politics was an intrinsic feature of the post-colonial state in the region, the successful elections in Tunisia and Egypt indicate that this period has been overcome.[5] From the perspective of the new leaders in Cairo and Tunis, the colonial predicament that was inscribed with so much vehement violence onto the geography of the 'global south' and into the consciousness of the people must seem like a bygone era now. There is a lot of enthusiasm in the Arab and Muslim world for these newly liberated spaces of dissent and the new politics of democracy that they have provoked. We are on the cusp of an era that promises to allow for an emancipatory politics marked by self-determination that has been achieved through national struggles for independence from 'indigenous' post-colonial states. The battles were primarily directed against domestic systems that aided and abetted nepotism, authoritarianism and corruption rather than the 'imperial motherland' as in the battles of the early and mid-twentieth century. This is a pivotal fold in history that promises a shift away from the post-colonial state to a new form of governance that is almost devoid of the colonial residues associated with the heydays of western imperialism.[6]

Secondly, if previously the colonial administrators decreed that there was 'to be one centre of authority, issuing standard rules and regulations,'[7] the Arab revolts have accentuated political pluralism. Republican dictatorships exemplified by Muammar Gaddafi's *Jamhariyya* (state of the masses) or the political systems that sustained the one-man rule of Zine El Abidine Ben-Ali in

Tunisia and Hosni Mubarak in Egypt have already been reassembled. Similar outfits such as Bashar al-Assad's Ba'athist state in Syria are fiercely contested and the tribal monarchies on the Arabian peninsula, in particular Bahrain, Kuwait and Saudi Arabia, are increasingly challenged by internal dissent and mass demonstrations in favour of social justice and political reform.

Thirdly, if colonial policy implied forging 'an alliance, implicit or explicit, with the large landowners and, in some cases, the tribal shaikhs who controlled much of the rural areas',[8] the Arab revolts have challenged engrained client–patron alliance patterns in the region. If western colonialism exploited 'sectarian, ethnic and tribal divisions, generally for the purpose of some strategy of "divide and rule"',[9] the Arab revolts have emphasised inclusivity – national causes within an internationalist, networked context. And finally, if the colonial economists 'left little money for development other than the small amounts spent on public works projects like roads, railways, ports and improved irrigation',[10] if fiscal and monetary policies were tightly controlled by the centre, the Arab revolts have accentuated the redistribution of national wealth and less economic dependency on the west.

None of these initial transformations that I have carved out so far are clear-cut of course. I find the changes momentous, but there is no naive enthusiasm for this hopeful moment here. Too many intellectuals have been caught up in the excitement of this historical juncture and have been too quick to call for the end of salient international systems. For instance, neo-liberal policies and dependencies on the financial core continue to be in place, but they are also repeatedly resisted. What is striking, nonetheless, is that the Arab revolts, like all great revolts in human history, have questioned the truth conditions that lay so heavily on the political and socio-economic systems in the region. The protests have challenged long-standing norms, symbols and practices, and they have rattled the political and socio-economic order in the region and beyond. By definition, a fold in history scatters foundations and as we will see these momentous changes are not confined only to the Arab and Muslim worlds. The slogans of the protesters that have reverberated in the streets of Tunis and Cairo, Manama and Sana'a reveal universal aspirations: 'Justice, Freedom, Human Dignity.' In that regard, the protests in Arab capitals in 2010 and 2011 did not seem very different from those in London, Peking, Moscow, New York, Madrid, Athens and Paris. In all of these global protests spanning the period of two years, calls for freedom, social justice and political empowerment have been central.

Judging from my conversations with Arab intellectuals, activists, scholars and decision-makers, there continues to be a lot of sober pessimism about the unfolding events. The many voices one hears from Cairo and Tunis after the revolts resemble a cacophony rather than a well-tuned orchestra. For sure, the transformational politics that we are experiencing as I write these lines are rather anarchic and not adequately institutionalised yet. But the very fact that so many voices *are* heard is indicative of the pluralistic spaces from which they trumpet their respective causes. Gone are the days when they had to fine-tune their notes in strict accordance with the deterministic script of one master-conductor. In the resounding festival of voices that this rupture in the politics of the Arab and Muslim world provoked, the cries of dissent may continue to be confined, but they are certainly not decisively silenced. These strengthened agents of change have the opportunity to inscribe their agendas into the unfolding political events, they point to human rights abuses, contest constitutional amendments that threaten to subdue the goals of the revolt and contribute to the content of fiery parliamentary debates. Non-governmental organizations continue to operate under strenuous circumstances, but they too have found their own ways to take advantage of the newly gained impetus toward democracy and social justice. For instance, NGOs banned in some of the restrictive Gulf monarchies have established offices in Tunis, where activists support human rights causes in Syria and Bahrain.[11] My point is that norms such as human rights, democracy and social justice have become the yardstick according to which political legitimacy and success is measured. In the long term, no political leader in the region can be oblivious of these norms without jeopardizing his or her political future.

In order to stress the global interconnectedness of those contemporary manifestations of power and resistance, I will focus on two central methodological and empirical themes that bind together the essays in this book: First, I will assess the impact of the Iranian revolution of 1979, including the recent tremors of Iranian politics, and the Arab uprisings between 2010–2012, on our understanding of power and resistance. I am departing from the hypothesis that we have entered a new form of universal politics that reveals itself in a distinctly global field that is densely networked. Appreciating the broad contours of this globalized space, I discuss how the Arab revolts are shifting our perception away from the idea that the Arab-Muslim 'other' is ultimately different. To that end, the next interregnum charters the flawed premises underlying the 'clash of civilisations thesis' and deliberates how the current transformations in the region promise to foster a cosmopolitan spirit that feeds into a new form of globalized resistance.

In order to substantiate this claim, the second interregnum to the current events departs from several recent battles between state and society and puts them in their proper global-comparative perspective. This interregnum discusses why the Arab revolts in Tunisia and Egypt were successful and why other resistance movements that occurred at the same time, for instance the various 'Occupy' demonstrations in western capitals, failed. It paves the way for the following, third interregnum that sketches the strengths and weaknesses of existing approaches to forms of power and resistance that have been dominant both in theoretical debates and in practical political terms. This interregnum carves out the commonalities and differences of some of the most influential schools of thought ranging from post-colonial studies (Bhabha, Sartre, Fanon, etc.), (post)Marxism (Gramsci, Žižek, Laclau and Mouffe, Hardt and Negri) and theories of civil disobedience developed by Gene Sharp and others. In a second step, I will set out how the current revolts differ from our traditional understanding of resistance politics. It is argued that there is no coherent or primordial dynamic that moves populations against their governments that could be defined in monolithically 'culturalist' terms. In other words, while forms of protest around the world may appeal to local norms, symbols and cultures, there is nothing particularly 'identitarian' about the resistance against real and perceived injustices. As such, this section sets the stage for the theoretical opening that is offered in the fourth interregnum.

We can conceive of resistance as a truly universal phenomenon that shapes and is shaped by the cultural context in which it occurs. So the starting point of the analysis must be far more general than most theories of power and resistance appreciate: People resist when they feel that there is an opportunity to stand up for a just cause that affects their lives and when they think that they cannot make progress on central issues without acting in word and deed. For instance, when gold medallist Tommy Smith and bronze medallist John Carlos raised their fists in solidarity with the black power movement as the US anthem began to play during their medal ceremony at the 1968 Olympics in Mexico City, their symbolic act of resistance was at once local and universal. It was 'local' because raising the fist was a symbolic act associated with the black power movement in the United States and it was 'universal' because the two athletes wanted to make an even more substantive point about racism and the self-empowerment of minorities. As Carlos himself said in a rare interview:

> Today, if an athlete doesn't have a view of their history before them, then they have a view of just that big cheque in front of them. It's not the responsibility of the oppressor to educate us. We have to educate ourselves and our own. That's the difference between Muhammad Ali and Michael Jordan. Muhammad Ali will never die. He used his skill to say something about the social ills of society . . . And because he spoke on the issues, he will never die. There will be someone else at some time who can do what Jordan could do. And then his name will just be pushed down in the mud. But they'll still be talking about Ali.[12]

Such acts of resistance – indomitable, yet rare as they are on the public stage – reveal a human default position that is provoked whenever a sense of normative or material injustice prevails. In order to theoretically locate this statement the fourth interregnum discusses how forms of power act upon resistance via a dialogue with the influential ideas of Michel Foucault and Edward Said. The suggestion that it is power that acts upon resistance and not the other way around, as Max Weber famously argued, does not imply the liberal myth that agency can be divorced from structure, that we are entirely autonomous in our political decisions. Carlos and his fellow black power activists were embedded in a political culture that was brimming with racism on the one side, and the powerful counter-cultural narratives of Martin Luther King Jr and Malcolm X on the other. Their activism was constrained and aided by that given context in which they forged their ideas and strategies. In other words, individual choices including acts of resistance cannot be separated from structural opportunity and constraint. Resisting in London is very different to resisting in Tehran, in terms of method, opportunity and repercussions. Neither are we mere products of the structures surrounding us, as if culture can ever be totalitarian or all-encompassing. Agent and structure, individual and culture, are implicated in each other; their relationship is entirely dialectical. They quite literally constitute each other. We are both culture maker and culture taker; we both produce 'reality' and are produced by it. Accordingly, this interregnum calibrates theoretically the constitution of power and resistance and the dialectic between individual and structure addressing the pivotal question of whether 'subaltern' agency exists. By necessity it is bulkier, more philosophically guided, written with a heavier pen than the other sections of the book.

In order to position the preceding conceptual conclusions on a wider empirical footing, the fifth interregnum offers a meta-historical analysis of radical resistance in Iran. It discusses (a) the theoretical and methodical difference between radicals and revolutionaries with a particular emphasis on contemporary 'radical subjectivity' in the country, (b) the dialectics between state and society in contemporary Iranian history, which created a new form of revolutionary politics in the 1960s and 1970s and (c) how out of the depth of the political disillusionment with the Pahlavi monarchy, radicalism turned to revolutionary action yielding the Islamic Republic in 1979. This interregnum will also discuss forms of contemporary resistance to the Iranian state and the 'disciplinary powers' that it enforces ranging from security measures, religious ordinances and judicial decrees. In addition, I will further identify, at once cautiously and tangentially, aspects of the Iranian case that merit theoretical deduction. To that end, I reengage with the conclusions offered in the first sections of the book and present the differences and commonalities between what happened in Iran in 1979 on the one side and the events after the disputed re-election of President Ahmadinejad in 2009 on the other.

The penultimate interregnum deepens the comparative, historical analysis of contemporary Iranian politics within the framework of the relationship between discourse, power and resistance in Iranian–American relations. It will zoom into the discursive field charting the interactions between the two countries and the reasons why relations are strained. As such, it presents a micro-analysis of the way Iran positions itself within a self-ascribed 'axis of resistance' to 'western imperialism' that spans from Tehran, Damascus and southern Lebanon to Caracas, Havana and La Paz. At the same time, this section of the book will further the thesis that power and resistance are entirely intertwined. I discuss how the hyphen setting the two terms Iranian–American apart cannot be a sign of unbridgeable difference, despite the immense efforts on both sides to convince us that Iran and the United States are essentially different entities. But upon closer inspection the hyphen reveals itself as a conjunction, a grammatical particle, a via media that indicates that in the word formation 'Iranian–American' nothing is detachable, autonomous, at liberty. We are confronted with a particular form of disjunctive synthesis that symbolizes the interdependence of Iran (mad mullahs) on the one side with 'America' (great Satan) on the other. Ultimately, within the discursive field we are looking at, each of these terms signify a common discursive field, and a conjoined cognitive region in which the 'self' is dependent on the 'other'. From this perspective, the idea that a discourse accentuating difference yields separation reveals itself as a fallacy.

The final chapter expands on two central conceptual arguments of the book. First, it re-emphasizes that power and resistance are intertwined, and secondly that a policy and discourse of enmity does not beget detachment or manifest independence. In order to substantiate these claims, I start with a discussion of the Palestinian–Israeli conflict in light of Levinas' conception of the 'neighbour'. I show how in the case of this conflict self and other are not detachable, how Israelis and Palestinians inhabit a common epistemological territory. In light of this linkage, the interregnum concludes with a new 'neighbourhood policy' between 'us' and 'them' that appreciates the neighbour as friend and not as a potential enemy. I am revisiting the hypothesis that relationships of self and other are social, but that 'sociality' can be violent, neutral, intimate or friendly; it could be charged with negative or positive energy, but it always remains the loci within which shifts from enemy to friend or ally to foe can be signified. The analysis in that final interregnum merges into a significant conclusion: The twenty-first century reality is that security cannot be safeguarded on a national or 'civilizational' basis, and that the viable and rational option is to make diplomacy and multilateral engagement a priority. The security threats emanating from the global system require a strategy that moves beyond notions of nationality, territoriality and ideological cohesion, and embraces as far as possible a non-militaristic approach to world politics. To these ends, emphasizing and then moving beyond the linkages between us and them rather than any artificial dichotomy is vital.

The theoretical signposts of the book shall not mean that the approach and style is inaccessible to undergraduate students or interested lay readers with some basic understanding about the politics and history of the area. The book is addressed to an audience beyond the traditional purview of academia and it is written accordingly. While each chapter is a relatively freestanding discussion of a particular issue affecting our understanding of power and resistance in light of the Arab revolts and the Iranian revolution, there is a common methodical and empirical concern binding them together: the ambition to further critical theories of power and resistance on the one hand and the analysis of contemporary politics of the Arab and Muslim worlds on the other.

INTERREGNUM 1

Our Revolting Neighbours

Good rulership is equivalent to mildness.

Ibn Khaldun, *Al-Muqaddimah*

The other side of us

A few metres from my office at the School of Oriental and African Studies in the heart of London's Bloomsbury area is the Senate House of the University of London, a remarkable neo-classical colossus of a building that functioned as the headquarters of Britain's Ministry of Information, where George Orwell worked occasionally during the Second World War. The building's influence on Orwell is apparent in his dystopian novel *Nineteen Eighty-Four*, which powerfully evokes a lobotomized society controlled by Big Brother, whose Thought Police dominate a brainwashed populace while torturing anyone guilty of 'thoughtcrime' into submission. Winston Smith, the tragic hero, is charged with the daily task of altering the historical record to conform with whatever the current position of the regime (Oceania) happens to be in relation to its counterparts (Eurasia and Eastasia); he works at the Ministry of Truth, which Orwell drew on his wartime experiences of Senate House to depict. The novel is most often viewed as a political satire of the totalitarianism of the era (especially Soviet, as the Fascist regimes had fallen by the time the book was written) and an indictment of ultra-controlled illiberal societies. Among the most memorable themes is its emphasis on the state's use of mass media to establish complete power over language and thought. Orwell elaborates this theme via the concept of 'Newspeak', the language of the ruling Party, used to smooth over any complexity in favour of easy and clear dichotomies: 'goodthink' versus 'thoughtcrime'.

Orwell writes elsewhere, in a famous essay, that '(political) language – and with variations this is true of all political parties, from Conservatives to Anarchists – is designed to make lies sound truthful and murder respectable, and to give an appearance of solidity to pure wind'.[1] In this non-fictional context, Orwell seems to be acknowledging that thoughtcrime is not limited to Soviet and Fascist regimes, that the distortion of reality is a feature of politics in general and that the media is complicit in the assault on independent thinking. The word Orwellian has itself become as instantly recognizable in modern media and political discourse as its description of a world of lies, propaganda and indoctrination. Its connotations seem to become even more sinister when it is used to identify, not direct and overt deceit, but the kind of thought control that operates in advanced capitalist societies: more ciphered, clandestine, opaque, flatly networked, horizontal, penetrative, global and politically transcendent than that in the intensely vertical and vulgar top-down form indicted in *Nineteen Eighty-Four*.

This current form of thought control can be seen operating in relation to many politicized topics, but it is particularly apparent in depictions of 'Arabs' and 'Muslims', especially after the terror attacks on the United States in September 2001. As I have argued in *A Metahistory of the Clash of Civilisations*, the outburst and jingoistic vitriol against individuals and issues considered to be remotely 'Islamic' was the surface effect of a cultural constellation that runs deep in the subliminal consciousness of western Europe and North America. In order to accentuate that this 'Islamophobic' assemblage is dense and historically anchored I called it a clash regime, a system that reproduces Islam as unique, deviant, violent and ultimately different to 'us'.[2] This is not to say that there is an all-encompassing anti-Islamic culture in Europe and the United States of course, but to accentuate that Islamophobia continues to be exploited politically by powerful strata of western society, exactly because there exists a cultural constellation that is amenable to such manipulation. It is this regime of truth, nurtured by influential doyens of our contemporary culture, which compels 'us' to believe in some inevitable, cosmic battle with 'them'. It is such norms, institutions and ideologies that fortify boundaries that are turned into trenches of war during times of crisis. And it is in this way that murder in the name of civilization continues to be accepted and legitimated as an international *modus operandi.*[3]

It is one of the central purposes of this book to cut through some of the representations of the Arab and Islamic world as ultimately different. To that end, I am taking as a point of departure the recent events in the Arab world, which spread like wildfire through the Mediterranean encompassing capitals in North Africa and southern Europe. I start by arguing that the uprisings are indicative of a post-modern form of globalized politics that reclaims the universality of norms such as social justice, independence, freedom and democracy. For a decisive period for the future of world politics, the 'power of the powerless' has been on display. Not since the uprisings that brought down the Iron Curtain and facilitated the demise of the Soviet Union in the early 1990s, has there been such an interconnected outpouring of public dissent with decisive political consequences. At the time of writing, three of the longest standing dictatorships in the region, those of Zine El Abidine Ben-Ali in Tunisia, Hosni Mubarak in Egypt and Muammar Gaddafi in Libya, have been swept away by the sheer determination of the people; in the case of Libya accompanied by a period of armed conflict between the state and the opposition who were partially aided by NATO. These leaders, whose legitimacy was not democratic, but geared towards the authority of the military establishment and the ideal of the charismatic and strong leader, have followed the fate of the Shah in Iran and Saddam Hussein in Iraq. Despite the residues of the authoritarian regimes that continue to be part of the political culture in West Asia and North Africa (WANA), it is safe to argue that demands for democracy, independence and social justice have become the common currency of the societies in the region. Irresistible as it would be to assume that the stereotype of Arabs and Muslims as unique, deviant and ultimately different has been overcome, the revolts have shown nonetheless that they are not simply reducible to targets in the 'war on terror,' that Orientalist depictions of them as the irreconcilable other are outdated and of questionable analytical value.

In that sense, the Arab revolts have given impetus to a trend that started in the middle of the Cold War with intellectual movements such as the *dependencia* school in Latin America, the New Left in Europe, post-colonial studies, feminism, critical theory and other forms of counter-cultural movements that were galvanized by the '68 generation'. Undoubtedly, this period opened up new opportunities to think politics in a critical mode and challenged the Euro-Americo-centric legacies in the western social sciences and the humanities. This is the topic of a recent analysis in the emergent field of global history, which establishes that in 'contrast to the beginning of the twentieth century, today critiques of Western bias have become a more common repertoire in many academic communities throughout the world'. At the same time, it is acknowledged that 'global hierarchies' continue to exist, that those challenges to the canon do not 'mean that Eurocentric structures and mentalities have disappeared from the global academic landscapes'.[4]

While it is true that today subjugated knowledge is more readily recognizable, that the other has a presence in the curriculum, to argue that Eurocentric knowledge has been subdued is too optimistic. If anything, the immediate presence of the other has provoked a hostile reaction, which transmuted into a counter-movement that has established its own power base within academia and beyond. After all, the theory of a 'clash of civilisations' reinvented by the late Samuel P. Huntington, who was also one of the main advocates against the 'hispanization' of the United States, continues to occupy a central, if also contested place in the curriculum of many political-science and international-relations departments in North America and, to a lesser extent, in Europe. This is detrimental to a better understanding, especially of world politics exactly because 'international theory does not so much explain international politics in an objective, positivist and universalist manner', as Hobson argues in a recent study, 'but seeks, rather, to parochially celebrate and defend or promote the West as the proactive subject of, and as the highest or ideal normative referent in, world politics'.[5]

But the effects are detrimental not just to scholarship. The clash narrative has become far more than a mere theoretical or scholarly construct, for it has entered the ideology and practice of political groups, including rightwing parties that have secured seats in the parliaments of many European Union countries; for example, the influential Dutch politician Geert Wilders has brought the clash thesis to life by making vulgar attacks on Islam the foundation of his career. Even at the centre of power, the idea of an inevitable clash between 'the west and the rest' can function as a political device to rally support for military intervention against the latter; for example, Britain's former prime minister Tony Blair deployed the notion in evidence to the

Chilcot Inquiry into the war in Iraq to, in effect, call for military action against Iran. 'At some point the west has to get out of what I think is a wretched policy or posture of apology, believing that we are causing what the Iranians are doing, or what these extremists are doing', he said.[6] Blair elided the adversaries of the west in characteristically sweeping fashion: 'They disagree fundamentally with our way of life, and will carry on unless met with determination and, if necessary, force.'[7]

The power of the idea of an inevitable clash of civilizations between the west and the rest is thus evident; it is too optimistic to argue that most consumers of the clash regime cease to be socialized into accepting the dominant narratives permeating their societies. Thought-control in advanced liberal-capitalist societies is practised in a much more subtle and clandestine way than even George Orwell imagined. A single example of what has been written and said about Islam at the same time as the Arab uprisings were unfolding illustrates the point. Thilo Sarrazin, a board member of Germany's *Bundesbank* and a former senator of finance serving in the Berlin government, published a book titled *Deutschland schafft sich ab* (Germany Does Away with Itself), which argues that high birth-rates among Turkish and Arab communities in the country mean that Germany will soon be ruled by 'Muslims,' and that 'Turkish genes' are responsible for lowering the level of intelligence in the country.

The great success of Sarrazin's book, helped by huge press exposure, prompted the leading political magazine *Der Spiegel* to ask why Sarrazin has become a national hero. Sarrazin's phobia corresponds to what is happening elsewhere in Europe, such as the electoral success of Geert Wilders in the Netherlands, the minaret ban in Switzerland, neo-Nazi terror cells responsible for the murder of immigrants in Germany, the massacre committed by Anders Breivik in Norway in the name of a 'global anti-Islamic crusade', and the emergence of ultra-nationalist parties in several European Union member-states such as Hungary, Sweden and in the United Kingdom in the form of the anti-Muslim English Defence League. Thilo Sarrazin's words contain residues of a persistent racist myth that was central to the cod-science of the Nazis (among others): that intelligence is ethnically codified. The obscure American pastor called Terry Jones who raised a furore when he threatened to burn a Qur'an in protest at the proposed establishment of an Islamic community centre in Manhattan (two blocks away from ground zero, the site of the 9/11 attacks) reflects another expression of social attitudes towards the other: that Islam functions as a formula to aggregate Muslims even more tightly under the label of terrorism. The social and geographical distance between these two men suggests that, while there is no all-encompassing anti-Muslim consensus, such attitudes are capable of reaching widely across the political cultures of the contemporary world.[8]

It was, for example, another prominent English novelist, Martin Amis, who in 2006 gave expression to the cultural persistence of the clash regime to say that Muslims should 'suffer until they get their house in order', in a sequence of measures: 'deportation – further down the road. Curtailing of freedoms. Strip-searching people who look like they are from the Middle East, Pakistan, until it hurts the whole community and they start getting tough with their children.'[9] Amis's friend, the late Christopher Hitchens – who had written widely on George Orwell – in 2007 linked what he called 'the fascistic subculture' in Britain to 'shady exiles from the middle east and Asia who are exploiting London's traditional hospitality' and to the 'projection of an immigrant group that has its origins in a particularly backward and reactionary part of Pakistan'.[10] All the individuals mentioned have (or in the case of Terry Jones, been given) privileged access to the media, and their tendentious and in some cases inflammatory views are readily disseminated across the world-wide-web. As one astute observer noted: 'The recent spike in anti-Muslim sentiment in the United States and Europe is not the result of a naturally evolving climate of scepticism.' Islamophobia is not coincidental. Rather it is a 'product that has been carefully and methodically nurtured over the past decade and is only now in the second decade of the twenty-first century reaching its desired peak'.[11] The US film industry is complicit too. At the time of writing a US hit series called 'Homeland' presents Arab characters that are either rich and licentious or ragged and violent. The plot revolves around sleeper cells in the United States, who have been 'turned' by al-Qaeda into the invisible enemy within. In the cacophony that invariably ensues when 'culture' is produced in this way, the voices of reason and empathy tend to be quelled.[12]

These narratives also sketch the contours of a new strategic enemy, which exists as a projection from the mind of its makers rather than as reality. An insidiously divisive discourse promotes the idea that 'Muslimness' is equivalent to an all-encompassing and reductive signifier. The toddler is the Muslim. The neighbour is the Muslim. The prostitute is the Muslim. The gay-rights activist is the Muslim. The prisoner is the Muslim. The worker is the Muslim. The feminist is the Muslim. The disabled person is the Muslim. The lover is the Muslim. Muslim – and nothing more. The waste of opportunities for understanding and dialogue here is obvious. But even on their own terms, if writers such as Martin Amis and Christopher Hitchens are seeking to distinguish forms of 'Islamic radicalism' from a notional 'good Islam' then to talk of Muslims and Islam as if they are integrated entities is self-defeating. Even more as their discourse pronounces the unity and singularity of Islam, and renders coherent what is diversified, differentiated and molecular. The resemblance here is to the views of the leaders of al-Qaeda, who fervently believe that Islam is an all-encompassing totality which determines everything, all the way down to a person's individual character traits. In their shared flattening of complex realities, these imagined adversaries collude in a dangerous myth of truly Orwellian proportions.

This makes it all the more important to question the underlying bipolar assumption on which the clash regime is based. For in reality, there are no such boundaries or 'bloody borders' separating a western entity from an Islamic bloc. To think in such dichotomous terms is a residue of a Cold War mentality that seems ever less fitting to the complexities of the post-modern disorder of the early twenty-first century. After all, the contemporary world more and more challenges the supposedly mutually exclusive categories of the clash thesis. For example, the everyday experience of major cities in the western hemisphere pervaded by hybridity and a cosmopolitan spirit, where many other cultural formations (including a sort of Islamo-European-American amalgam) are present.[13] On an anecdotal note, one could refer to personal experience in my current hometown of Cambridge, where a mosque operates almost immediately adjacent to a traditional public house (pub) where one can cherish a good pint of traditional Ale. At no stage has there been any disturbance or agitation. The two manifestations of lifestyles in Britain shadow dance with each other in mutual respect on an everyday basis, despite occasional tensions which have remained the exception rather than the norm. In light of this intertwinement of lifestyles, policy attempts to 'fix' the division between entities – which have been a feature of British government reactions to the attacks of July 2005 in London, and of subsequent anti-extremist initiatives such as the 'Prevent' strategy – are misconceived and anachronistic. They assume the existence of a west that is ideologically unified, provincial and devoid of cosmopolitan spirit and intercultural heritage. In today's globalized world order this assumption no longer has purchase, for the west and its correlates (east, south, north) are *inside* each other, part of an emerging post-modern constellation.

The consequences of this development are profound. First, the fact that the west has no clear boundary anymore (inner or outer) creates security interdependencies. The global terror campaign of al-Qaeda has made abundantly clear that no foreign war can be waged without some serious blowback. Second, the globalized world order fuels a particular kind of transnational solidarity exemplified by the opposition across the world to the invasion of Iraq in 2003 or the global support for a Palestinian state. This in turn is connected to the evolution since the 1990s of a sort of global public sphere in which local forms of political activism are woven into a borderless structure of resistance. The world-wide-web makes it easier to connect, organize and fuel diverse political struggles, and gives them a multi-polar and decentralized character; an influence that can be seen from the uprisings in Bahrain, Egypt, Tunisia and Syria through campaigns in Britain against steep increases in university tuition-fees to protests in Stuttgart, Germany, against the destruction of a valued railway station. This interconnected and unified field of global politics is a challenge to those who cling to language and mindsets that belong to an era that has passed. Many will ignore it, because (like Geert Wilders or extreme Islamists) an us-versus-them logic that demonizes the other is fundamental to their strategy of exclusion. But many more could be persuaded that the west does not exist as a separate, monolithic entity, and that both domestic politics and international relations need to be reconstituted accordingly. To that end, the canon of the western social sciences and humanities have to be opened up even further to critical approaches which appreciate different cultural experiences within a common universality.

Critical theory as democratic resistance

In this particular appreciation of the interrelationship between theory and praxis, the present book connects with the idea that intellectuals are the guilty man of our political and socio-economic reality. Practical people, journalists and pundits, who believe themselves independent of any theoretical/intellectual impact, are most of the time the product of some political theory or norm spun by an oblique scholar in the solitary of his/her study. Karl Marx's bohemian existence in nineteenth-century Soho is merely a prominent example of that impact, but there are many more which have been less publicized. Naturally, there are trajectories according to which ideas penetrate the consciousness of people. But none of us thinks politics in a vacuum, even if the tradition of Anglo-American positivism has habituated many to assume that a political consciousness can float freely, that politics is objective rather than objectified. To put it crudely: The idea comes first.

The German critical theorist Max Horkheimer links this propensity to divorce theory from praxis to the residues of the Enlightenment in general and Cartesian thought in particular. This 'inability to grasp in thought the unity of theory and practice and the limitation of the concept of necessity to inevitable events,' he argues, 'are both due . . . to the Cartesian dualism of thought and being'. From this perspective, to assume that theory and praxis are divorced is false and hypocritical, directed against the transformative and liberating opportunities that critical theory promises. 'The idea of a theory which becomes a genuine force, consisting in the self-awareness of the subjects of a great historical revolution', Horkheimer notes, 'is beyond the grasp of a mentality typified by such dualism'. The dangers of such thinking for scholars and intellectuals is apparent, for if they 'do not merely think about such a dualism but really take it seriously, they cannot act independently'.[14] Their theories would be confined to the lecture room and their everyday life would be played out in private without any linkage between thought and daily action. They would say one thing to their students and audience and act in very different ways in their own lives. Resistance and critique would be mere academic talk and not a daily project. The consequences for society would be acute, because cloistering critique to the ivory tower translates into confining democratic praxis, which is why 'those who profit from the status quo entertain a general suspicion of any intellectual independence'.[15] As Theodor Adorno adds: 'Critique is essential to all democracy. Not only does democracy require the freedom to criticise and need critical impulses. Democracy is nothing less than defined by critique.'[16] It must follow, then, that this dialectic between theory and praxis has to be explicitly embraced as an intellectual and normative necessity, in particular in a study like the present one which is concerned with mechanisms of power and modes of resistance, that is, the stuff out of which history and our political truth conditions are made in the first place.

If critique is meant to create politically independent subjects who would contribute to the democratic culture of society, critical theory must be considered a form of resistance. Adorno makes this very clear when he says that critique delivers a politically mature society which manifests itself 'in the power to resist established opinions and, one and the same, also to resist existing institutions, to resist everything that is merely posited, that justifies itself with its existence'.[17] The second theme of this book takes seriously this notion of critique as resistance through a theoretical survey which is informed by current revolts and demonstrations in West Asia, North Africa and to a lesser extent in Europe and the United States.

The sketch of the trajectories of these events informs the argument that resistance begets power, that is, that power acts upon our inclination to resist injustices and confinements to our individual liberties. I think these forms of resistance are innate, deeply rooted in the human psyche and transcendent of cultural or ethnic particularities. To my mind then, resistance to injustice is a human trait. Adorno and Horkheimer do not say much about the sources of resistance within society. But when they present critical theory as a strategy of resistance, they must have assumed that it could appeal to certain internal dispositions within the individual. If critical theory 'has for its object men as producers of their own historical way of life in its totality', and if the desire to resist can be constructed by such critique, then it must follow that the ability to resist can be internalized, that critical theory lodges into an internal disposition.[18] There seems to be something within us that triggers action in resistance to authority, to power, that provokes a radical subjectivity that may turn individuals into revolutionaries. Academic conventions and the middle-class attitudes that permeate the contemporary university culture in the west, trivialize the raw anger and ferocity that drives such radical and revolutionary subjectivity. 'At the very centre of revolution', it is rightly argued in this regard, 'lies an emotional upheaval of moral indignation, revulsion and fury with the powers-that-be, such that one cannot demur or remain silent, whatever the cost'. This kind of radical subjectivity interrupts the common order; it creates a fold in the humdrum affairs of history. 'Within its glow, for a while, men [women, transsexuals] surpass themselves, breaking the shackles of intuitive self-preservation, convention, day-to-day convenience, and routine'.[19]

This agent-centred dynamic can be expressed in more general terms: If it is the case that 'desire only exists when assembled or machined', as Deleuze and Parnet suggest, then there must be internal, bio-political triggering devices which are prompted by such an assembled desiring machine.[20] To put it simply: There must be something on the inside that is provoked by incentives from the outside; the desire to act out resistance must have exogenous linkage. This dialectical link between power and resistance is the interrelationship between the interior, ideational conditioning of the psyche (cognition) and incentives of the outside, the social realm. The action thus produced is the effect of a 'resistance drive' of some sort. Power is therefore internalized in a process of ideational repatriation. It acts on the subjectivity of the agent and provokes an action which is not merely a rebound or a reaction to power, but a genuinely productive force in itself. Such resistance is as productive and promiscuous as power, which is why both are coterminous – resistance is where power is.

Naturally, all of this does not mean that I am proposing a 'psychology of resistance', that I am trying to identify and dissect 'organs' within the human body that would explain the reasons why we resist. But it means that politically conscious individuals have internalized certain norms; that they act in accordance with a sense of justice. These norms are derived from the outside of course, but they have found a place on the inside. As such, it is imperative to find out how resistance is assembled and which power mechanisms act upon the 'resistance drive'. I will discuss this dialectic between the inside and the outside, individual and system, agent and structure in more detail in the fourth interregnum, which focuses on Michel Foucault and his writings on the revolution in Iran in 1979 and to a lesser extent when I discuss Edward Said. Suffice it to say at this stage that structure and agency are co-constitutive. This idea posits that power and resistance function in very similar ways in Jakarta, Beijing, Paris, Beirut, London, New York and Athens, that there is no profound, historically primordial difference between power and resistance in the western/northern and eastern/southern hemisphere. In light of the current globalization of protest movements from Cairo to Madrid, Athens to New York, the present book departs from the hypothesis that post-modern power and resistance, post-modern radicalism has changed from the familiar forms we have known so far. This is not to say that there has been a major rupture with the methods of previous revolts and revolutions. Neither do I imply that violence and hierarchies have been entirely absent in what is happening. It is the nuances of these contemporary movements that I find illuminating and which signal changes in the dialectics between power and resistance that the book will bring out. It is striking, for instance, that none of the demonstrations we are witnessing were geared to a Weberian charismatic figurehead embodied so emotively in the persona of Lenin, Mao-Zedong, Castro or Khomeini in the build-up to the Russian, Chinese, Cuban and Iranian revolutions respectively. Even the main movements that brought about the downfall of the European states of the Warsaw Pact were led by powerful individuals, for instance Lech Walesa in Poland or Vaclav Havel in the former Czechoslovakia.

Material and ideational signposts

What analytical signposts and preliminary conclusions does the preceding discussion offer us at this stage? First, if previously, iron-clad ideologies and charismatic leaders were the driving forces of the masses, today mass politics has opened up wider spaces across the ethers of the world-wide-web and satellite TV stations. In accordance with this, revolts cannot be monopolized easily by one party or an avant-garde anymore. Post-modern resistance reacts to post-modern power in a distinctly decentralized manner demonstrating a shift away from authoritarian forms of political organization to flat-out networks that diversify authority across interlinked nodal-points. The protesters in Cairo and Tunis not only demanded democracy and social justice, they enacted their ideals internally by creating a self-sufficient system of protest that was devoid of an authoritarian hierarchy. In a symbolic act, the demonstrators in Cairo even organized their own cleanup operation during the final days of the first wave of the revolt. Outside the national museum which is just adjacent to Tahrir Square, volunteers laid back stones that were dislodged from the pavement. Others scrubbed graffiti, posters and paint off the walls. Egyptians wanted to show that after Mubarak they will be building a new Egypt and that they are quite capable of organizing themselves without a central authority commanding them to do so. This was not only about re-conquering the public spaces from the authority of the state, it was also about active self-empowerment.

It is true, as Asef Bayat argues, that daily 'anti-order' practices and activities such as setting up 'illegal' street businesses in main squares, squatting in public parks and tourist hubs or challenging moral sensitiveness through provocative dress have always been part and parcel of public life in the region and beyond.[21] But these 'non-movements' are decisively morphed into a political upheaval during revolts exactly because the anarchic, daily actions that questioned public order are suddenly coordinated and enriched with political symbols and imagery that promise a better future for the people. Under the pressure of such an event, daily routines that rupture public order transform into active detachment from the demands of the state: The street vendor marches to the public square to demonstrate; the squatters set up camps with the help of organized student movements; and housewives sabotage infrastructure as a part of a grand strategy to overcome the oppression of society. In other words, daily dissent transmutes into a revolt with transversal capability that challenges both established norms within society (horizontal movement) and the truth conditions held up by the state and the normative order of the international system (vertical movement). The revolts in Tunisia and Egypt were exactly multi-dimensional in this sense. As the Lebanese political theorist Ali Harb correctly argues in a recent book published in Beirut: These uprisings comprised civil, political, economic, technical and ethical realms and engendered an irresistible momentum that was both Arab and global.[22]

Second, until Tunisia and Egypt erupted, the dominant narrative was that Arab and Muslim societies are beset by radicalism and that al-Qaeda is a viable political force. Over the past decade, the fight against 'Muslim radicalism' (or what Bernard Lewis infamously called 'Muslim rage') has seen huge resources allocated to the wars in Iraq and Afghanistan; to the regime-change strategy in Iran, Lebanon and Gaza; and to huge military budgets and many national-security papers.[23] Now, a deep transformation is exposing the failures and follies of this approach. The current uprisings in the Arab world and beyond are a key agent of this process of renewal. Perhaps for the first time since the violent rupture of colonialism, the range of discourses signifying the meaning of resistance in the region is geared towards universal aspirations for freedom and democracy. Today then, Arab and Muslim societies are equipping themselves with a political language that could institutionalize those norms systematically and for the long run.

Third, with the departure of Ben-Ali in Tunisia and the demise of Mubarak in Egypt we witnessed the second coming of independence, which promises to do away with the residues of the post-colonial state. Today, Tunisia and Egypt are on their way to becoming 'non-colonial'. The post-colonial consciousness may be finally relegated to the archives of history. As Rashid Khalidi notes: 'What distinguishes the revolutions of 2011 from their predecessors is that they mark the end of the old phase of national liberation from colonial rule, and are largely inwardly directed at the problems of Arab societies.'[24] The main factors behind the revolts in the Arab world are familiar – dictatorship, oppression, nepotism, social inequality, structural poverty and demographic changes. The centres of the revolts, Tunisia and Egypt, shared several structural features in that regard. Both Mubarak and Ben-Ali were pro-western, emerged out of the ranks of the military and headed authoritarian *mukhabarat* states that did not rely on public accountability (or even populist ideology), but systematic coercion. Both leaders instituted economic policies premised on neo-liberal reform under the auspices of international financial institutions such as the World Bank and the International Monetary Fund (IMF). In turn, these policies merely benefitted an oligarchic coterie attached to the whims of the presidential palaces, rather than the middle classes and the lower-income strata of society. Both leaders were seen as subservient in their foreign policies, and often acted in compliance with US demands (and in the case of Mubarak Israeli coercion), rather than the national interest of their societies.

In the absence of popular accountability, Ben-Ali and Mubarak coalesced with outside forces, primarily successive US governments and the IMF and the World Bank, in order to secure their power base. In 2010 – that is, one year before the demonstrations forced Ben-Ali out of the country – a State Department cable indicated that the 'United States and Tunisia have an active schedule of joint military exercises'. Relations were said to be wide-ranging and productive: 'U.S. security assistance historically has played an important role in cementing relations. The U.S.-Tunisian Joint Military Commission meets annually to discuss military cooperation, Tunisia's defense modernization

program, and other security matters.'[25] The 'war on terror' buttressed this
security relationship. As a result, in Tunisia the anti-terror act of 2003 worsened
the human rights abuses in the country especially for inmates with Islamist
persuasions.[26]

Several state department cables released by wikileaks show that Mubarak's
regime too became a trusted partner in the war on terror and actively aided and
abetted the extraordinary rendition regime which effectively internationalized
the torture of al-Qaeda suspects.[27] A similarly problematic relationship emerges
on the economic front. Ignorant or purposefully silent about the decadent
lifestyle of the Ben-Ali family clan, their patronage system and the political
oppression in the country, the former IMF managing director Dominique
Strauss-Kahn praised the economic reforms in 2008 which were deemed
'the best model for many emerging countries'. Tunisia was thought to make
'impressive progress in its reform agenda and its prospects are favourable.'[28]
The statistical indicators published by the World Bank seemed to support
this view. The poverty headcount ratio at the national poverty line decreased
from 7.7 per cent in 1985 to 3.8 per cent in 2005. Access to water sources and
electricity, the Gross National Product (GNP) and life expectancy increased
as well.[29]

However, such statistical indicators gloss over the realities on the ground.
Human sentiments are not quantifiable in numeric terms; changes in
macroeconomic indices were not meaningful to the average Tunisian labourer.
Yet in the world of neo-liberal economics, always rather devoid of political
acumen, Tunisia under Ben-Ali was deemed a success story. In particular
the IMF supported and commended Ben-Ali's policies that were deemed
conducive to enhancing the business environment in Tunisia and 'improving
the competitiveness of its economy'.[30] In line with the neo-liberal ideology
of the WTO, the IMF and the World Bank, Tunisia was commended for
pursuing several preferential trade agreements with West Africa, the free trade
agreement with the Central African Economic and Monetary Community
and bilateral negotiations with the European Union including a free trade
agreement for industrial products. The problem was that these de-regulative
measures, which went hand-in-hand with large scale privatization efforts,
merely reinforced the economic grip of the Ben-Ali family (especially his
wife Leila Trabelsi) who were in the advantageous position to dominate, if

not to monopolize, those sectors of the economy that were privatized under IMF supervision. Lucrative foreign dealerships were all controlled by a tight clan around the Ben-Ali family. Moreover, IMF-sponsored economic policies, such as cuts to the social security system, especially the pension fund, lowering subsidies of food and fuel products and reducing the tax rate for business and offsetting this reduction with an increase of the standard VAT rate, directly hurt the poorest strata of Tunisian society.

Comparable to Tunisia, Egypt tried to liberalize its economy under the supervision of the IMF and the World Bank for decades starting with the *infitah* (open door) policies of Sadat implemented in the late 1970s and adopted by Mubarak after the assassination of Sadat in 1981. Its central aim was to transform Egypt from the state-centred Nassirite economic system to a neo-liberal economy, a move much endorsed by the United States and international financial organizations. Again, in the neo-liberal world of mainstream economics, Egypt's economic reform programme spearheaded by Hosni Mubarak's son Gamal was deemed 'successful'. The country registered GDP growth rates of 7.1 per cent in 2007 and 7.2 per cent in 2008; at the height of the global economic recession in 2009, GDP continued to increase to 4.7 per cent. Comparable to Tunisia, Egypt was lauded for the reforms that were implemented more systematically since 2004, including the large-scale privatization of state-owned companies and assets which were said to turn the country into an attractive place for foreign direct investment.[31] Yet in Egypt too these reforms merely benefitted a few to the detriment of the majority in the country. As an editorial in *Al-Ahram* put it: 'the *infitah* policy effectively set Egypt on a path of reliance on conditional financial aid, with abysmal results on the ground. Illiteracy skyrocketed, infrastructure deteriorated, the poverty rate climbed and high unemployment levels became the norm.'[32]

Mubarak was overtly reliant on outside support in political terms as well. A cable from March 2009 shows that the United States provided Egypt with US$1.3 billion annual foreign military finance (FMF). Ironically, this amount was allocated for the purchase of US weapons and defence equipment. In other words, the United States provided Egypt with military finance to purchase US weapons. The FMF also secured a 'strong military relationship' which was said to have 'supported peace between Egypt and Israel and ensured critical Suez Canal and overflight access for US military operations'. Indeed, both sides seemed to be rather nonchalant about admitting that the FMF purchased Egypt's silence on the Palestinian question: 'President Mubarak and military leaders view our military assistance program as the cornerstone of our mil-mil relationship and consider the USD 1.3 billion in annual FMF as 'untouchable compensation' for making and maintaining peace with Israel.'[33] As Adam Shatz implied in the *London Review of Books*, part of the military aid garnered for border security was used by the Mubarak regime to reinforce the blockade of Gaza.[34] It was US finance then that was used by Mubarak to fortify the blockade, in particular after the electoral victory of HAMAS in 2006 and even through the devastating Israeli assault on Gaza in 2007–2008. In light of this subservience, an editorial in *Time* magazine exemplified the anxiety in Washington that the impending fall of Mubarak caused: 'Having tolerated and abetted Mubarak's repressive rule for three decades precisely because of his utility to US strategy on issues ranging from Israel to Iran, Washington could be deprived of a key Arab ally with his fall from power.'[35] In a similar vein, Steven Cook of the US Council on Foreign Relations warned that 'a successful Islamist push for power in Egypt would result in a fundamental shift in the regional order that would pose a far greater threat – in magnitude and degree – to U.S. interests than the Iranian revolution.'[36] From this perspective, then, Mubarak's Egypt was deemed central to safeguarding US strategic preferences in the region: 'Egypt is a difficult yet critical US ally', Cook contended. 'Along with Saudi Arabia, Jordan, Morocco, and the smaller Gulf states, Egypt has helped create a regional order that makes it relatively inexpensive for the United States to exercise its power.'[37]

The signposts and consequences of the interconnected revolts that have questioned that order are the topic of the following interregnum. I will show more closely how the successful Arab revolts in Tunisia and Egypt, comparable to the Iranian revolution of 1979, have accentuated independence from foreign dictates. As I have started to discuss at the end of this interregnum, when Mubarak sustained the blockade of Gaza during the war with Israel in 2007–2008, he was on the wrong side of history. When he and Ben-Ali colluded with the inhumane rendition regime administered by the Bush dministration, during a period when the Abu Ghraib prison scandal broke and pictures of dead Iraqis and Afghans were beamed around the world, they lost a decisive amount of legitimacy among their populace. There is precedence for such strategic mistakes. It was the Shah's Status of Forces bill of 1964 that granted US military personnel diplomatic immunity for crimes committed on Iranian territory that gave impetus to a mass rebellion which ushered Ayatollah Khomeini to the political scene.[38] The Shah, for right or for wrong, was perceived and represented as a puppet of the United States by the Iranian revolutionaries and his behaviour and pro-western rhetoric provided ample breeding ground for such ideas to fester. Equally devoid of democratic legitimacy, Ben-Ali and Mubarak repeated the mistakes that the Shah made. Ultimately, they paid a similar price. While neither the Iranian revolution nor the Arab revolts were anti-American per se, they were geared to norms and symbols that accentuate independence from the preferences of the United States and Israel in favour of self-rule and emphasis on national interests.

Between Power and Resistance in Praxis

No, painting is not made to decorate apartments. It is an instrument for offensive and defensive war against the enemy.

Pablo Picasso

Global insurgencies

Tehran, June 2009. Iranians have voted in the tenth presidential elections after the revolution of 1979. Amid massive demonstrations in Tehran and other cities throughout the country, the leaders of the opposition, former parliamentary speaker Mehdi Karroubi and ex–prime minister Mir Hossein Mousavi, declare the elections null and void. Flanked by the former presidents Mohammad Khatami and Ali-Akbar Rafsanjani, they accuse President Ahmadinejad of fraud calling for a recount. According to the mayor of Tehran and former commander in the Revolutionary Guard Mohammad Baqer Ghalibaf, the voice of approximately three million peaceful demonstrators reverberates in Iran's capital. Not since the Islamic revolution of 1979, which swept away the monarchy of the Shah, has Iran and the world witnessed such an outpouring of popular dissent. The colour green is chosen as a symbol of defiance; the so-called Green Movement is born. The official calendar of the state, marked by rallies against western imperialism, religious festivals and in support of the Palestinian cause, is turned into a calendar of protest.

On Jerusalem Day, instituted by Ayatollah Khomeini the late leader of the revolution of 1979, demonstrators clash with the Baseej. The Baseej is a huge voluntary movement whose security wings are under the loose control of the

Revolutionary Guards, the main military force of the state. The demonstrators are young, the club and gun wielding Baseejis too. There are violent clashes on 7 December 2009 (National Students' Day), and on 27 December – Ashura, one of the holiest days in the calendar of the Islamic Republic and the Shi'i-Islamic world in general. On Ashura, which commemorates the martyrdom of the Shi'i Imam and grandson of Prophet Mohammad, Hossein Ibn Talib, eight protestors are killed including Seyyed Ali Mousavi, the nephew of Mir Hossein Mousavi, one of the protagonists of the Green Movement and the main challenger of Ahmadinejad in the election. Previously, on 20 June 2009, a young student identified as Neda Agha-Soltan is shot dead on the streets of Tehran. The horrific scene of her murder is captured on camera and the video is widely distributed on YouTube in a distasteful display of the fetishization of death. The state shirks its responsibility to protect all its citizens. For the first time after the devastating Iran-Iraq war (1980–1988), the national security of the country is in danger. Yet again, the Revolutionary Guard claim the legitimacy to safeguard the system. They defended the country against the forces of Saddam Hussein during the first Persian Gulf War (Iran-Iraq war, 1980–1988), now they consider it their duty to defend the country against what they perceive to be a 'soft colour revolution' from within. As one official close to the Revolutionary Guard told me: 'We saw our brothers perish in the bloodied war trenches of Khuzestan and Basra. We stood against the pharaoh of the age and his foreign supporters. Do they really think we will abandon the country like the Shah did?'[1]

The shadow of Khomeini looms large, even two decades after his death, which brought millions of Iranians to the streets in mourning. When his picture is torn apart by demonstrators, or possibly by agent provocateurs, in a well-choreographed scene, the loyalists evince their power more trenchantly. From their perspective, the Green Movement reflects the preferences of the nouveaux riche, the Northern Tehranis who are besmirching, if not desecrating, the legacy of their revered Imam. This is a one-sided depiction of course. The protest movement encompasses a broad spectrum of Iranian society, if largely concentrated around the middle class, and it was not anti-Islamic. This was not a class war or a war of ideologies. The ongoing clashes in the country epitomize a Machiavellian struggle for power and a battle over the future direction of the revolution of 1979.

The pro-government supporters are supplied with refreshments and sandwiches. The opposition is beaten, bruised and incarcerated. Yet throughout the summer of 2009 and well into January 2010, the battles for the street flare up regularly. At the height of the violence, the Iranian state makes it abundantly clear, in word and deed, that it will battle out, with organized ferocity, any challenge to the system. I talk to Iranians on both sides. A member of the Baseej tells me with a shaky voice that he recognized his older brother among the demonstrators he was confronting. 'It was shocking, I couldn't react and I left the scene.'[2] A demonstrator supporting the reform movement appears similarly distraught. 'I would never have thought that they would beat up unarmed women on the streets. But I saw it with my own eyes and it was terrifying.'[3] Once again in contemporary Iranian history, brothers and sisters are pitted against each other, while the state fortifies the boundaries between enemy and friend to the detriment of all Iranians.

There is no doubting the complicity of influential sections of the state in the violent, and at times brutal, breakdown of the demonstrations. But at the same time there was criticism from within the system which almost translated into the impeachment of President Ahmadinejad by the parliament in 2011. One prominent parliamentary deputy, and the son of the late revolutionary cleric Ayatollah Morteza Motahhari, criticized the authorities in this way:

> If they had been granted several assembly permits, they would have lost their supporters and, for example, only 100,000 people would have remained at the end who wanted to cause destruction and set [places] on fire. Then they could have been seriously confronted. I saw [with my own eyes] that they [government forces] beat up on the people with batons right from the first day. We viewed the problem from a security/intelligence angle, not political and social, and acted based on the intelligence [gathered on the opposition], whereas we should have calmed the common people until they went home. In reality, we did not separate the common people from the leaders of the crisis.[4]

To make matters worse for a critical understanding of Iranian politics, influential segments of the international media routinely distort the lucrative 'Iran story'.[5] At the height of the demonstrations, the most obscure theories float around aided by the flawed testimony of predatory analysts with a pro-war agenda.[6] As an example, the *Telegraph* of London reports that the current

Supreme Leader of Iran, Ayatollah Ali Khamenei, whose position is part of an intricate constitutional system,[7] has 'accumulated a sprawling private court that stretches across six palaces, including Niavaran, the former resident of the Shah in Tehran'. The Niavaran palace complex, including the gardens, adjacent buildings, the museum, etc., is open to the public and is visited by thousands of tourists every year. I for one never saw Khamenei there, but perhaps he was in the 'deep, reinforced concrete nuclear bunkers said to be capable of withstanding nuclear attack' which presumably sprawl like a mysterious Oriental labyrinth below the nineteenth-century marble structure of the palace? If we are to believe the authors of this news story, Khamenei would revel there in his 'bejewelled pipes', indulge in eating 'caviar and trout' and treat 'bouts of depression . . . in part by audiences with a mid-ranking mullah who tells vulgar jokes'. We are encouraged in all seriousness to imagine Khamenei sitting there wearing a cloak 'said to be woven from hair of specially bred camels'.[8] And in a final affront to serious, investigative journalism, *Radio Netherlands* distributes a report based on a forged document in which it was alleged that Iran's Supreme National Security Council was organizing the departure of Ayatollah Ali Khamenei to Russia.[9] The story is widely distributed on social networking sites, particularly Facebook.

The complexities of the situation remain underappreciated in the media frenzy that routinely envelopes events in Iran (I noted an average of 30 calls/e-mails by journalists per day over the period of one month between June and July 2009). Only when the state organizes counterdemonstrations that draw millions of Iranians into every urban centre in the country is there some recognition that the state is supported too. Quite suddenly, the verdict turns and the idea of a revolution is deemed a fantasy, for instance by Fareed Zakaria, who was adamant that the system in Iran would be falling during successive screenings of his CNN programme GPS, but who suddenly changes his mind once reality kicked in.[10] Revolutionaries make revolutions. Revolutionaries know how to quell revolts. In order to do so, they turn from Che Guevara to Machiavelli. Four years after the demonstrations the streets of Iran are eerily calm. Politics has returned, state and society continue to tinker on the Iranian polity. Despite the ongoing confrontations, or rather exactly because of them, the 'pluralistic momentum' in Iranian politics continues to dissect the system from within.[11] In June 2013, Iranians overwhelmingly vote for the moderate cleric Hassan Rouhani as the next President. The era of Ahmadinejad is over. The reformists are hoping again.

Sidi Bouzid, Tunisia, December 2010. As a part of his daily routine, Muhammad Bouazizi, an unemployed street vendor, makes his way to the local market where he would sell fruits and vegetables from his cart in order to provide for his family. The Tunisian authorities did not grant him a license, but selling the produce is his only source of income, so he continues with his routine despite the regular harassment by the police. On 17 December 2010, the authorities confiscate his goods and humiliate him in front of his peers and colleagues. In an act of desperation, at once tragic and heroic, Bouazizi drenches himself in gasoline and sets himself on fire outside the office of the local governor. Spontaneous demonstrations follow and quickly spread to the capital Tunis. Bouazizi is transferred to a hospital where he would succumb to his wounds on 4 January 2011. In a desperate attempt to garner support and contain the mass protests against his corrupt regime, Tunisia's pro-western dictator Zine El Abidine Ben-Ali visits Bouazizi in the hospital a few days before he passes away. The demonstrations encompass the whole country. Tunisia trembles and the system falters. Ten days after the death of Bouazizi, on 14 January 2011, Ben Ali and his family flee the country to Saudi Arabia. The departure marks the end of a presidency' that lasted 24 years. Bouazizi's act of self-immolation reached the comparable political impact that the same act by the Vietnamese Buddhist monk Thich Quang Duc provoked. Duc set himself on fire in Saigon in 1963 in protest at the persecution of Buddhists by the Roman-Catholic government in South Vietnam. This thoroughly political act has become a powerful symbol: A photo of his death, taken by the Pulitzer prize–winning photographer Malcolm Brown, appeared on the cover of the music band Rage against the Machine's bestselling debut album in 1992.

The end of Ben-Ali marks the end of a particular form of post-colonial governance and mentality. Ben-Ali was a product of the militarized post-colonial order that was typical not only for the Arab-Islamic world, but also for Latin America and sub-Saharan Africa. Tunisia became a French protectorate in 1881 after the treaty of Al-Qasr as-Said, which effectively sanctioned indefinite French occupation of the country. As in Algeria and other places, the violence of colonialism was countered by anti-colonial resistance movements nurtured by a mixture of nationalist ideology and, to a lesser extent, Islamic imagery. In the early twentieth century the anti-colonial resistance movement was institutionalized in the Destour (constitution) party which metamorphosed into the neo-Destour in the 1930s when it came under the sway of Habib Bourguiba. Bourguiba was not a revolutionary, no Che Guevara. He was a gradualist who wanted to bargain his way to Tunisian independence. In the end, it was not his strategy that was successful, however, but the increasing material and immaterial costs that the anti-colonial resistance provoked. For the French state, it ceased to be economically viable to keep the colonies in North Africa. The intense resistance in Algeria, which is so beautifully eulogized in the movie *The Battle of Algiers*, was very consequential to that end. Not that the colonial functionaries did not try: the resistance movement was countered by the French with immense brutality including sustained campaigns of rape and other forms of sexual violence.[12] In the end, in both Tunisia and Algeria, it did not help: Tunisia became independent in 1956 and Algeria six years later.

The militarized state that Bourguiba presided over was typical for post-colonial politics in the Third World. It emerged out of the intense turmoil that the colonial order provoked and it was secured primarily by the military establishment and an oligarchic coterie surrounding it, which was entirely tied to the global capitalist market. Ben-Ali followed in Bourguiba's footsteps when he took over the presidency in 1987 in a peaceful transition of power. Educated and socialized in the authoritarian structures of the French military schools in Saint-Cyr and Chalons-sur-Marne and the Senior Intelligence School in Maryland and the School for Anti-Aircraft Field Artillery in Texas, Ben-Ali's rule exemplified the cliché associated with tin-pot military dictatorships that would hold fragile post-independence states together with an iron fist. Here lies the significance of the events in Tunisia. Today, Tunisians are writing their own script, their own history, for the first time in their modern history. Events are not constituted by either the colonial system or post-colonial dictators such as Bourguiba and Ben-Ali anymore. In that sense, we are witnessing a truly historical event: the beginning of the end of post-colonialism.

Tahrir Square, Egypt, December 2010. Tens of thousands of Egyptians gather. Inspired by the events in Tunisia and the ouster of Ben-Ali, Egyptians from all strata of society take to the streets to force their own dictator out. There is a carnivalesque atmosphere in Tahrir Square. Families picnic, young Egyptians play music, Woodstock meets Scheherazade. Hosni Mubarak had ruled the country at the helm of a pro-western state since 1980. He is determined to hold on to power. Saudi Arabia and Israeli Prime Minister Benjamin Netanyahu lobby the Obama administration to support Mubarak lest he faces the fate of the Shah of Iran who was deposed after the Iranian revolution in 1979. The fate of the Shah looms large in the mind of the struggling dictators and their supporters in Washington, DC and Tel Aviv. A US embassy cable released by wikileaks indicates that Mubarak himself fosters this analogy between revolutionary Iran and Egypt. 'We have heard him lament the results of earlier U.S. efforts to encourage reform in the Islamic world', it is stated in a cable dated 19 May 2009. 'He can harken [sic] back to the Shah of Iran: the U.S. encouraged him to accept reforms, only to watch the country fall into the hands of revolutionary religious extremists.' Another cable, dated 6 December 2010, that is, a month before Mubarak's regime fell, describes a meeting between the chairman of Joint Chiefs of Staff Admiral Michael Mullen and Egyptian General Intelligence Service Chief Omar Suleiman, who would take over from Mubarak in February 2011 to form an interim government. In the cable Suleiman is quoted as saying that Egypt has 'started a confrontation with Hezbollah and Iran' and that the Mubarak regime 'will not allow Iran to operate in Egypt'. In an apparent effort to outline the geopolitical utility of Egypt to ward off Iranian power in the region, Suleiman further stressed that 'Egypt had sent a clear message to Iran that if they interfere in Egypt, Egypt will interfere in Iran, adding that EGIS had already begun recruiting agents in Iraq and Syria'. This geostrategic competition should compel the US government to work closer with Egypt. Iran must 'pay the price' for its action and not be allowed to interfere in regional affairs. 'If you want Egypt to cooperate with you on Iran, we will', Suleiman made clear, 'it would take a big burden off our shoulders'.[13]

Iran is presented here as the main source of Islamist anti-Americanism. Mohamed Tantawi, who was then defence minister and would go on to lead the military council that took power after Mubarak and until he himself was ousted by new President Mohammed Morsi in August 2012, adopted a similar position on Iran in a meeting with a visiting delegation from the US congress. In reply to a question by Republican Senator Mitch McConnell (KY), Tantawi stressed that 'Iran was a "danger" for Egypt and the whole region'. While he cautioned against military action, he was quick to use the 'Iran threat' to lobby the congressmen for access to 'advanced US weapons systems'. In the same meeting, Tantawi was adamant to point out that Egypt is doing everything it can to enforce the Israeli embargo of Gaza.[14]

Comparable to Ben-Ali and the Libyan leader Muammar Gaddafi, Mubarak repeatedly stressed that the options are limited to either the status quo, however repressive it may be, or an anti-American Islamist state, a dysphemism for the prospects of an independent Egypt. Successive US administrations and generations of CIA analysts accepted that narrative, which is why they turned a blind eye to the systematic suppression of the Islamist opposition in the country (and Tunisia). Like the Shah of Iran, Mubarak was their man, described as 'a tried and true realist, innately cautious and conservative', an authoritarian leader who 'has little time for idealistic goals'. The alternative to him would be the Muslim Brotherhood, which Mubarak continuously misrepresents as fanatically anti-American and potentially pro-Iranian. They are said to 'represent the worst, as they challenge not only Mubarak's power, but his view of Egyptian interests . . . In Mubarak's mind it is far better to let a few individuals suffer than risk chaos for society as a whole.'[15]

A culture of flawed intelligence permeates the perception of the political elites in the United States and affects how events in the Arab/Muslim world are perceived. The mainstream media of the country, largely compliant, and an armada of analysts, lobbyists and 'embedded academics' are equally culpable for the lack of understanding of the complexity of international affairs. It is not at least due to this politico-cultural habitat that the United States has suffered strategic defeats in the region, from the 'loss' of Iran to the disastrous wars in Afghanistan and Iraq. So it does not come as a surprise that on Mubarak, the Obama administration got it wrong too. One year before he was ousted it was deemed 'inevitable' that he would win the next presidential elections scheduled for 2011, if 'he is still alive'.[16] Comparable predictions were made about the stability of the Shah's Iran, undoubtedly based on similarly flawed 'intelligence'.[17] In December 1977, a few weeks before the departure of the Shah, former US president Jimmy Carter deemed his Iran 'an island of stability in one of the more troubled regions of the world'. The Shah and his wife Farah Diba toasted him with champagne. A year later they departed into exile.

In a comparable manner, Hillary Clinton deemed Mubarak's Egypt stable as late as in January 2011. A few weeks later, on 10 February, Mubarak was forced to hand over the presidency.[18] On 11 February, Vice President Omar

Suleiman announced that Mubarak was stepping down and that the country would be ruled by the military's supreme council. The resistance proclaims a historic victory. Previously banned parties such as the Muslim Brotherhood are directly involved in the power politics of the country again. The military continues to discipline and punish and the Muslim Brotherhood positions itself close to power in an uneasy relationship of convenience with the remnants of Mubarak's security apparatus. The demonstrations go on, civil society continues to resist. The Arab *nahda* is in full swing. On 30 June 2012, Mohammad Morsi, the candidate of the Freedom and Justice Party, an offspring of the Ikhwan, becomes the first president of the new Egypt. As one demonstrator told me with exuberance and passion: 'After Mubarak, nothing will be the same again!'[19]

Athens, December 2010. The largest public sector union of Greece, ADEDY and the largest private industry union, General Confederation of Labor (or GSEE), are spearheading strike action. Flights are grounded, the ports come to a standstill and public transport is phased out. Protesters clash with police in Athens. In May 2010, amidst worsening economic conditions, socialist Prime Minister George Papandreou was forced to accept a package of 'emergency loans' from the International Monetary Fund and the European Union in the amount of 110 billion Euros. Germany and France are particularly adamant. The bailout is linked to massive cuts in wages, pensions and public services and begets higher taxes. Within a couple of months, Greek workers lose one-third of their disposable income. Periodic strikes are combined with demonstrations across Syntagma Square, the glitzy shopping area of the Greek capital that is taken over by the demonstrators in a symbolic act of public defiance. Tens of thousands protest on a regular basis. The square is turned into a 'resistance camp'. Even after one year the socialist government does not manage to cut a gaping deficit. The protests continue, and the violence too. In June 2011, several demonstrators are injured during clashes with the police who make ample use of their baton sticks and tear gas. Athens in June 2011 resembles Cairo and Tunis during the heydays of the Arab uprising. The hospitals in the Greek capital are filled with injured protesters, some of them with life threatening head wounds.[20] The protesters chant 'bread, education, liberty', again with a similar emphasis on the delivery of social services, public goods and freedom from the authoritarian arbitrariness of the state that permeated the revolts in the Arab world and in Iran too. In April 2012, a desperate father shoots himself in Syntagma Square in protest against the austerity measures implemented under the supervision of the European Union. At the time of writing, Greece is still rattled by massive demonstrations against the draconian 'austerity' measures decreed by the European Union and international financial organizations. The desperation of the people can be measured by the wave of suicides that has hit the country in the past couple of years.[21]

Parliament Square, London, December 2010. In the streets of the British capital, students, civil rights activists, scholars and others demonstrate against plans to allow for an increase of tuition fees for university students by over 270 per cent within two years. There are tens of thousands, some of them organized by the National Union of Students, others by the worker's unions, or grassroots organizations such as UK Uncut. Egyptian and Palestinian flags abound. Oxford Street is turned into a site of resistance. Major retail chains such as Topshop, Dorothy Perkins and Burton, owned by Sir Philip Green's Arcadia Group, are accused of tax avoidance.[22] For many demonstrators, Green represents everything that is wrong about the alliance between consumer capitalism and political power. The main target is the coalition government, however. The demonstrations come during a period of economic calamity, triggered by the banking crisis which spread like a malignant cancer from the other side of the town, the City or London's financial centre. For some of the demonstrators, it is the arrogance and anti-social attitude of the political establishment itself that needs to be challenged. A general election in May 2010 had produced a coalition between the Conservative Party and the Liberal Democrats and with David Cameron the first Tory prime minister since 1997. Before the general election, Nick Clegg, the leader of the latter, junior partner in the coalition, had promised that his party would oppose any move to increase tuition and fees. Once in power as deputy prime minister, he makes an undignified U-turn.

In protest the students mobilize, they shout, they resist, largely non-violently. Some of them are beaten, some are arrested. The police employ a tactic termed 'kettling' – students are herded into manageable groups and sealed off for hours without the opportunity to break out of their cordon, a form of temporary corralling associated with the enclosure and control of sheep, cows and other livestock.[23] A disabled young activist and blogger by the name of Jody MacIntyre is pulled out of his wheelchair, dragged along the street and dumped on the pavement. In a patronizing interview with the BBC, he is asked if he was a threat to the baton wielding policemen that were surrounding him. 'There's a suggestion that you were rolling towards the police in your wheelchair', BBC's Ben Brown asks in all honesty, 'Is that true?'[24] After a couple of months, the demonstrations subside. In 2011, all of the 123 universities in England have applied to charge at least £6,000 per year in tuition fees from autumn 2012. The majority of them intend to charge the maximum amount of £9,000 per annum.[25] At the same time, there are some headlines about the pay package of the chief executive of the Royal Bank of Scotland, one of the banks that were bailed out by the UK government who owns 83 per cent of the company. The pay package is worth £7.7 million for 2010. The bank registered losses of £1.2 million in the same year.[26] There is no patronizing interview on the BBC. In August 2011, London is shaken by the worst riots since the 1980s. Within days the riots spread to other major cities in England.

Columbus, Ohio, February 2011. An estimated number of 15,000 workers gather in the main hall of the statehouse in Columbus. They are taking up the fight for their pensions which started in Wisconsin where students boycotted classes and embarked on a protest march to the capital where they joined union activists and members of several grassroots movements operating in the area.[27] In Wisconsin, Republican Governor Scott Walker promotes an austerity bill. It would limit the bargaining rights of workers, the right of strikes for teachers and force them to contribute more to their pensions and health care premiums. Members of the 'Tea Party' demonstrate in favour of the cuts. They are entrenched at the far right wing of the neo-conservative coterie in the United States. Academics, teachers, students and workers are pitted against them. It is estimated that 44 states and the District of Columbia have to deal with a US$125 billion deficit for the fiscal year 2012.[28] The sum is more than the aggregate Gross Domestic Product of Syria and Libya.[29] In the end, the protests are simply not widespread and big enough to force a standoff. The state Senate's Insurance, Commerce and Labour Committee approves the bill by a vote of 7 to 5. All the four Democrats sitting on the committee and one Republican vote against the bill, but to no avail.[30] In March, the Ohio Senate passes the bill that curbs the collective bargaining power for government employees. The Center on Budget and Policy Priorities reports that 'as of June 27, 32 states have enacted their budget for the coming 2012 fiscal year. Three-fourths of these states – at least 24 of 32 – are making major cuts to important public services.'[31] The country is in recession, and as in the United Kingdom and elsewhere, it is primarily the workers who are paying for it.

Madrid, May 2011. The Spanish demonstrate against 'austerity' measures by their government that are largely dictated by the European Central Bank under the aegis of German chancellor Angela Merkel and former French president Nicolas Sarkozy. On 15 May, the first day of the protests, people are arrested. On the following day, the demonstrators gather in defiance. Due to the sheer number of people showing up, the police keep their distance. Inspired by the revolts on the southern side of the Mediterranean, in Tunis and Cairo and to the East in Athens, Spaniards mobilize throughout the country. Following the Tunisian-Egyptian model, they occupy the central squares in major cities. For instance, the central Puerta del Sol square in Madrid is turned into a self-sustainable resistance camp. The demonstrators set up portable toilets, furniture, tents, mattresses, a canteen, a library and solar panels that generate enough electricity to keep the facilities going. They have their own democratic committees where daily duties such as cleaning and child-care are organized. The last time the Spanish mobilized in such numbers was in protest against the decision by former prime minister José María Aznar to support the George W. Bush administration in the invasion of Iraq in 2003. At the height of the demonstrations in June 2011, eyewitnesses count tens of thousands.[32] The protesters refer to themselves as *los indignados*, the indignant ones. They demand judicial reform, direct democracy and social justice. The politicians of the country remain fractured along party lines, which do not represent the desires of the protesters. Neither the conservative People's Party, nor the left-leaning socialist party of Prime Minister José Luis Rodríguez Zapatero are trusted. They are indicted for failing to stem the corruption in the banking sector and to lower the rate of unemployment which stands at 21 per cent in 2011, the highest rate in the European Union.[33] Municipal elections at the end of May topple the Socialist Party of ruling Prime Minister Zapatero in favour of the People's Party, even in the traditional strongholds of the socialists. After one month, the resistance camp at Puerta del Sol plaza is dismantled by the protesters.

But the demonstrations continue. On 15 June 2011, dozens of demonstrators are injured after clashes with police in front of the Catalonia regional parliament in Barcelona where lawmakers were deliberating about cuts to social services. Instead of gathering in squares, the demonstrators adopt a new tactic. Six groups of protesters march through the city starting at the same time from the north, south, east and the west. To that end, instant messaging, on the Internet and/or on mobile phones, accelerates the communication between the group leaders. Likewise, and in another parallel to the events in Iran in 2009 and in the Arab world in 2010 and 2011, grassroots organizations such as *Democracia Real Ya* (Real Democracy Now) serve as a platform to mobilize the demonstrators through social networking sites such as Facebook and Twitter. The Internet is turned into a tool for political organization, yet that does not mean that it is only the youth who are on the streets. There are housewives and students, workers and academics, pensioners and teenagers. Apart from the leading businessmen of the country and mainstream politicians, all strata of society are well represented. This is a spontaneous, non-violent resistance movement that has caught politicians and even the unions by surprise.

There are many more examples of resistance in the short time span under focus here. In the Arab world, from Morocco in the west to Bahrain in the east, people have been standing up in defiance of arbitrary rulers, whose legitimacy is based largely on patronage and force, rather than on popular legitimacy and the ballot box. Events are still unfolding rapidly as I write these lines. In Libya, an armed insurrection, supported by NATO air bombardments, ended the rule of Muammar Gaddafi. In Syria, the dictatorship of Bashar al-Assad is shaken by recurrent outburst of massive protests that are met with crushing violence. The degree of human losses in both countries is immense. A similar, if less violent, scenario unfolds in Bahrain, where the rather more hawkish wings of the al-Khalifa monarchy managed to crush a revolt in favour of social justice, economic empowerment and a constitutional monarchy. Saudi Arabia sent troops to the tiny kingdom, lest the majority Shi'i population manages to install a government that would be close to Iran. In Saudi Arabia itself, brave women are defying the ban on driving cars and they are linking up with other forms of defiance that are engulfing the kingdom. Islamic thinkers such as Salman Al-Awda are devising paradigms that attempt to bridge humanism and the salafi/wahhabi norms permeating the country, a seemingly gigantic effort of intellectual reconciliation. In Yemen, President Saleh was the victim of a bomb planted in his palace by the opposition who were protesting against his two decade long 'Presidency'. Forced to flee to Saudi Arabia, which has bankrolled his dictatorship, Saleh manages to install his cronies in Sana'a forestalling the calls for reform by Yemeni society. In June 2012, after a year-long uprising, bulldozers dismantled the main protest camp near Sana'a University. Since then the Yemeni capital has been relatively calm.

The art of resistance

Power and resistance: Between 2009 and the production of this book, world politics have been shaken by recurrent battles that have given theorists and activists ample material to reflect upon and theorize. What are some of the conceptual lessons that we can learn from these protests? What do they tell us about the politics of radicalism, power and resistance? Can we discern new tendencies in the way people revolt? The first striking aspect addressing these questions is that from Tehran to Athens, Cairo to Madrid, Tunis to Ohio people were not moved by all-encompassing ideologies. It was not Marx who drove the people onto the streets. Neither was there in the Arab-Muslim world a particularly Islamic ideology with a totalitarian claim that gave the revolts momentum. The bulk of the demonstrators carrying the events were not morphed into one ideological group with an all-encompassing claim by an avant-garde or a charismatic point of fixation for the masses. These were not modernist ideological projects, in the sense that they were not trying to advocate total revolution of some sort. The grievances were geared to very specific socio-economic issues and political demands. In short, these were 'bread and butter' revolts as much as movements for political emancipation, rather different from the revolutions of the twentieth century in Russia China, Cuba and Iran which brought about more abrupt and immediate changes to the ancien régimes in place.

Secondly, the revolts and demonstrations played out on a broad canvas, as none of the protests movements sketched out above were provincial or cloistered locally. While the demonstrators organized in confined spaces – major streets, squares, public areas – their demands and activities were spread out on a vast plane permeated by molar lines, interspersed mental images, scattered political activities and economic agendas dispersed within globalized, networked polities. In this respect, online networks certainly made the organization of protests more efficient because they multiplied the recipients of information who had instant access to updates about where to gather and how to organize. They caused a domino effect on the Internet which galvanized a large number of followers in a relatively short time. This facilitated the recruitment of protesters and their identification with the cause in a decentralized yet highly efficient and pluralistic way. The absence of physical headquarters, a centralized politburo that would organise the resistance, is an important departure from previous revolts and revolutions and it is indicative of the post-modern context within which contemporary resistance reveals itself.

While online networks are very functional for organizing and coordinating social movements, they do not automatically translate into a political dividend. For instance, the Occupy Wall Street movement in the United States and the Occupy London demonstrators that set up a 'tent city' around St. Paul's cathedral in the capital for weeks did not achieve decisive political concessions from the state. The online networks and the occupation of public spaces elicited a lot of support and media attention, but the very fact that there was no intellectual framework to the movements or an effective decision-making process to articulate the aims of the protesters is a part of the explanation as to why they failed in their efforts to bring about lasting political and socio-economic changes. The daily assemblies in the occupy tent towns that were leaderless were very functional to simulate radical democratic politics, a communal utopia that resembled an anarcho-egalitarian order, but the minimalist consensual agendas that came out of these meetings were devoid of political stamina. Post-modern modes of resistance cannot be oblivious to the determinations of power. Within a regime of truth that is as intrusive as in advanced liberal-capitalist societies in the west, the nodal points of resistance need to be coordinated in order to produce effective demands and a political infrastructure to translate them. What is needed to combat a politics of 'truth' that delimitates political choice is a counter-cultural politics of resistance that transcends different strata of society and their cultural loci.

Moreover, online technologies may be efficient tools to organize the initial phase of resistance – the politicization of the protesters, their physical aggregation in public spaces and the constant reminder that the revolution has started, a message that can be easily visualized through online TV channels such as YouTube. But in the occupy movements this initial phase did not translate into a political agenda or a viable political infrastructure of resistance that would transmute the demands of the protest movement into norms and institutions powerful enough to relay them to the state. The resistance remained without the ideational and material scaffolding necessary to withstand the whims of state power which came down on the protesters with sinister force. As Naomi Wolf wrote in the *Guardian* at the height of the crackdown of the Occupy Wall Street demonstrations in the United States:

> US citizens of all political persuasions are still reeling from images of unparallelled police brutality in a coordinated crackdown against peaceful OWS protesters in cities across the nation this past week. An elderly woman was pepper-sprayed in the face; the scene of unresisting, supine students at UC Davis being pepper-sprayed by phalanxes of riot police went viral online; images proliferated of young women – targeted seemingly for their gender – screaming, dragged by the hair by police in riot gear; and the pictures of a young man, stunned and bleeding profusely from the head, emerged in the record of the middle-of-the-night clearing of Zuccotti Park.[34]

Pluralistic democracies, as opposed to authoritarian regimes, have better mechanisms to counter resistance. This is not only because they are more adept at co-opting dissidence through non-violent means, but because post-modern forms of control are densely modulated and flexible. In the post-industrial west, the Fordist machinic power of the pre-war generations was complemented and partially substituted in the 1950s and 1960s by computerized forms of discipline and control that assault political subjectivity and agency through generatively networked bio-systems. Biometric passports and genetic databanks come to mind as two recent examples, the linkage of mortgage decisions to 'criminal' convictions including public order offences (handed out rather generously by police during the occupy demonstrations in the United Kingdom) would be another. This is the kind of 'liquid' power that is represented in Aldous Huxley's *Brave New World* where it appears as diffuse, subliminal, fluid, whereas George

Orwell's *Nineteen Eighty-Four* simulates the dictatorial variant that dominated the Soviet Union. The former bio-political forms of power that are present in western democracies can only be challenged through forms of resistance that are transversal: that is, that go beyond several restrictions set up by the state at the same time. Such forms of resistance already exist aided and abetted by the Internet as indicated. But in the various occupy movements they did not create transversal *discursive* dynamics that would connect in a multitude of interdependent fields, including multi-modal forms of political expression from pamphlets and university action groups to mass demonstrations and union support. In short: The protests did not decisively amalgamate with other sites of resistance to constitute a denser structure within the well-supervised realms of US/British society.

Here lies one of the differences to the fall of the Berlin Wall in 1989. The momentous events that contributed to the disintegration of the Warsaw Pact and the demise of the Soviet Union were precipitated by Hungary's decision to open its borders, Gorbachev's *glasnost* and *perestroika* reforms, mass demonstrations in East Germany and Lech Walesa's *solidarność* (solidarity) union movement. In other words, the Wall fell in a pan-Soviet space that was densely interconnected by various forms of power and resistance. The same applies to the Arab revolts in Tunisia and Egypt which erupted in a multi-connected pan-Arab space as we will see in the following paragraphs. The occupy movements were linked up globally, but they did not create a political subjectivity that could traverse opposing discourses, conflicting identities and cultural systems. There did not emerge a radical subject out of the resistance camps that would have been powerful enough to sustain the resistance politically and to forge a dialogue beyond class and ideological affiliation. The battle was fought out on a broad canvas, but the nodal points dotted onto it remained scattered; they were not connected to shrink the blank spaces into the contours of a political symbol with transversal capability. In Europe and the United States, the saturated middle classes kept away from the demonstrations and the poor were not included in the struggle in a systematic way. Conversely, in Egypt in the weeks leading up to the mass protests against Mubarak at Tahrir square, youth activists from several opposition parties connected with Cairo's Bulaq al-Dakrour slum district whose march towards the centre of the town snowballed into the massive demonstrations of 28 January 2011. These were galvanized by the Friday prayer congregations, mobilized by the Muslim Brotherhood. Whereas in Cairo in January 2011, the nodal points along which the protests coalesced multiplied, the occupy movement in London and the violent riots that rocked parts of the British capital in the summer of the same year remained politically unconnected.

I have argued that the events in Tunisia and Egypt erupted within a densely interconnected space. Satellite TV and the Arabic blogosphere contributed to expanding Arab tropes that were not dominated by the propaganda of the state, opening up new spaces for dissent. Until the 1990s, citizens in the Arab world had to rely either on western news sources or the heavily censored news outlets in their own countries. The first pan-Arabic satellite TV station to change this was the Middle East Broadcasting Centre which was launched in London in 1991.[35] Several independent broadcasters followed, many of them based in the British capital. But it was not until the launch of Al-Jazeera in 1996 in Doha that the international media landscape changed on a global scale creating a counterbalance to the dominance of the BBC and CNN. The Iranian owned Al-Alam news network and the Saudi owned Al-Arabiya followed in 2003, adding further layers to an increasingly multifaceted, highly politicized Arabic news sphere.

There is no suggestion here that the pan-Arab field I am delineating is entirely new. Of course, there had been an Arab consciousness before the recent changes. Such an Arab 'nodal point' around which several narratives coalesced was compounded by a common Islamic history, modern experiments such as Ba'thism and Nassirism and a common cultural and artistic realm that reaches from the Egyptian diva Umm Kulthum, whose iconic songs were broadcasted by the official Egyptian media alongside Nassir's anti-imperial proclamations, to the poetry and writings of Noble Laureate Naguib Mahfouz and the Palestinian Mahmoud Darwish. In the political realm, pan-Arab nationalism was articulated in the pamphlets and writings of Michel Aflaq and Sati al-Husri among many others. They were widely distributed in the Mashreq in the twentieth century, especially in Syria and Iraq, where their ideas advocating pan-Arabism became a part of the national educational curriculum.[36]

Furthermore, the modernist Arab nationalist message of yesterday was embedded in new artistic movements. In Egypt, the Contemporary Art Group founded in 1946 and the Group of Modern Art established a year later used a folkloric and populist style to invent and facilitate the growth of a politicized national consciousness in the country which was meant to have a pan-Arab appeal. Under the growing influence of Nassirism, especially after the successful coup of 1952, artists such as Abdel Hady El-Gazzar, Hamed Nada and Hamed Owais put forward a socialist-revolutionary utopia that was aestheticized through 'artistic propaganda'. Images of bulky peasants, workers and women in revolt who would serve the nation on their path to national development were meant to simulate an alternative form of Arab modernity. This was art in the service of power which was framed during the 1940s and 1950s by notions of Arab nationalism that partially harked back to pre-Islamic myths and imagery. In Egypt, this kind of nationalism evoked a pharaonic style, in Iraq a form of 'Mesopotamian art' and in Syria 'Assyrian' imaginations. All of this was geared to secularized state politics and was detached, by ideological necessity, from centuries of Islamic art. Counter-cultural movements were not entirely muted by this wave of modernist artistic propaganda, however. For instance, in Egypt, resistance to state-sponsored art came from audacious women such as Inji Eflatoun, one of many who were imprisoned due to their radical critique of the politics of the day.[37] Indeed, state sponsored art was monolithic, rigid and an easy target for resistance art which repeatedly challenged the fixed narratives propagated by the political elites tied to the state with immense artistic vigour and innovation.

The purpose of this short and incomplete foray into the politics of art is to indicate that art in the service of power, central to constructing identities and national narratives amenable to the politics of the state, has provoked counter-movements that are innovative and radical. Such expressions of resistance art are particularly apparent in Palestine of course, for instance in Laila Shawa's 'Walls of Gaza' series which depicts the graffiti images, symbols and messages that were used by Palestinians to communicate amongst each other and to send messages to the Israeli soldiers during the successive intifadas in the occupied territories.[38] Resistance art is not only meant to challenge power, in this case the oppressive power of the Israeli state, but it contributes to a political subjectivity that defies the status quo. In this sense, it creates urgency, reinforcing an idea of art as an insurgent act of trans-cultural mobility. Thus, it promises to refigure the practical translation of resistance in the occupied territories into a new space that is exactly in between politics and aesthetics. As Bashir Makhoul argues in an interview on the cultural colonization of contemporary art co-published by the Tate Museum in Liverpool: Resistance art can and perhaps should be as tactically agile as strategies of resistance pursued by radicals on the ground. According to him 'this idea of tactical agility is something that can be used at many levels, from military resistance to making a painting but perhaps most importantly at the level of identity'. Makhoul refers to the movements that resistance art should provoke, in this case movements within the idea of Palestinian-hood. A constantly shifting idea of the meaning of Palestine would not only reflect the reality of the interrupted and dispersed national narrative that Palestinians grapple with, it could complement a flexible resistance strategy that would outmanoeuvre the enemy:

> If we think of an important attribute of a resistance such as its ability to appear and disappear in the background – something you can't do with a column of tanks. What creates fear and insecurity for the occupying force is not knowing where or who their enemy is . . . What could be more threatening to the national identity of a rigid nationalistic state such as Israel than an enemy that cannot be pinned down whose identity is also constantly shifting?[39]

The focus of Makhoul on the dialogue between art and identity is an interesting reminder that resistance art promises to turn the individual into an entangled transit hub connecting her to a vast, universal network of stations, switches and crossings. But what is underestimated here is the penetrative fluidity of post-modernized forms of power that are geared exactly towards identifying, cloistering and ostracizing that kind of radical infrastructure. The policy of identification manifesting itself in the tightly woven administrative web that Israel has spun across the West Bank and Gaza serves as an example here. Israel has set up a centralized hierarchy of commands and responsibilities that effectively incorporates the region into Israel's body politic. Such bureaucratic incorporation was matched by supervisionary strategies aimed at enumerating, monitoring and surveying as many Palestinian 'objects' as possible.[40] In 1970, for instance, the Israeli military delivered a detailed report on the 'Palestinian economy and population, listing the precise number of licensed carpenters, printing presses, fire trucks, and water wells'.[41] Each Palestinian received a numbered card from the state that had to be carried at all times, facilitating the military's ability to track dissidents and rebels. This rationalization of administrative control over the population has been a key source of Israel's supervisionary power in Palestine until today.

Through its aesthetic syntax and transcendental message, resistance art has the power to cross such structural constraints and to cut through the confinements that they are meant to fortify. Resistance art creates an immediate intervention in rigid systems; it can contribute to the momentum that cuts through ideological and historically structured causalities, in this case Zionism. It is for this reason that the poetry of Mahmoud Darwish has been so central to the re-figuration of Palestinian identity. The poetry of Darwish not only transverses the ideology of the Israeli state, it also creates a particular form of desire in the Fanonian sense that promises to link up to a universal possibility that defies narrow spatialization. 'As soon as I *desire* I am asking to be considered', Fanon wrote famously. 'I demand that notice be taken of my negating activity . . . insofar as I do battle for the creation of a human world – that is a world of reciprocal recognitions.'[42] Comparable to Fanon's writings and anti-colonial activism, the resistance poetry of Darwish empowers its addressees, heaving them into a new space beyond the oppressive status quo. For the colonized, confined spaces, even the idea of Palestinian nationalism in the case of Darwish, always also means imprisonment. The trans-spatial spirit that defies provincial definitions of Palestine is encapsulated in the ending of one of Darwish's most prominent poems, titled *Madeeh al-Thill al-'Aaly* (In Praise of the High Shadow):

> How large the revolution,
> How narrow the journey
> How grand the idea
> How small the state![43]

Darwish wrote the poem on the deck of one of the refugee ships carrying Palestinians from Beirut to Tunisia in the aftermath of the devastating Israeli invasion of Lebanon in 1982. His own *hegra* exemplifies that resistance art in this irresistibly humanistic mode begets an invasion of space, structure, regimes of truth; it creates the opportunity for emancipatory effect. This is resistance art at its best: combative, syncretic, iconographic, transversal. Yet in much of the western world, art has succumbed to the whims of the market, it is organized by what Adorno and Horkheimer so aptly termed the culture industry. Many see the pop creations of Andy Warhol 'who boasted he could produce as many works of art in a day through mechanical reproduction as Picasso could in a lifetime', as an early symptom for this commodification of art.[44] Today market-oriented artists such as Damien Hirst are worthy heirs to the apolitical nausea of Warhol. Who could imagine him to step up and identify himself as a revolutionary as Pablo Picasso (1881–1973) did upon his accession to the French Communist Party (PCF) in 1944? 'Yes, I am aware of having always struggled by means of my painting, like a genuine revolutionary', Picasso famously stated.[45] In today's politically correct art world dominated by western galleries, museums, dealers and auction houses such a statement seems highly improbable. As Jonathan Harris correctly implies in that regard, through the domination of the 'culture industry' by the west

> a decisive and *illicit* re-description or translation of meaning and value takes place . . . this is what 'cultural colonisation' or 'curatorial imperialism' essentially amounts to: the removal of an artefact's initial and authentic identity, and, by association, the true identity of its makers.[46]

This identity theft of non-western art and its concomitant sanitization in the culture industry has left a void for artistically inspired political activism which was central to the avant-garde in the 1950s and 1960s. For the various occupy movements this lack of an artistic culture of resistance constituted yet another dilemma: there was simply no counter-cultural infrastructure that could have taken up their cause and that the protesters could have lodged into in order to disseminate (and aestheticize) their message more effectively. Conversely, the Arab revolts achieved such transversal dialogue beyond cultures and beyond different strata of society through an eclectic melange of graffiti art, rap music and poetry, all geared to the common aim of revolution. Consequently, at least in Egypt and Tunisia, the demonstrators created a semiotically diverse disruption of public order, a disorderly collage of different styles that were anti-systemic and that communicated beyond generations. The art and activism of the talented Ahmed Basiony who was gunned down by snipers from the Egyptian Police Force in January 2011 serves as a tragic example here.[47] The rap songs of Hamada Ben Amor in Tunisia and the radical lyrics of the Alexandrian rap group Revolution in Egypt are others. These artistic vibes resounded with and echoed the resistance poetry of twentieth-century romantics such as Aboul-Qasem Echebbi (1909–1934) to create a unique sampling act that defied the prevalent norms and aestheticized the message of resistance, effectively communicating it to society and the state. The poem *Ila tughat al-'alam* (To the Tyrants of the World) written by Echebbi (Al-Shabbi) during the French occupation of Tunisia at the beginning of the twentieth century encapsulates this culturally diverse space that the revolts opened up. During the second Palestinian initifadah in 2002, the title was picked up and turned into a successful song and music video by the Tunisian vocalist Latife in opposition to the policies of Ariel Sharon and George W. Bush. In a grand synthesis of processed memory and creative resistance, the verses of the poem were chanted both in Tunisia and in Egypt in defiance of Ben-Ali and Mubarak respectively, and in solidarity with the universal cause for social justice and political empowerment. The poem itself is self-explanatory:

Hey you, the unfair tyrants

You the lovers of the darkness

You the enemies of life

You've made fun of innocent people's wounds; and your palm covered with their blood

You kept walking while you were deforming the charm of existence and growing seeds of sadness in their land

Wait, don't let the spring, the clearness of the sky and the shine of the morning light fool you

Because the darkness, the thunder rumble and the blowing of the wind are coming toward you from the horizon

Beware because there is a fire underneath the ash

Who grows thorns will reap wounds

You've taken off heads of people and the flowers of hope; and watered the cure of the sand with blood and tears until it was drunk

The blood's river will sweep you away and you will be burned by the fiery storm.[48]

The revolts in Tunis and Cairo transposed this poem of Echebbi from the anti-colonial battles in the beginning of the twentieth century to the battle against oppressive post-colonial states today in a grand display of the intrusive powers of cultural memory. Such resistance poetry did not stand alone during the revolts. It was flanked by the slogans of graffiti artists, the samples of rappers and the rhythmic chants of the demonstrators. The calls for 'a revolution of freedom and dignity' (*thawrat al-hurriyyah wa al-karamah*) was not only communicated in narrow political terms then; it was recited within a rich culture and resonated with pre-existing memories. Ultimately, the Arab revolts rekindled an audible mixture of resistance poetry, music and art which circulated sonorously through all strata of society.

Between Islamutopia and Islamocracy

I have suggested that the Arab revolts unleashed immediate transversal movements that cut through several layers of state and society. These transversal movements cannot only be observed in the participation of different strata in the demonstrations and the resistance art of the radicals, for it also buttressed significant shifts within the discourse of Islam. At this historical juncture in the Arab and Muslim world, we witness a mixture of Islam, democracy, cosmopolitanism, and nationalism superseded by stringent calls for democratic representation and social justice. Within this space a hybrid, post-modernist 'Islamocratic' politics is emerging. One significant debate about the role of Islam, as a cultural and political force, illustrates this core of what is happening in West Asia and North Africa: a truly innovative evolution that enmeshes universal principles of freedom, democracy and social equality with what I call 'Islamutopia'.[49] The revolts were after all taking place in Muslim-majority societies, where massive demonstrations were held after Friday prayers, prayer-rugs were laid out in front of tanks, and nationalist sentiments and slogans were permeated by Islamic symbols. But what is striking about this moment is that this entire Islamic complex is now directed towards democracy and social equality. Islam is realizing its latent social and cultural force, transforming itself into a 'post-modernised Islam' that is a significant departure from the deterministic, totalitarian 'Islamism' of previous generations which continues to linger on at the margins of the political mainstream.

To contextualize these current changes some historical background is needed. Whenever contemporary Islamists ponder their own genealogy, there are two pivotal figures that invariably come up to invigorate their imaginings. These two reference points of contemporary political Islam are

Sayyid Jamal al-din al-Afghani (or Asadabadi) and his disciple Mohammad Abduh. Afghani and Abduh lived through a tumultuous period for the *umma* whose decline as an organized political entity they tried to prevent in theory and in praxis. They were battling against the inevitable, however, and did not live long enough to witness the abolishment of the caliphate in Turkey in 1924. Now with the Arab revolts yielding a new spring for the (neo)Islamists, parallels to these pioneers of the Islamic revival are being dusted down. Are we at the dawn of a new Islamic era in West Asia and North Africa? With the Muslim Brotherhood winning both the parliamentary and presidential elections in Egypt, the electoral victory of Ennahda in Tunisia, the emergence of 'neo-Ottoman' politics in Turkey, 'neo-Shi'i' authoritarianism in Iraq and the continued influence of the Islamic republic in Iran the headlines almost write themselves. There is no doubt that there is something Islamic about what is happening. But what is it exactly?

Intellectuals and scholars have been generally uncomfortable engaging with Islam as a subject matter, lest they would compromise the secular dictum of the social sciences. Few in burgeoning disciplines such as International Relations (IR) would accept that belief systems such as Islam are valid units of analysis. This bias reveals a distinctly Eurocentric orthodoxy that permeates the curricula of many of our universities, a topic that has recently been tackled in books by Arlene Tickner and David Blaney on the one side and more progressively by Meghana Nayak and Eric Selbin on the other.[50] Yet a secular analysis of political discourses of Islam, systematic ideational inventions that use Islamic symbols, norms, metaphors, and imagery for ideological and political purposes, is very necessary to understand the trajectories of Muslim-majority societies. We are currently witnessing the birth of a post-modernized Islam, an eclectic experimentation, new interpretations being tried and new forms of legislations being experimented with, all within a discursive field claimed to be authentically Islamic. And yet in most interpretations of what is happening, from the opinion pieces of pundits in the mainstream media, to recent novels and movies, Islam as politics is either trivialized and occulted or demonized and exaggerated. As such, the meanings of discourses of Islam are disguised to the detriment of our understanding of what is happening in West Asia and North Africa at the very moment I am writing these lines.

It was a feature of the modernist precursor of the current experiment in the late nineteenth century that it yielded extraordinarily new forms of Islamic thinking even as it failed to deliver politically the utopia of a pan-Islamic renaissance. Abduh and Afghani re-opened the gates of *ijtihad*, or independent reasoning, questioning the orthodoxy of the clergy and the anti-philosophical leanings of the most prominent Islamic institutions, including al-Azhar in Cairo in the case of Abduh, and the Shi'i seminaries in the case of al-Afghani. Their discourse was pregnant with an 'Avicennian Islam', imbued with the dialectical musings of the classical Islamic philosophers, doyens of political thought such as al-Farabi, Ibn Sina, Ibn Rushd and Ibn Khaldun. And yet in Abduh and Afghani we also find the beginnings of something else, traces of the violent ruptures of modernity exemplified by their emphasis on the ideological merit of Islam – *Islam din wa dawla*, Islam as religion and governance. It is the promise of this Islamutopia, not merely a desire to conquer the state, that motivates many rank and file Islamists to venture into the realm of Machiavellian politics in many ways until today.

The decline of the Caliphate in 1924 and the emergence of authoritarian, militarized and semi-dependent post-colonial states was a caesura so traumatic that even today's politics, Islamist and other, continue to be affected. It is not too far-fetched to generalize that for the modernist Islamists from Abduh to Khomeini, Qutb to Mawdudi, al-Banna to Iqbal, Islam was the answer to the social, political, economic and cultural decline of the *umma*. These modernist Islamists invented many Islams. They were assembled to be suitable enough to function in the modernist mode, as agendas for socio-economic organization, governance, cultural policies, or in the case of a famous *fatwa* of Ayatollah Khomeini, to provide jurisprudential cover for transsexual surgery.

Moreover, opening up the gates of *ijtihad* de-monopolized the authority of the orthodox clergy. Suddenly, laymen such as al-Banna and Qutb, the engineers of the *Ikhwan* in Egypt, proclaimed an authentic Islam that would transgress the interpretation of the clergy questioning their institutionalized power and sovereignty. Likewise, Ali Shariati in Iran and Mohammad Iqbal in the sub-continent deemed their poetics of politics intellectually superior to the prevalent clerical jurisprudence. Centuries of *tafsir*, the interpretation of the Qur'an and *fiqh*, or Islamic jurisprudence, were superseded by the necessities of the politics of the day which required formulations of Islam that were amenable to ideological mobilization, almost as if Islam is what one makes of it. Trends in the opposite direction were discernible too. Clerics such as Ayatollah Khomeini in Iran and Ayatollah Baqir al-Sadr in Iraq tried to galvanize the clerical class into political action in opposition to the quietist tradition among the Shi'i *marja'a al-taghlid* (sources of emulation) represented by influential clerics such as Ayatollah Kho'i in Iraq who kept abreast of politics. This was also an effort to close down the epistemic community, to monopolize authority in the hands of the clerical class, to control the anarchy of *ijtihad* that Abduh and al-Afghani's intellectual revolution inadvertently brought about.[51]

The differences in what is happening today become further visible by comparing the political thought of the founders of the Muslim Brotherhood in Egypt with that of the movement's current leaders and other neo-Islamists. Modernist Islam had a radical connotation, expressed in what I call a Qutbian syntax. For Qutb, Islam 'is a revolutionary concept and a way of life, which seeks to change the prevalent social order and remould it according to its own vision.'[52] In response to western imperialism and authoritarian states in the Arab world, Qutbian Islam did away with philosophy in favour of ideology. In a radical twist of meanings, 'the word Muslim became the name of an international revolutionary party that Islam seeks to form in order to put its revolutionary programme into effect.'[53] Jihad was not the individual's spiritual path to God. In the Qutbian discourse, it 'signifies that revolutionary struggle involving the utmost use of resources that the Islamist party mobilises in the service of its cause.'[54] Islam as revolution; Iran in 1979 experienced it as I will explain further in the fifth interregnum.

The first generation of the *Ikhwan*, which was established by Hassan al-Banna in 1928, defined Islam as an all-encompassing ideology, an instrument to realize explicit political aspirations – an approach that was shared by later figures such as Sayyid Qutb and (allowing for some doctrinal differences) Ayatollah Khomeini and his followers in Iran. Modern Islamism was equipped with enough political vigour, radical fervour and doctrinal content to fight on two fronts. The first was to battle with the authoritarian states that emerged after the demise of the Ottoman Empire following the First World War, and within the context of the imperial system enforced primarily by Britain and France. In the period of intense upheaval and political uncertainty that followed, the paternalistic post-colonial state in West Asia and North Africa (and elsewhere in the global south) was born.

In this context of insecurity, the military emerged as the primary force in the making and preservation of state power. This had nothing to do (as some western Orientalists argued) with any particular Arab or Muslim propensity for a strong state. It was rather rooted in the historical circumstances of the end of the Ottoman system, and the emergence of nation-states with weak bureaucracies and minimal institutional support. The Islamists who contested the new settlement understood themselves to be facing an adversary with two aspects: the militarized state itself, and the neo-imperial intrusions into domestic affairs that continued even after the formal retreat of European imperialism. The Islamists' credo was *Islam din wa dawla* (Islam is religion and state), a dominant version of the faith that encompassed both the conception of an independent, self-sufficient state and a comprehensive religious system that could satisfy the individual's spiritual needs.

This imagined Islam – partially modelled on a modern version of the *salaf*, the pious compatriots of the Prophet Muhammad – was pitted against an equally imagined west, reduced to a materialistic, invasive and largely evil construct. Occidentalism versus Orientalism; a homogenous alien force counterposed to an elusive, longed-for *homo islamicus*; a minimalistic, dense and total Islam seen against a similarly distorted, monolithic west. This discourse was to impose itself in Iran in 1979, a revolutionary event that (along with the struggle against Soviet forces in Afghanistan in the 1980s) helped open the great, politicized retrieval of Islamic politics that followed.

Today, the context in which Islams reveal themselves is rather different. In the political arenas of Egypt, Iran, Tunisia and Bahrain, they do not function as revolutionary programmes. There is no Khomeini at their head; no Islamist manifesto driving people's actions; no headquarters topped by a green flag coordinating things. Post-modern Islam is diffuse, networked, differentiated, multi-institutional and (in the sense that it is neither paternalistic nor primarily feminist) 'transsexual'. Post-modern Islam floats freely on the world-wide-web, and links up with the universal move towards democracy, social equality and resistance to political tyranny. It has put a new face to the book, one that is far less angry and more empathetic to the demands of society and other political actors than was 'Qutbian Islam'.

Post-modern Islam can afford the luxury of being democratic because it is formed in a context that is less fluid and insecure than that in the early twentieth century when 'Islamism' was born. Islamism was raw, unmitigated and apostolic in its political prescriptions; by contrast, post-modern Islam

matured within the nascent and latent civil societies in West Asia and
North Africa, and is filtered through a pluralistic space permeated by many
institutions. Today, the *Ikhwan* itself is in no way a vanguard movement of the
kind envisaged by Sayyid Qutb. It is an amalgam of charitable organizations,
social endowments and political factions: a pluralistic abstraction rather than
a substantive, driven, totalitarian movement. The deities of yesterday are
being questioned and partially dethroned. As the brother of Hassan al-Banna
recently conceded in an interview:

> Hassan al-Banna was before anything else an educator and his principles and
> his teachings went in this direction. With time, it seems that [the *Ikhwan*]
> have started forgetting his instructions and for now, it is obvious that they
> are adopting a different approach than the one presented by my brother. But
> the realities of life impose certain actions and things never go the way you
> expect them to. The world is changing and the MB [Muslim Brotherhood]
> should not treat Hassan al-Banna as a god. The events that went on during
> his time are long gone and if there is need for changes, these changes are
> welcomed.[55]

As a consequence of this pragmatism of the neo-Islamists, there is no Qutbian
vanguard that is specific and deterministic about the contours of the 'Islamic
state'. Rather, there is an 'Avicennian political realism' that is utilitarian and
cautious, indeterminate in its prescriptions and post-ideological in its political
syntax. In this emerging discourse, prescriptions such as 'Islam is . . .' and 'Islam
must be . . .' are succeeded by formulations such as 'Islam may add . . .' and
'Islam could be . . .'. This is a profound shift, one that is discernible in many
speeches of the leaders of the *Ikhwan* in Egypt and the *Ennahda* (Renaissance)
party in Tunisia as well as by proclamations and strategic papers of some of the
reformists in Iran.

As a consequence, current inventions of Islam revert to an Avicennian
realism that is characterized by pragmatic politics, quite contrary to the radical
upheaval demanded by people like Mawdudi, Khomeini and Qutb. If for the
latter, Islam was a revolutionary panacea to western imperialism and tyrannical
regimes, today Ghannouchi talks about dialogue, pluralism, democracy and
women's rights, for instance in his first interview when he returned from exile
to Tunisia in 2011 after the successful ouster of Zine El Abidine Ben Ali: 'There
is no limit to political pluralism other than the condition of rejecting violence,

and giving anyone the right to found the party', Ghannouchi emphasized. 'There is full acceptance of the full legal rights of women . . . We recognise that Tunisians have the freedom to believe in anything, to leave or embrace any faith, as faith is a personal matter . . . For the Tunisia that we are working towards, one in which women enjoy equality, people can establish and join any party and they have the freedom to adopt any faith.'[56] On the gender question there has been a considerable shift too. Ennahda has not moved to abandon the Personal Status Code in Tunisia which was introduced by Habib Bourguiba in 1956 (amended in 1993) and which abandoned polygamy and secured several matrimonial rights for women, including a judicial process for divorce. In the first free elections of the new Tunisia in October 2011 after the downfall of the Ben-Ali regime, 49 women were elected to the 217-member constituent assembly or parliament; out of those 42 represent Ennahda.

Contemporary (neo)Islamists have departed from the totalitarianism of yesterday (and their personal radicalism in the past). Socialized into the politics of the Arab and Muslim world, they were certainly fascinated and imbued by the revolution in Iran and the radical politics of independence that sustained it – Ghannouchi dedicated one of his books to Khomeini and the Egyptian presidential candidate Mohamed Selim El-Awa gave several keynote speeches at pan-Islamic conferences in Tehran – but despite persistent proclamations by Iranian leaders, including Ayatollah Ali Khamenei, to the contrary, none of the current movements have contemplated adopting the Iranian model which developed in lieu with modern Shi'i political thought and here especially Khomeini's re-conceptualization of the Usuli school towards the doctrine of the *velayat-e faqih*, the guardianship of the Supreme Jurisprudent.[57] While it is true that in Iran in 1979, as in Arab capitals in 2010, people carried their demonstrations with slogans 'against despots . . . against dictatorship' and in support of the 'dignity of individuals . . . freedom and democracy . . . [and] ethical and moral values' as the Iranian Foreign Minister Ali Akbar Salehi recently stated,[58] it is equally true to argue, certainly from the perspective of a large section of Iranian society who continue to resist the theocratic elements of the Iranian state, that those norms have not been achieved, that many deemed the Islamist takeover after the revolution a betrayal of those initial goals and that the Islamic Republic has not ensured an inclusive order that would safeguard the human dignity of all Iranians irrespective of their political persuasion. So really the narrative of the Iranian state that the Arab revolts were 'Islamic awakenings' against authoritarianism and in favour of democracy and freedom is an ironic reminder that these lofty goals are still to be attained in Iran itself. As some Iranians pondered on social networking sites: 'chera Tunis tunest, va Iran natunest?' (why did Tunisia do it, and Iran could [did] not?).

If Khomeini spoke of the legitimate leadership of the clerics, El-Awa organized his failed presidential bid in Egypt around his theory of a 'hermeneutical Islam'. This includes six signposts that are typical for the political agendas of Muslim democrats today: First, al-Awa argues that governance in an Islamic state is not predetermined given that in 'neither the Quran nor the Sunnah does Islam prescribe a specific system of government . . . In the political field, this is compatible with the nature of Islamic legislations which are characterised by complete flexibility.'[59]

Second, citizens are considered to be both subjects and objects of their laws which they are free to amend in accordance with the necessities of the period. Accordingly, the 'ummah (community) should be able to exercise its free will in choosing and appointing the ruler. The actual procedure is left for the community to determine, and may therefore differ from time to time and from one place to the other.' Islamic democracy should be engineered in theory and in praxis through 'the election of the head of state and of the people's representatives through direct free elections.'[60] There should not be a Supreme Jurisprudent ultimately nominated for life as in the Iranian case or any provision about the religiosity of the candidates, who are, in Iran, vetted for their Islamic credentials by the Council of Guardians, a Supreme Court of some sort. Rather, 'all citizens should have the right to participate, and appointment to the office should be for a limited period. No group or individual should be excluded from the process or deprived of the right to nominate themselves or elect others.'[61]

Third, and typical for the interpretative twist and turns of other democrats with a Muslim persuasion such as the late Mohammad Arkoun and Abdol-Karim Soroush in the Iranian context, al-Awa deems freedom 'an indispensable Islamic value, guaranteed and considered to be instinctive'. In particular, 'political freedom in Islam, is a branch of a general fundamental right: the freedom to choose'. The fact that throughout the centuries Islam's language and syntax has been constructed around duties rather than rights is turned into an advantage: 'Voicing one's opinion is not just permissible but is an Islamic duty,' al-Awa argues. 'Scholars of *usul* (fundamentals) define a *wajib* (duty) as being 'the action that is imperatively demanded' and consider a person who fails to execute such an action to be a sinner.'[62] A fourth and fifth right is added to this set of values: 'Equality before the law and equity in the treatment of citizens and in the assessment of their rights and liberties are essential Islamic values.' The Qur'anic phrase 'Let there arise out of you a band of people inviting to all that is good, enjoining what is right and forbidding what is wrong' is turned into a normative obligation to engineer and sustain a social and political order that is just.[63]

The sixth point that al-Awa puts forward indicates another difference to the Iranian model. In Iran, in the conservative interpretation of the role of the *vali-e faqih* (the Supreme Jurisprudent), Ayatollah Khamenei is ultimately accountable to God. Conversely, self-proclaimed Muslim democrats such as al-Awa argue that the prophet Muhammad did not endorse absolute governance or hereditary rule by the Household of the prophet or the *ahl-e bayt* as the conservative wings of the Shi'i *ulema* in Iran and elsewhere among the Twelver Shi'i argue. Rather, 'rulers are accountable to the community and are responsible for looking after its affairs . . . No ruler succeeding the Prophet has the right to claim an immunity that the Prophet himself did not enjoy.'[64]

So here Islam is not presented as unchangeable, total, fundamentalist, yet instead it is reinvented as a relative system of thought that needs to be constantly reinterpreted to fit the current circumstances. Islam is primarily considered a cultural force and source of identity that follows politics rather than predetermining it. Hence, the new Islamists are entirely promiscuous in their choice of strategies and allies. There are almost no taboos when it comes to this new mode of Islamist politics. While there is an absence of an anti-imperial discourse and an explicitly pro-Palestinian agenda at least at this stage, there is an emphasis on national independence which is likely to yield a rather more distant relationship to the United States and bolder proclamations regarding Palestinian statehood in the long term. Differences notwithstanding, I think it is this type of post-modernized Islam that fuels the mainstream politics of the Islamic parties in Egypt, that rules in Turkey in the form of

Erdogan's AKP, that governs Tunisia and that feeds into the reform process in Iran and elsewhere in the region too. The molar shifts from the apostolic, intransigent, opprobrious postulations of 'Qutbian Islam' that were geared to radical change, if not revolution, to the post-modernized mode is not absolute. Quite literarily there are residues of modernity in post-modernity. But the context of politics in the Arab and Islamic world has changed and so have the forms of political expression and organization: US hegemony is very different from British imperialism. There is no formal control of what is happening in the Arab and Muslim world anymore. The current leaders of Ennahda in Tunisia and the Ikhwan in Egypt do not have to fight British and/or French colonialists as Abduh and Afghani felt compelled to do during the Urabi rebellion in Egypt (1881–1882) and the Tobacco revolt in Iran (1891) respectively. And yet, US power, more abstract, clandestine, molar and eclectic (and thus more difficult to detect), continues to impinge on a lot that is happening in West Asia and North Africa.

So in tone and syntax this type of post-modernized Islam has departed from mainstream Muslim politics of the twentieth century and the revolutionary Iranian variant. Here as well I am not speaking of strictly delineated periods, but paradigmatic shifts in the way dominant discourses of Islam are expressed and rendered useful for politics. For instance, in Egypt al-Awa and the reformist wings of the Ikhwan built upon the work of luminaries such as Sheikh Muhammad al-Ghazzaly (1917–1996) whose voluminous scholarly works critiquing Qutbian Islamism expressed a democratic politics of Islam that resonates with many contemporary ideas, even those of some of the secularists in Egypt and beyond.[65] On the other side of the spectrum, there is the work of Nasr Hamid Abu Zayd (1943–2010), whose hermeneutical reading of the Qur'an is comparable to the political thought of other critical theorists such as Mohammad Arkoun. The point I am making is that the current historical juncture has provided the opportunity for these 'secular-Islamic' approaches that emphasize a continuous politics of *islah* (reform) and the concomitant virtue of *sulh* (peaceful action) and *amal salih* (pious deed), terms that are central to the syntax of the Qur'an, to come to the fore more prominently. At the same time, current events are not entirely unrelated to what happened in the twentieth century and in particular in Iran. The regional impact of the Iranian revolution may be compared to the opening that the Cuban revolution in 1953 provided to Central and South America. The emphasis on national independence by the Castros and Guevara may have been a symptom for the future politics of the region but it did not determine the emergence of the Chavezes, da-Silvas, Moraleses and Ortegas of this world. So while the revolution in Iran was a symptom of a potential post-American future of West Asia and North Africa, the current revolts in the Arab world are geared to different dynamics. Consequently, they have yielded politics that are less radical than Iran's in 1979 and that do not, at least at this stage, trump the Palestinian cause or decisively erode US claims to hegemony in the region. What seems to be certain in all of this is that the utopia of Islam, re-imagined by those yearning for it centuries later in the tumults of their own time, has been cast by generations of Islamists as one of justice, prosperity and power, animated by spirituality and by the mythical bravery of heroic figures. This Islamutopia still irradiates the politics of the Arab and Muslim world today and informs contemporary manifestations of power and resistance in a very immediate way.

Between Power and Resistance in Theory

Grip tha canon like Fanon and pass tha shells to my classmate
Lyrics of US group *Rage against the Machine*

Transversal struggles and the terror of modernity

In this interregnum, I present a detailed discussion of some of the theoretical approaches that engage with forms of power and resistance with an eye on the argument of the previous section and the conceptual propositions I have made. I have started to argue that the revolts in Tunisia and Egypt engendered transversal movements that were dispersed in different directions within and beyond society and which attacked the main tenets of the state. Transversal movements are neither characterized by hierarchy, pyramidal structures that are held together by a charismatic leader on top, a Castro, Khomeini, Lenin, or Mao, nor are they purely horizontal, devoid of an infrastructure that can relay political demands beyond the event (mass demonstrations, resistance camps, etc.). The definition of transversality offered by Felix Guattari is instructive in this regard:

> Transversality is a dimension that strives to overcome two impasses: that of pure verticality, and a simple horizontality. Transversality tends to be realised when maximum communication is brought about between different levels and above all in terms of different directions.[1]

Transversality appears here as a unifying difference. In politics a transversal movement conjoins heterogeneous discourses under a unifying agenda (revolt, revolution), which resists being moulded into a totalitarian monolith.

Transversal struggles are not premised on the politics of terror and violence, all encompassing ideologies, systematic militarism or the sole leadership of a charismatic figurehead. As such, they are productions of the an-archical condition of post-modernity, rather different from the essentialist and Cartesian certitudes that 'traditional' revolutions offered.

One way of fleshing out some of those suggestions is to look at previous forms of resistance in lieu with some of the major theoretical concepts that have been used to explain them. It is striking, as a starting point for this discussion, that the revolts in Tunisia and Egypt were not drenched in a 'blood orgy'; there was no ideological momentum that would legitimate a politics of terror. This is different from modernist revolutions. France in 1789 resembled Petrograd in September 1917 in one important way: The terror of the ancien régime was countered in word and deed by the terror of the revolutionaries. In other words, the modern European model for revolution was premised on the French *regime de la terreur* enforced by Robespierre and his followers. In fact, for Robespierre revolution was synonymous with terror: 'If the mainspring of popular government in peacetime is virtue, amid revolution it is at the same time virtue and terror.' This implies that a revolutionary process requires systematic violence; terror and virtue are co-constitutive, they feed upon each other, they are necessary components of the revolutionary order that promises freedom. In Robespierre's own words: 'Terror is nothing but prompt, severe, inflexible justice; it is therefore an emanation of virtue. It is less a special principle than a consequence of the general principle of democracy applied to our country's most pressing needs.'[2]

The Bolsheviks in Russia effectively applied a similar model. For Lenin, violence was a necessary and inevitable component of the historical dialectic of the communist revolution. The object of violence is restricted to the ruling classes, but violence and terror continue to be equated with the act of resistance itself. The Comintern handbook was clear on this issue:

> For the proletariat, armed insurrection is the highest form of political struggle . . . *Denial of the inexorable necessity for armed insurrection or, more generally for armed struggle against the ruling classes on the part of the proletariat, means automatically denial of the class struggle as a whole. It means denial of the very foundations of revolutionary Marxism and its reduction to an idious* [sic] *doctrine of non-resistance.*[3]

Resistance is equated here with violence which is deemed entirely 'rational' and necessary in order to bring about the communist utopia. Conversely, non-violent movements are not deemed authentic or revolutionary. In communist Russia, terror was not only thought a necessary strategy: the historical dialectic that was decreed in order to yield the proletarian revolution was presented as inevitable. As Maurice Merleau-Ponty famously stated in his apology for Stalinist terror published in 1946: 'The man who repudiates terrorism in principle – i.e. repudiates measures of suppression and intimidation towards determined and armed counterrevolution – must reject all ideas of the political supremacy of the working classes and its revolutionary leadership.' From this perspective violence had to target everyone objectively opposed to the revolution, with terror as the prerequisite for a just order: 'The man who repudiates the dictatorship of the proletariat repudiates the socialist revolution, and digs the grave of socialism.'[4]

Such notions of terror and rationalized violence were major products of a particular juncture of European modernity that was central to theories and practices of resistance for a long time. To be more precise: It was the *zeitgeist* of the Enlightenment with its immensely hubristic positivism and the ideological perversions that it provoked – in particular Fascism and Communism – that gave the terrorist subject the adequate habitat to function. It was after all this desire for the real, science, perfection, always also intertwined with the passion for purification, that characterized the Enlightenment. As Alain Badiou rightly argues: It was that penchant for purity that preceded and abetted both Nazism in Germany and Stalinism in Russia.[5]

If methods of terror and rationalized violence were characteristic of the French and the Russian revolution, guerrilla warfare is associated with the revolutions in China and Cuba. If terrorism emerged out of the French model, guerrilla warfare was a product of the non-western world. When Mao Zedong spearheaded the triumphant march of the People's Liberation Army on Beijing and proclaimed a People's Republic on the ruins of the Kuomintang regime in 1949, China's communists popularized guerrilla warfare as a viable form of resistance that could yield a revolution. Generations of self-proclaimed freedom fighters in the Third World drew their inspiration from the theories of Mao and the events in China. Guerrilla warfare was deemed a legitimate and effective liberation strategy. Movements in Vietnam, inspired by the

writings of General Vo Nguyen and current Maoist rebellions, for instance in
the border region separating Nepal (ruled by a Maoist government) and India,
have continued to be premised on this model of resistance.

The Cuban revolution embellished the model of guerrilla warfare further
and gave it a distinctly 'romantic' edge. With the successes in China, Vietnam
and Cuba in 1958 it appeared that this method of resistance would deliver
the promise of a just order and the development of viable political systems
responsive to the demands of the people. As such, at least in the post–Second
World War period, guerrilla warfare became the model for armed resistance
throughout the non-western world. From the perspective of the late Fred
Halliday, the reasons for this prevalence are sociological and structural. He
identifies the radicalization of the intelligentsia and the emergence of a new
class of uprooted peasants as primary sociological factors. The stalemate
created by Mutually Assured Destruction (MAD), on the other side, 'inhibited
outright war between states in the two blocks of the Cold War' necessitating
guerrilla war as a 'means of pursuing military conflict without this leading to
an outright nuclear confrontation'.[6]

Halliday is right to point out that in the absence of a hot war between the
Soviet Union and the United States, guerrilla wars were supported in order to
battle out proxy wars on the vast turf of the 'non-aligned world'. But he fails
to discuss the distinct intellectual habitat that gave meaning and sustenance
to such forms of violent resistance. To that end, the literature in post-colonial
studies is instructive because it engages with the ideas of Frantz Fanon, Jean-
Paul Sartre and Ernesto Che Guevara who espoused both the concept of
armed insurrection and guerrilla warfare. In their manuals and proclamations,
violence is presented as a necessary strategy to combat colonial oppression and
dependent governments in the name of a higher ideal. Fanon is particularly
straightforward and practical in that regard. According to him, revolutionary
change would be brought about not by the 'westernised proletariat' as
Marxists would have it, but by the poor peasantry, 'the wretched of the earth',
who constitute the real revolutionary class in the non-western world. In this
dialectic between the oppression of the colonizer and its oppressed subject,
violence was deemed inevitable. In the words of Fanon himself: '[V]iolence
of the colonial regime and counter-violence of the native balance each other
and respond to each other in an extraordinary reciprocal homogeneity.'[7] From

this perspective, the colonized subject does not have the luxury to choose between non-violent resistance and violent insurgency. Fanon suggests that the violence of the colonized is an effect of the violence of colonial oppression and the authoritarian rule of the bourgeois, westernized natives tied to that system. Here, he used his insights into psychotherapy to argue that violent resistance is the only way to counter the cognitively penetrating abuses of the colonialists. There exists, then, a dialectic, a sort of abusive reciprocity, between agent and structure, subject and object, native and colonizer, that makes violence inevitable.

Fanon wrote *The Wretched of the Earth* during a period when colonialism was a reality in most of sub-Saharan Africa. He was trying to gauge why the successful anti-colonial movements in Guinea-Bissau and in Algeria had not been replicated there. As Edward Said notes: 'Fanon is unintelligible without grasping that his work is a response to theoretical elaborations produced by the culture of late Western capitalism, received by the Third World native intellectual as a culture of oppression and colonial enslavement.'[8] To the psychotherapist Fanon, the colonial system must have felt callously penetrative, both in terms of physical encroachment (i.e. the colonization of territory) and cognitive abuse (e.g. the colonial mindset, torture, rape). Confronted and enveloped by this abusive system, Fanon argued that violence is intrinsic to the dialectics of history and that this violence had to be disseminated throughout the Third World to all those who were objectively opposed to revolution. Traces of Merleau-Ponty are apparent here. More specifically, Fanon advocated a strategy that would 'bleed out' the colonizers and that would make it economically unviable to retain the colonies. If imperialism transformed colonies into markets for the 'motherland', turning these markets into arenas of protracted warfare renders obsolete the profit rationale to keep them. To that end, it is not enough to get engaged in spontaneous acts of sabotage. What is needed is a systematic campaign of armed insurrection including a strategy of guerrilla warfare that would make the colonies ungovernable.

In the 1960s, Fanon drew inspiration from the Mau Mau revolt in Kenya and the peasant-led campaigns in the Congo to argue that a revolutionary party would grow out of the guerrilla campaigns recruited from the peasant class under the guidance of a revolutionary intelligentsia. Fanon was immersed in the revolutionary culture of the late 1950s and early 1960s, an immensely disruptive period when ideas of armed resistance floated freely in a transnational space dotted by the battles against the remnants of western imperialism. Traces of the rump theory on guerrilla warfare advocated by Fanon can be found in Che Guevara's manual on the same subject. Guevara defines the guerrilla band as an 'armed nucleus, the fighting vanguard of the people' that would draw its main strengths 'from the mass of the people themselves'.[9] Yet in contrast to Guevara, who was almost mechanical in his prescriptions, Fanon also included a metaphysical momentum to the struggle for independence. In *Black Skin, White Masks*, for instance, he argues that through anti-colonial violence, the native can reclaim his lost authenticity: 'At the level of individuals, violence is a cleansing force. It frees the native from his inferiority complex and from his despair and inaction.'[10] Violence is presented here as a cleansing ritual to rescue the 'self' from the exploitation of the 'other.' It must follow logically that Fanon rejected non-violent resistance as entirely 'inauthentic'.

As indicated, Fanon was writing during a period of massive violence. His direct experiences of the French massacres in Algeria and the abominations of imperial power in sub-Saharan Africa must have had an impact on the way he conceptualized his ideas on armed anti-colonialism. But there were also direct intellectual influences on him, in particular the writings of the aforementioned Maurice Merleau-Ponty (especially *Humanism et Terreur*, 1947) and the works of Jean-Paul Sartre, especially his play *The Devil and the Good Lord* and the voluminous *Critique of Dialectical Reason*. In the latter, Sartre affirms the dialectic of violence that was central to the methodical grid underlying the argument in *The Wretched of the Earth*. Sartre presents here, perhaps for the first time in such an elaborated fashion, a theory that entangles the forces of power and resistance with violence. In Sartre, the mechanical distinction between the two is pulverized in a grand display of dialectical rigour. If it is the 'crucial discovery of dialectical investigation that man is "mediated" by things to the same extent as things are "mediated" by man', as he argues, then the violent force of the imperial embrace must provoke its own counter-violence, not as a coincidence of history but per definition.[11]

Objectively, according to Sartre, violence creates indissoluble bonds. Violence does not sever the ties between colonizer and colonized, oppressed and oppressor; it binds together subject and object in an abusive embrace. This inter-relationship is elaborated in an intelligent paragraph on the dialectics between group solidarity and deviant behaviour in the middle sections of *Critique of Dialectical Reason*. In this part of the book, Sartre shows how violence begets fraternity. He starts by explaining the contingency of the group and the self-fulfilling prophecy thus ensued. He defines this 'fraternity' of the group as '*the right of all* through everyone and over everyone. It is not enough to recall that it is also violence, or that it originated in violence: it is violence itself affirming itself as a bond of immanence through positive reciprocities.'[12] 'Positive reciprocities' refer here to actual and real reciprocities rather than to a *normatively* 'positive reciprocity' as something 'commendable'. In other words, whether we like it or not violence has constitutive powers; violence is creative, it binds us together. Consequently, acts of violence by the group against the traitor do not divorce the two. The traitor cannot be 'excluded from the group; indeed he himself cannot extricate himself from it. He remains a member of the group in so far as the group – threatened by betrayal – reconstitutes itself by annihilating the guilty member . . . by discharging *all its violence* onto him.'[13] Such is the creative power of violence that it reaffirms that bond because the 'exterminating violence' of the group is 'still a link of fraternity between the lynchers and the lynched in that the liquidation of the traitor is grounded on the positive affirmation that he is *one of the group*; right up to the end, he is abused in the name of his own pledge and of the right over him which he acknowledged in the Others.'[14] The act of violence both reconfirms and constitutes a linkage between the lynchers, who reaffirm their fraternity and love for each other in the act of killing, and the lynched who is the object of violence exactly because he is a member of the group. If it was the aim to divorce him from the group once and for all, the deadly embrace does not keep its promise; it creates linkage not severance. 'In other words, anger and violence are lived both as Terror against the traitor and (if circumstances have produced this feeling) as a practical bond of *love* between the lynchers. Violence is the very power of this lateral reciprocity of love.'[15]

Starting from those theoretical propositions, Sartre charters the ways violence functions as a strategy in the colonial system. He proposes three 'levels of action' according to which the French operated in Algeria and elsewhere in the Muslim world: First, the 'physical liquidation of a number of

Muslims and the dissolution of their institutions, while they were not allowed to "enjoy" ours'; second, 'depriving indigenous communities of land ownership and transferring it to the newcomers through the brutal and deliberately over-rapid application of the civil code'; and third 'establishing the true bond between the colony and the metropolis (sales of colonial products at minimum prices, and purchases of manufactured goods from the metropolitan power at high prices) on the basis of systematic super-exploitation of the native'.[16] This is how the colonized is born into a system of oppression and violence that creates resentment and anger. Crucially, Sartre points out that the colonizer is implicated in the same colonial system that provokes similar symptoms of rage and compulsion. 'The son of the colonialist and the son of the Muslim are both the children of the objective violence which defines the system itself as a practico-inert hell.'[17] Sartre remains loyal to his dialectical analysis which is inspired by the famous reciprocity that Hegel attributed to the relationship between master and slave, apart from the synthesis that Hegel allows for in his dialectical musings. Much in that spirit, Sartre does not divorce oppressor and oppressed. Colonizer and colonized are trapped in the same cycle of violence of the colonial system. Both come out of it mentally damaged.

Comparable to violence which creates the group and the outlaw, self and other, as two protagonists involved in the drama of killing, the colonial system positions both the colonizer and the colonized on one stage. Sartre reiterates this productive dialectic of violence in his introduction to *The Wretched of the Earth* where he likens the book to 'the moment of the boomerang', when the violence of the oppressors comes back to haunt them.[18] All of this is far from arcane and irrelevant to contemporary culture. For instance, the emotive image of violent resistance is echoed in the alternative music world. In a track entitled 'Year of tha Boomerang' on their 1996 bestselling album *Evil Empire*, the US band *Rage against the Machine* makes reference to Fanon. The phrase 'grip tha canon like Fanon and pass tha shells to my classmate' exemplifies an unmistakeable aestheticization of the 'beauties' of violent resistance, much in the same way as Fanon and his contemporaries imagined it over five decades ago.

What kind of general discussion points can we discern from the conceptual suggestions with which I started this chapter and the theories of power and resistance that I have perused so far: First, it is safe to argue that today we have largely passed the period when guerrilla warfare is the dominant tactic to achieve political ends. It is striking that neither theories of terror nor guerrilla warfare have played a particular part in the revolts in Egypt and Tunisia and the unsuccessful upheaval in Iran in 2009. In the so-called Arab Spring the political event is not constituted through a protracted period of warfare between classes and regular and irregular armed units that would organize in the provinces. Today, mass movements are largely urban based and do not enact or move in accordance with a grand ideology. There are pockets of guerrilla warfare in places such as the India–Nepal border region, where Maoist groups continue to subscribe to armed insurrection, or in the Kurdish areas between Iran, Iraq and Syria. But these are exceptions, remnants of a bygone era. The common denominator of a majority of political struggles today is democracy and social justice and these demands are increasingly reflected in the vertical organization of the internal structures of the movements. At the same time, we are witnessing, perhaps for the first time in human history, the emergence of a universal, radical democratic space in which the resistance in one part of the world is linked to the resistance in a geographically distant area. The examples from different continents sketched out in the previous interregnum exemplify those linkages and the contagion of protests that spread around the world within a short period of time. This implies an important conceptual conclusion: There is nothing particularly Iranian or Arab about these revolts and nothing European, western or American about demands for democracy and social justice.

Liberal imaginations

Non-violent resistance, sometimes in lieu with limited armed confrontations, became more prevalent in Latin America in the 1980s and throughout West Asia and North Africa in the twenty first century. In Europe it was the non-violent resistance strategies of Mohandas Gandhi and Martin Luther King Jr that were espoused by leading dissidents such as Adam Michnik, Jacek Kuron and Lech Walesa in Poland, Vaclav Benda and Vaclav Havel in Czechoslovakia and Gyorgy Konrad in Hungary. There are at least two sets of literature in comparative politics and international relations that address such forms of non-violent resistance. The first approach may be termed 'liberal-functionalist'. It refers to the influential work of Gene Sharp, Peter Ackerman, Jack Duvall and more recently to the writings of Kurt Schock and Stephen Zunes among others.[19] The smallest common denominator of this approach is an emphasis on non-violent resistance or what Zunes and Schock term 'unarmed insurrections'. Schock defines unarmed insurrections 'as organised popular challenges to government authority that depend primarily on methods of nonviolent action rather than on armed methods'.[20] There is then a clear distinction between armed resistance and unarmed insurrections that reject violence as a form of protest. There is a second premise that derives from this: non-violent resistance to authoritarian regimes is necessary and viable and it must be the outcome of a utilitarian strategy. According to Schock: '[U]narmed insurrections typically involve pragmatic rather than principled nonviolence. Pragmatic nonviolence is characterised by a commitment to methods of nonviolent action due to their perceived effectiveness.' In other words, Schock puts particular emphasis on strategy and method rather than on the ethics or the morality of the struggle. From this perspective, pragmatic nonviolence is 'an attempt to inflict nonphysical pressure on the opponent during the course of the struggle to undermine the opponent's power, and an absence of nonviolence as a way of life.'[21] Ackerman and Duvall argue along similar lines. According to them, the simple fact that Mohandas Gandhi and Martin Luther King Jr, the most celebrated leaders of non-violent action, had a religious background does not mean that non-violent action is primarily driven by moral preferences. The true effectiveness of non-violent action is not linked to the climactic event, the spontaneous outpouring of popular sentiment. Rather, the power of the people is 'less theatrical than technical. It has little to do with shouting slogans and putting flowers in gun barrels. It has everything to do with separating governments from their means of control.'[22]

The liberal-functionalist approach draws heavily on a theoretical opening suggested by Gene Sharp almost four decades ago. Drawing on the writings of Mohandas Gandhi, Gustav Landauer and Leo Tolstoy, Sharp argues that the power of the state is never really total, that it cannot sufficiently function from the top-down without the acquiescence of the populace. To put it simply: The power of the state is dependent on the obedience of the people; power is sourced from the bottom-up or in the words of Sharp, 'obedience is the heart of political power'.[23] Sharp seems to contradict the orthodox Weberian notion that power claims and achieves obedience. Weber defined power as the 'probability that one actor within a social relationship will be in a position to carry out his own will despite resistance, regardless of the basis on which this probability rests.'[24] Sharp departs from this traditional view. He argues that power is only synonymous with control, oppression and inequality if people comply with it. As such, Sharp flips Weber around: Don't ask how power controls and moulds. Ask what it is you are doing that allows power to do so. For Sharp, power is only all-encompassing if there is no resistance to it.

At the same time, Sharp remains loyal to the functionalistic Weberian tradition that accentuates pragmatism over questions of morality and ethics. From this perspective, resistance to power is entirely goal oriented: the aim is to sever the sources of state power in order to transform a political system. There is no metaphysics or romanticism involved in the act of resistance, no poetics of martyrdom. Despite this absence of drama, strategized methods of non-violent action can produce revolutionary outcomes. If the power of the state cannot be sustained through brute force and violence, the argument goes, it can be unhinged if the regime is detached from its sources of support within society. Hence, Sharp suggests six major sources of power and lists 198 ways to counter them under the following categories: non-violent protest and persuasion, social economic and political non-cooperation, and psychological, social, economic and political intervention. More recently he argued:

> As I was completing the next to final chapter on the operation of nonviolent struggle, I was startled that nonviolent coercion was produced by restricting or severing those same sources of power. That confluence brought to nonviolent struggle the basis of potential political realism, and thereby facilitated the development of political policies employing this technique.[25]

Political realism is represented here as the counter-position to utopianism which is misunderstood as referring to goals that are by definition 'unrealistic' and hence impossible to pursue. In that vein Sharp writes in 1980:

> Far from being utopian, nonviolent sanctions build upon crucial parts of our past and present reality. Past cases, however, are only the crude beginnings of alternative nonviolent sanctions. These could be refined and developed to increase their power potential, and adapted to meet society's genuine need for sanctions. One of the major tasks before us is to learn better how nonviolent sanctions can be used more effectively in place of violent sanctions to preserve and defend societies.[26]

Non-violent action is presented here as a break-out strategy from the vicious cycle of violence. According to Sharp, even a brutal political system can be transformed by non-violent means if society is mobilized in that direction. As such, the liberal-functionalist position is at the opposite end of (neo)Marxist approaches that remain dominant in post-colonial studies. The latter tend to continue to sanction violence and guerrilla warfare as viable modes of resistance to tyrannical regimes, while the former categorically reject them: 'In distinct contrast to Marxist-inspired theories and praxis, which suggest that the state apparatus must be captured through force, or theories and praxis of guerrilla warfare which suggest that the state's capacities for violence must be worn down over time through a "people's war" of attrition,' Schock emphasizes, 'the nonviolent action approach maintains that methods of nonviolent action can produce "revolutionary" political change despite the state's superior coercive capacities'.[27] Referring to the ideas of Hannah Arendt, who denounced strategies of violence as inadequate to secure the power of the state in the long term, Ackerman and Duvall too argue against the 'nostrum of many would be revolutionaries, distilled by Mao Zedong in his famous aphorism, "power grows out of the barrel of a gun", which could as easily have been a line from Hitler's *Mein Kampf*. According to them, 'people power in the twentieth century did not grow out of the barrel of a gun. It removed rulers who believed that violence was power, by acting to dissolve their real source of power: the consent or acquiescence of the people they had tried to subordinate.'[28]

The liberal-functionalist approach can be positioned on one end of the power/resistance spectrum. On the other end, almost diametrically opposed, there is the set of literature that accepts war as an instrumental strategy. Proponents of non-violent resistance such as Ackerman and Duvall have a short fuse when it comes to such prescriptions. They reject both Fanon's seemingly quixotic idea that gangsters, pimps and prostitutes would be at the helm of the anti-colonial struggle and Sartre's 'promethean feat' that 'mad fury' and 'irresistible violence' would deliver the oppressed from the yoke of imperialism.[29] For Ackerman and Duvall, power and resistance are not in a dialectical relationship to each other, certainly not to the degree that the agency of the individual would be threatened. To put it in simple terms: Individuals are seen as almost entirely autonomous in their choice of resistance. The colonial system does not beget violence as Sartre and Fanon argue. It remains an individual choice to be violent *or* non-violent. According to this view, the orphan whose father was tortured and killed in prison and whose mother was raped in front of his eyes has the same choice as the middle-class boy whose only worry is if Santa delivers his Christmas wish list.

Lest the previous paragraph presents a one-sided analysis of the liberal-functionalist approach, let me differentiate my argument, for some theorists of non-violent action criticize the idea that we are at liberty to choose our strategy of resistance. Schock concedes in this regard that 'discursively embedded systems of exclusion and oppression such as statism, militarism, patriarchy, capitalism and bureaucracy (not to mention their mutual enforcement), cannot simply be overthrown through popular dissent'.[30] Individual choice may exist in theory but 'in reality tradition, ideology, socialisation, and social structures constrain people's knowledge of and capacity for individual choice, and it is very difficult for people to escape from their regularised patterns'.[31] As indicated, on a theoretical level the reciprocity of individual (agent) and systems of oppression (structure) is central to Fanon and Sartre. It is one of the great shortcomings of the literature on non-violent action that the theoretical openings offered in post-colonial studies and neo-Marxist approaches have not been taken seriously. There are many side jabs like the one by Duvall and Ackerman mentioned above, but there is no engagement on a theoretical level. There is, I believe, a good degree of liberal arrogance at play here.

Neo-Marxist musings

A group that I would call 'latent neo-Marxists' such as Michael Hardt, Ernesto Laclau, Chantal Mouffe, Antonio Negri and Slavoj Žižek are unlikely candidates to address that shortcoming, but they have gone furthest in comparing the different theoretical experiences and engaging the liberal argument on an intellectual level. Žižek in particular has been a prolific opponent of liberal ideas, especially when it comes to contentious issues such as immigration and Islam. A couple of questions in his book on violence point the way to his mode of argumentation: 'Is there not something suspicious, indeed symptomatic, about this focus on subjective violence – that violence which is enacted by social agents, evil individuals, disciplined repressive apparatuses, fanatical crowds?' he asks. The second question is rather more conspirational: 'Doesn't it desperately try to distract our attention from the true locus of trouble, by obliterating from view other forms of violence and thus actively participating in them?'[32] Žižek implies here that the liberal premise that violent resistance can be entirely subjective or driven by individuals unaffected by structural constraint and opportunity is a myth. According to him, it is the objective violence of the prevalent capitalist order that provokes, even necessitates, counter-violence in theory and praxis. Žižek challenges the liberal blind-spot that overlooks this diffusion of counter-violence that theatres of power and resistance provoke with an allegory:

> According to a well-known anecdote, a German officer visited Picasso in his Paris studio during the Second World War. There he saw *Guernica* and, shocked at the modernist 'chaos' of the painting, asked Picasso: 'Did you do this?' Picasso calmly replied: 'No, *you* did this!' Today, many a liberal, when faced with violent outbursts such as the recent looting in the suburb of Paris, asks the few remaining leftists who still count on a radical social transformation: 'Isn't it *you* who did this? Is *this* what you want?' And we should reply, like Picasso: 'No, *you* did this! This is the true result of *your* politics!'[33]

Žižek is right to allude to the hypocrisies involved in liberal thinking. After all, the hot and cold wars for 'humanity' fought by 'liberal democracies' in Iraq, Afghanistan, southern Lebanon and Palestine have killed and maimed more civilians than any other contemporary conflict. Not that liberal theory condones or advocates war. The problem with liberal theory is that it claims a moral high-ground that legitimates exceptions to the rule, for instance wars that are fought to bring about 'liberty' in foreign countries. Too often, in the name of such lofty ideals, liberal theorists turn into liberal crusaders, for instance Bernard Henry-Levy who kept *stumm* when US army officials stacked Iraqi prisoners and made them perform obscene sexual acts or when NATO soldiers posed with corpses of dead Afghans and posted the 'trophy' pictures on the internet. This silence of self-proclaimed liberals in the face of barbarism has precedence in history. It resembles the apologies of Tocqueville for the French massacres in Algeria, the aversion of Mill to Indian independence, and the racist calls of Spenser for a campaign of ethnic cleansing in Ireland, as Said explains.[34] Moreover, it was not the French liberals who protested when women associated with the Algerian FLN were gang raped in front of their husbands and when 'French soldiers took trophy photographs of their exploits in a standard pose that consisted of two mates "sharing" a naked woman who stands like a prisoner between the two men'.[35] The protests against French colonialism were driven by the French Communist Party and leftist intellectuals such as Sartre.

But Žižek is not primarily concerned with this side of western liberalism, despite his short historical reference to the 'humanitarian intervention' by self-proclaimed liberals such as Belgian king Leopold II whom Žižek finds responsible for the 'Congo holocaust'.[36] Žižek seems to be more concerned about liberal acknowledgement of 'otherness', especially the liberal tendency to tolerate the 'violence' of 'Muslims'. 'For the Western liberal', he writes, there is the 'problem of the brutal and vulgar anti-Semitic and antichristian caricatures that abound in the press and schoolbooks of Muslim countries'. No reference is given. Elsewhere, Žižek attacks 'Muslims' for reacting to caricatures of the prophet Muhammad published by the Danish newspaper *Jyllands-Posten*: 'Some of the Western partisans of multiculturalist tolerance' are criticized for displaying understanding for the Muslim reaction and their 'murderous violence at first aimed at Denmark, but then expanding to the whole of Europe and the West'.[37] According to Žižek, this 'Muslim rage' should not be seen within the context of imperialism, the occupation of Palestine, anti-Americanism, etc. Liberals are merely presenting such contexts as apology and to divert attention away from the 'TRUE cause,' that is Islam as a whole. Citing Oriana Fallaci, whose writings must be deemed racist even by the most tolerant standards of contemporary intellectual thought, Žižek concludes that the 'enemy is not the political misuse of Islam, but Islam itself. The danger from within is the compromising attitude predominant in Europe.'[38]

From the perspective of Žižek, then, Islam and multicultural liberalism are two sides of the same coin. Effectively, he is calling for a politics of identity that would evaporate cultural differences in a strange mixture of Eurocentric communism and populist belletristic. Here lies the poverty of his argument. He is attempting to recover particularly European norms and symbols in the name of a communist universality. But as a communist he is meant to argue the other way around: from the universality to the ways the European experience fits into it, from the international to the local. By starting with a warped understanding of European-ness he is essentializing what it means to be European a priori. As such, he is denying what Said aptly called 'overlapping territories' or what we have worked out as dialectics via Fanon and Sartre.[39] Žižek reveals himself as neither a Marxist nor a humanist, but as a Christian-democratic conservative.

It is not so much Europe that is the problem here, but the politics of difference that Žižek pursues. Hard pressed for a normative judgement, I would agree that compared to other areas of the world, Europe today has safeguarded a degree of tolerance, human rights and democratic transparency. In many ways, Europe is what the United States always wanted to be, but never really achieved. But the problem with Žižek is that he seems to think that such norms and their institutional manifestation (courts, governments, NGOs, etc.) are particularly European and that they have to be celebrated as such. All of this serves a central ideological purpose to subsume the 'other', in particular Muslims, under the category of Europe (as defined by Žižek). Here is embedded the political message that he attempts to get across. From his perspective, resistance to the 'anti-immigrant wave' and support for 'multi-cultural' diversity should not be limited 'to the endless ritual of confessing Europe's own sins, of humbly accepting the limitations of the European legacy, and of celebrating the wealth of other cultures'. Rather, Žižek advocates – very much in line with ardent conservatives like Niall Ferguson – that we need a European *Leitkultur* or a dominant culture that moulds the European project into one. 'The best lack all conviction, while the worst are full of passionate intensity', he hijacks a phrase coined by Yeats. For Žižek this 'is an excellent description of the current split between anaemic liberals and impassioned fundamentalists, *Muslim as well as our own, Christian*'.[40] 'Muslim as well as our own Christian': the delineation of us versus them could not be clearer than in this patronizing sentence that separates Islam from Europe. Žižek does not want Islam. What he prefers are politicians such as Germany's chancellor Angela Merkel whom he praises for announcing that the 'multicultural approach, saying that we simply live side by side and live happily with each other, has failed'.[41]

What is missing in Žižek then is an understanding of Europe and the world as a dialectical surface effect of the common experience of humanity. Freedom, democracy, human rights and/or social justice are not the prerogative of one culture. Žižek does not appreciate such cosmopolitanism. His is a tacitly nativist project, which is why he never really talks about India, the civil rights movement led by African Americans or the anti-Apartheid struggle of Nelson Mandela. There is no room in his writings for the heroes of humanism of the non-western world. Consequently, Žižek is incapable of proposing a dialectic of power and resistance that is truly appreciative of the reciprocal complexities of the contemporary world order. Hence, his ideas about Europe share with conservatives a sort of hermetic sense of identity, which yields an approach to resistance that is not dialectical, but sectarian and partial.

There are more attractive alternatives on the Left, for instance the concept of a pluralist and radical democracy put forward by Chantal Mouffe and Ernesto Laclau which they think proves the most suitable way to organize and rationalize continuous resistance to the status quo. Alas, their writings are not sufficiently empirically grounded, but their theoretical formulas are worth noting. Their starting point is a radical re-conceptualization of political plurality: 'Pluralism is *radical* only to the extent that each term of this plurality of identities finds within itself the principle of its own validity, without this having to be sought in a transcendent or underlying source and guarantee of their legitimacy.'[42] The compelling quality of this definition is that it accepts plural identities, while it rejects the hegemonic claim of any identitarian construct. Be European, but don't prescribe to others to be what you think Europe is all about. Radical pluralism stretches identities so thin that they lose their overbearing claims to primordial and hegemonic legitimacy. We shall not resist in the name of a local identity, but in the name of manifold experiences that constitute the egalitarian structures on the plane of humanity. 'Hence, the project for a radical and plural democracy, *in a primary sense*, is nothing other than the struggle for a maximum autonomization of spheres on the basis of the generalization of the equivalent-egalitarian logic.'[43]

This approach not only re-dimensions the struggles of workers as Laclau and Mouffe suggest; it not only shows that the new worker's struggles in Europe in Italy and France in the 1960s were composed of different forces, from young workers to 'immigrants in France and southerners in Italy': they were a result of a plurality of relations which 'cannot be magically erased to constitute a *single* working class.'[44] Such notions of radical pluralism allow us to appreciate the wonderfully interwoven experiences of resistance without the pitfalls of nativism which appear in a tacit form in the writings of Žižek. To claim authenticity in the name of Islam, Europe, the west or liberalism is to accept hegemony and oppression of the other who would fall beyond the confines of our comforting ideational construct. The sites of resistance sketched in the previous interregnum, which were deliberately chosen from different continents, show that the sources of power and resistance are never really unitary. Power and resistance are everywhere. They form a part of our human existence which is common to the resistance both at Tahrir Square and Oxford Street.

Laclau and Mouffe's notion of radical and pluralist democracy as a heterogeneous experience which evaporates ideational claims to superiority corresponds very closely to Michael Hardt and Antonio Negri's theses about Empire and the new struggles of the 'Multitude.' For Laclau and Mouffe, radical democracy implies difference within the singularity of the collective. Differences can be mitigated; radical democracy digests social antagonisms and turns them into agonism, into an open field of political engagement: 'An adversary' is turned into 'a legitimate enemy, an enemy with whom we have in common a shared adhesion to the ethico-political principles of democracy'.[45] The singular is superseded, but not overwhelmed by the 'collective will'. With reference to Gramsci, Laclau and Mouffe do not squeeze this collective into a predefined universality such as the 'proletariat' which Lenin imagined as a unitary actor. Rather, the collective will is 'a result of the politico-ideological articulation of dispersed and fragmented historical forces'.[46] In the words of Gramsci himself: the creation of a 'cultural-social unity' can only be safeguarded if 'a multiplicity of dispersed wills with heterogeneous aims, are welded together with a single aim, on the basis of an equal and common conception of the world'.[47] This is very different to the notion that the western model or European norms are exclusive and primordial and that they are simply replicated elsewhere in the world. When Žižek advocates resistance to multicultural liberalism, he is asking for it in the name of his essentialized understanding of what Europe means. Equally, when Ackerman and Duvall write that the 'old Roman *civitas* has become the universal standard – and with a few exceptions, its enemies are gone', they are overlooking other universal standards in favour of a concept that is culturally familiar to them. Such hierarchies of 'good and bad' resistance are ultimately normative. They do not appreciate the pluralistic interpellation of contemporary resistance struggles which are fought from Athens to Sao Paolo as we speak.

We have established that in the world of Fanon and Sartre 'authenticity' is a necessary virtue in order to achieve independence from colonialism; violence emerges as an inevitable cleansing force. 'For the native', Fanon writes, 'life can only spring up again out of the rotting corpse of the settler'.[48] By definition, theories of non-violent resistance reject any application of force premised on the problematic assumption that human beings do not digest the violence of the system or culture that they are embedded in. The second shortcoming of this view, especially in relation to the approach of Sharp, is that he never really presents a theory of resistance that appreciates the de-localized politics characteristic of contemporary forms of power and resistance. Hardt and Negri are rather more forthcoming in that regard. According to them, 'political action aimed at transformation and liberation today can only be conducted on the basis of the multitude'. This multitude is not a unitary actor, neither does it represent the manifestation of a superior politics of identity. It is plural and multiple: 'The multitude is composed of a set of *singularities* – and by singularity here we mean a social subject whose difference cannot be reduced to sameness, a difference that remains different.'[49] Comparable to Mouffe and Laclau, then, Hardt and Negri imply that there is no unity in identity, but that there is unity in purpose. You and I are different, we are singularities. But we are members of the Multitude which allows us to resist as a communitarian force. 'From the socio-economic perspective', it is argued, 'the multitude is the common subject of labour, that is, the real flesh of postmodern production, and at the same time the object from which collective capital tries to make the body of its global development'. We are engaged in a bio-political war here, which turns our bodies into a site of the battle between power and resistance. Another dialectic, this time between the individual (as a part of the multitude) and the oppressive capitalist system ensues: 'When the flesh of the multitude is imprisoned and transformed into the body of global capital, it finds itself both *within* and *against* the processes of capitalist globalisation.'[50] The multitude is not overwhelmed by its implication in the capitalist system as long as it accepts that resistance is possible and necessary. It is acknowledged 'that the situations across the world are very different and they are divided by dramatic hierarchies of power and wealth'.[51] At the same time it is claimed that a 'common political project is *possible* . . . We are all capable of democracy. The challenge is to organise it politically'.[52] To that end, Hardt and Negri deem it imperative 'to remember that another world is possible, a better, more democratic world, and to foster our desire for such a world . . . Multitude is an emblem for that desire'.[53]

And yet, despite the emphasis on plurality and inclusivity, neo-Marxists do not go far enough beyond the global north or the west in their theoretical and empirical references. Marxism has developed in close liaison with events in Europe but the applicability of the European experience has been eclipsed by the independence movements of the twentieth century and current events in the Arab-Islamic worlds that have created their 'own' intellectual dynamics. Hardt and Negri are quick to dismiss Homi Bhabha and Edward Said along with post-modern theorists as symptoms of a bygone era. 'To a certain extent,' they assert, 'postmodernist and postcolonialist theories are important *effects* that reflect or trace the expansion of the world market and the passage of the form of sovereignty'.[54] They are necessary but not sufficient theories to understand the intensely networked and finely knotted de-centralized power of Empire encapsulated in a hybrid and penetrative capitalist system that orders world politics literally from everywhere. Post-modern theorists are criticized for focusing attention too 'resolutely on the old forms of power', those traditional forms of sovereignty that we inherited from the Enlightenment and that induce hierarchies between self and other, female and male, master and worker, colonizer and colonized.[55] Equally, post-colonial theorists are indicted for giving a 'very confused view of this passage because they remain fixated on attacking an old form of power and propose a strategy of liberation that could be effective only on the old terrain'.[56]

From this critique, Hardt and Negri take the wrong turn. In their empirical examples, the non-European world, the playing field of post-colonial theory, remains almost entirely absent. When there are references to major events such as the Islamic revolution in Iran, their empirical blind-spots translate into severe conceptual mistakes. This is how in *Empire* the Iranian revolution is deemed fundamentalist and culturally reactionary, 'an anti-revolution, resurrecting an ancient world order', while a few pages later it is considered the 'first postmodernist revolution' because of the revolutionaries' 'powerful rejection of the world market'.[57] This is not only contradictory – how can a revolution be ancient and post-modern at the same time? – it reveals a problem in the materialist logic underlying the argument of Hardt and Negri. First, the Iranian revolutionaries did not die for the 'price of watermelons' as Khomeini famously put it; the revolution was about values, social justice, norms, egalitarianism, identity, empowerment, power and Islam. And second, as one of the major oil producers of the world, the post-revolutionary Iranian state could never really abandon the world market. Till today, Iran's political economy remains tied into the global economic order exactly because of the rich hydrocarbon resources that the country offers to the world. So there could never really be a 'powerful rejection of the world market', as Hardt and Negri put it. A serious engagement with the political economy of Iran would have been needed to buttress that statement and to rescue it from its thin empirical base. Instead, Hardt and Negri entangle themselves in further contradictions when they designate Iran at the same time as an anti-modern, fundamentalist entity, a post-modern revolutionary state as well as a dictatorship under Russian influence.[58] If theory is employed without sound empirical knowledge as it is on this occasion, it tends to be condescending, even hegemonic.

As I have argued throughout the present book and in my previous publications: the indelible political articulations beyond the west have to be appreciated in their own right before they can inform critical theory. Forms of power and resistance are always both local and universal, steeped in the common experience of injustice all over the world. In summary, the theories perused in this chapter demonstrate problems in capturing such variations exactly because they are either enmeshed in the particularities of local dependencies (post-colonialism) or too abstract and steeped in misleading notions of theoretical universality (neo-Marxism, liberal theories). Egypt, Tunis and to a lesser degree Libya are the first examples of successful transversal struggles that made ample use of multi-modal forms of expressions, from social network tools, poetry and rap music to resistance camps, graffiti and satellite TV stations. These revolts were both local, permeated by the symbolism and imagery of nationalism and Islam, and universal, tied to a global multitude. What is needed to appreciate these molar horizontal and vertical movements that the revolts enforced is critical theory that is empirically sound, informed by the experiences and histories of the people on the ground. In order to contribute to this ongoing project, the following chapters delve deeper into the dynamics of power and resistance in the Arab and Muslim world with a particular emphasis on primary sources and other empirical data.

How the (Sub)altern Resists: A Dialogue with Foucault and Said

Resistance comes First

Le problème de l'islam comme force politique est un problème essentiel pour notre époque et pour les années qui vont venir. La première condition pour l'aborder avec tant soit peu d'intelligence, c'est de ne pas commencer par y mettre de la haine.

Shi'ism in the face of the established powers arms the faithful with an unremitting restlessness. It breathes them into an ardour, wherein the political and the religious lie side by side.

Michel Foucault

Foucault as a subject

In the last interregnum I have deliberately left out one of the most influential approaches to power and resistance which was developed by Michel Foucault and adopted so prominently by Edward Said in his seminal *Orientalism*. In this chapter, I will focus on this approach and present a dialogue with both thinkers along the theme of power and resistance and with a particular emphasis on Foucault's writings on the revolution in Iran. This will give additional conceptual depth to some of the themes discussed throughout the present study and calibrate theoretically the dialectics between power and resistance that I have traced so far.

Let me start with a simple premise that was coined so famously by Foucault: Where there is power, there is resistance. This phrase encapsulates the dialectic that he battled with almost throughout his scholarly life. In *Orientalism*,

Edward Said took seriously Foucault's ideas about the way knowledge is implicated in power. Yet, ultimately, he did not fully appreciate that for Foucault power cannot be total. When Said argues that through 'Orientalism as a discourse' European culture not only 'manages' the Orient but 'produces' it, he overemphasizes the productive force of power at the expense of the creative force of resistance. According to Said, Orientalism not only constitutes a particular discourse, it produces the Orient 'politically, sociologically, militarily, ideologically, scientifically, and imaginatively during the post-Enlightenment period'.[1] For both Orientals and Europeans then, there is no escaping the fictional world established by the Orientalist corpus. It follows for Said that Orientalism has muted the east intellectually and discursively. The object (the Orient) is ostracized from the discourse of Orientalism; it does not speak, it is not present within its articulation. Without the power to speak, the '(sub)altern' remains trapped in a self-fulfilling prophecy.

It is this strategy of marginalization through disciplinary power regimes that has been targeted by post-colonial theorists and subaltern studies to the advantage of several disciplines, especially Middle Eastern Studies.[2] But in the following discussion I intend to question and theoretically advance a very specific methodical premise that undergirds the argument of *Orientalism* in particular and post-colonial approaches in general. I argue that overemphasizing the power of the west, or a discourse such as 'Orientalism' not only threatens to contribute to muting the 'other', it confuses the way resistance affects power. To be more precise: A gigantic constellation such as Orientalism – even the west for which it functions – can never really shut down modes of resistance or counter-discourses. In earlier reflections on this, I have gone as far as to say that Said's overemphasis on western representations of the east threatens to negate resistance to Orientalism.[3] Ultimately, Said misunderstands Foucault when, years after the publication of *Orientalism*, he adheres to the common perspective that Foucault ascribes 'undifferentiated power' to the disciplinary regime of modern society. 'With this profoundly pessimistic view', Said criticizes him,

> went also a singular lack of interest in the force of effective resistance to it, in choosing particular sites of intensity, choices which, we see from the evidence on all sides, always exist and are often successful in impeding, if not actually stopping, the progress of tyrannical power.[4]

Immediately, one can return the critique and point to Said's own bias towards the power of the west which he highlights almost exclusively not only in *Orientalism* but also in *Covering Islam* and his extensive writings on Palestine. But the fact that Said did not spend much of his talent on the 'other' as an agent of history has already been sufficiently addressed.[5] What I am more interested in, and what has remained marginal in the post-colonial literature, is his methodical confusion about the dialectic between power and resistance that was a part of Foucault's method throughout his career. Said undervalued, like many other critics of Foucault, that discourses and their corresponding knowledge-power dynamics cannot be possessed, organized or shut down by one social agent (e.g. individuals, institutions or disciplines). They are, in this sense, gliding phenomena; heterogeneous rather than homogeneous, capillary rather than hierarchical, progressive rather than conservative. Said was mistaken to infer that a discursive constellation such as Orientalism can be all-encompassing. His argument in *Orientalism* is too structuralist; if the power of the west and its Orientalist conduit would have been truly totalitarian, the Arab revolts would not have produced a modified form of political subjectivity that has eroded the status quo. Neither would there be an Islamic Republic of Iran with its own rather unique governmental institutions. Foucault's notion of power was not deterministically structuralist as Said implied. Rather, Foucault draws attention to the diffusion of power, its 'relayed' locality within society, the individual and our psychological and physical existence. His approach to power and resistance is exactly post-structural and 'dialectic.' He clarified this view as early as in 1976 in his lectures at the Collège de France:

> Do not regard power as a phenomenon of mass and homogenous domination – the domination of one individual over others, of one group over others, or of one class over others; keep it clearly in mind that unless we are looking at it from a great height and from a very great distance, power is not something that is divided between those who have it and hold it exclusively, and those who do not have it and are subject to it. Power must, I think, be analysed as something that circulates, or rather as something that functions only when it is part of a chain. It is never localised here or there, it is never in the hands of some, and it is never appropriated in the way that wealth or a commodity can be appropriated. Power functions. Power is exercised through networks, and individuals do not simply circulate in

those networks; they are in a position to both submit to and exercise this power.[6]

In the way Said uses 'power', and at the latter stages of his career then criticizes Foucault, he leaves out a range of methodical nuances. True, if there is one central theme recurring in the different phases of Foucault's scholarly life, it is his emphasis on the birth of a series of disciplinary strategies which he deems central to the making of western modernity and its 'controlled' subject. According to Foucault, a genealogy of these 'disciplines' reveals societal norms that were slowly perfected, institutionalized and enforced through a network of prisons, clinics, asylums, medical organizations, educational routines, the penal system and jurisprudential practices. 'Each society has its regime of truth, its "general politics" of truth', Foucault famously stated in an interview in June 1976. It is these colossal regimes that determine 'the types of discourse [society] accepts and makes function as true; the mechanisms and instances that enable one to distinguish true and false statements; the means by which each is sanctioned; the techniques and procedures accorded value in the acquisition of truth; the status of those who are charged with saying what counts as true.'[7] In other words, discourses (such as Orientalism) not only represent a particular issue and not only produce meaningful knowledge about it which in turn affects social and political practices, they are a part of the way power operates, reveals itself and is contested. Once a particular discourse sustains its effectiveness via disciplinary constellations and in practice, it can be conceptualized as a regime of truth.[8]

Ultimately then, such regimes appear as particularly overbearing power constellations. But where does that leave the power to resist? In the same interview mentioned above, Foucault seems to indicate that resistance remains viable: 'The essential political problem for the intellectual is not to criticize the ideological contents supposedly linked to science, or to ensure that his own scientific practice is accompanied by a correct ideology',[9] he stresses at the end of the interview. The political task is to ascertain the 'possibility of constituting a new politics of truth'. It is not a matter of 'changing people's consciousness – or what's in their heads', but to tackle the 'political, economic, institutional regime of the production of truth'.[10] The main target, in other words, must be the political economy of truth-making, for it is here where the subject is moulded in accordance with the reigning norms of society. The battle is to be directed against the disciplinary systems that feed into that process of wilful distortion (e.g. universities) for instance by giving a voice to the powerless.[11] In the case of History, resistance to the canon would require 'a use of history that severs its connection to memory, its metaphysical and anthropological model, and construct a counter-memory – a transformation of history into a totally different form of time'.[12] And with regard to the legal system there exists the possibility of eliminating the judicial apparatus through 'anti-judicial guerrilla operations'.[13] The possibility of social engineering on the ruins of a deconstructed disciplinary regime is apparent here. This is not the strategic disposition of a 'realist conservative'.[14]

Between the possibility to resist and the disciplinary power governing the individual, Foucault places a vast and at times enigmatically paradoxical space that needs to be overcome in order to make possible the power of the powerless. It is here where we can locate one of the nuances that was not fully appreciated in Said's interpretation of Foucault. In order to flesh them out, I investigate what I call Foucault's 'power-resistance dialectic' emancipating his statement that resistance is immanent to power from the charge that it negates individual agency. This goes to the heart of the famous statement of Foucault – 'where there is power, there is resistance, and yet, or rather consequently, this resistance is never in the position of exteriority in relation to power' – exactly calibrating the 'dimension' in which he places the forces of resistance that constantly battle against the imposition of institutionalized regimes of truth (Orientalism included). I intend to pursue this argument in two principle ways: I will start by reinterpreting the power-resistance dialectic of Foucault in close liaison with the recent literature on the topic. Some of the material marshalled has been published in English and French after his death in 1984 and has remained largely untapped since then. In a second step, I will shift the focus to his writings on the revolution in Iran. Via a thorough reading of those articles, it is possible to achieve a better understanding of his approach to power and resistance. As such, this second part attempts to corroborate my suggestion that Foucault affirms transversal political agency in general and the possibility of radical resistance in particular. This implies that Said misunderstood the reciprocal battles at the root of the power-resistance dialectic that is under focus here.

Power to Resist, or Resistance to Power?

In a particularly striking section of James Miller's biography of Michel Foucault, the author describes a scene at the University of Vincennes on 23 January 1969, when Foucault participated in the occupation of the university's administration building in solidarity with the student movement triggering vociferous clashes with the French police. 'Police began their assault on the administration building in the predawn hours of January 24', Miller writes. 'Those still inside, including Foucault, fought back furiously. They clogged the building's stairways with tables, cabinets and chairs. The police in response shot tear gas through the windows.' Foucault and others did not surrender. Instead they fled to the roof of the building where they hurled bricks at the police gathering below. 'Witnesses recall that Foucault exulted in the moment, gleefully lobbing stones – although he was careful not to dirty his beautiful black velour suit.'[15]

Throughout his life, Foucault emphasized the necessity and viability of political action. This proclivity to resist is exemplified in his support of the student movement in France and the 'battles' at Vincennes, his assistance to persecuted students in Tunis, his engagement with the Gauche Prolétarienne, the establishment of the *Groupe d'Information sur les Prisons* (Prison Information Group or GIP), his endorsement of the gay rights movement in France and in his initial sympathy for the revolution in Iran in 1979. And yet his biography as an activist seems to stand in stark contrast to his scepticism as a scholar. Many of his critics have argued, including Said, that in his writings Foucault subdues agency, the power to act in a meaningful way, to the overwhelming force of all-encompassing, deeply penetrating power structures. Thus the synthesis between the activist and the critic, epitomized for a whole generation of French intellectuals by Jean-Paul Sartre, appears to be ruptured by the dissonance between praxis and theory that seems to open up so disjunctively with the emergence of Foucault on the stage of French philosophy. From the perspective of Foucault, it is often argued against him, the self is trapped in a 'terrifying' stalemate between power and resistance, frozen into a mere 'product of discursive structures and disciplinary regimes, which operate far above mere perception or feeling or individual control, and which d[o] not aim at moral uplift', as one critic put it.[16] In particular, historians have indicted Foucault's seeming antagonism towards History as a 'scientific' (or objective) enterprise and as a practice. This scepticism towards History and the corpus of the western 'human sciences' in general, is discernible from his earliest major writings, from *Madness and Civilisation* (1961) and *The Order of Things* (1969), and his 'middle period', signposted by the publication of *The Archaeology of Knowledge* (1969) and *The Discourse on Language* (1970). In his latter publications, that is, in *Discipline and Punish* (1975) and *The History of Sexuality* (1976), this scepticism is compounded by his fascination with the effects of power on the constitution of knowledge and subjectivity, and the fledgling instances of resistance that strategies of 'governmentality' provoke.[17]

Ultimately, Foucault was a reluctant yet subliminal dialectician; his concepts cannot be read in isolation from each other or within strict and uni-directional action–reaction schemata.[18] This is particularly true when it comes to the issue of 'agency' which poses a problem to Foucault in a very personal note and permeates, as a central dilemma, the main narratives holding together the structure of *The Order of Things*: 'What must I be', Foucault asks here, 'I who think and who am my thought, in order to be what I do not think, in order for my thought to be what I am not?'[19] This dilemma, elicited by the 'outside' pressures on the making of our 'self', links up with several central questions that Foucault grappled with throughout his scholarly life: Is it possible to think in detachment from the outside world? Are we at liberty to constitute our 'self' in independence? Of course, the answers to these questions indicate the viability of resistance, for if disciplinary regimes such as Orientalism penetrate all the way down to an individual's subjective constitution, then how can we act against it and defy it?

Critics of Foucault would point to his oeuvre and argue that in his writings, as opposed to his projects as an activist, he focuses almost exclusively on the strategies that mould us into subjects of power. As Said argued: For Foucault power seems 'irresistible and unstoppable'.[20] Foucault not only described how disciplinary constellations affect our thinking, the argument goes, but he also suggests that power is both physical and metaphysical; it acts on the body *and* the cognition of the subject. 'Foucault seems sometimes on the verge of depriving us of a vocabulary in which to conceptualise the nature and meaning of those periodic refusals of control that, just as much as the imposition of control, mark the course of human history', one feminist author complains.[21] 'From Foucault's perspective', another critic notes, 'the human sciences are a major force in the disastrous triumph of Enlightenment thinking, and the panoptical scientific observer is a salient expression of the subject-centred putatively universal reason which that thinking promotes'.[22]

It is true that Foucault spilled most of his ink on the overbearingly intrusive, carefully networked impact of disciplinary techniques that are deployed in order to contain any meaningful expression of resistance. In terms of his empirical research and theoretical treatises, Foucault prioritized disciplinary power over resistance, to the detriment of a better theory of political agency. But to conclude from this that Foucaultian 'postmodernism' has contributed to the denial of 'both agency and causal explanations of socio-cultural change' is problematic.[23] Foucault may have been more concerned with 'what is', than with 'what could be', but his theory of power and resistance does not suffocate the viability of radical dissidence. To say, as Said does, that Foucault is caught up in a paradox, that his 'imagination of power was by his analysis of power to reveal its injustice and cruelty, but by his theorisation to let it go on more or less unchecked',[24] only reveals one part of the dialectic. Criticism like this does not appreciate the theoretical thrust that Foucault ascribes to modes of resistance.

A paper authored by Gilles Deleuze provides a useful start to unravelling that accusation further. In this paper, Deleuze argues that there is no real rupture between the latter and early Foucault, that he continuously theorized the prospects of change, viz. the viability of resistance to power. This is particularly apparent, according to Deleuze, in the way Foucault conceptualizes the relationship between the subject and the outside world which creates its own dialectically constituted dimension in which the self can act. Within this dimension, which must be treated as a theoretical category, the subject resists disciplinary power, not entirely autarkic from the political economy of knowledge, but autonomous enough to enact radical change. Deleuze is alluding exactly to the dialectics (relationships or interdependencies) of self and other, subject and object, power and resistance to make this point: 'If the outside is a relationship, the absolute of relationships', he notes, 'then the inside is also a relationship, the relationship becoming subject'.[25] This subject has access to a dialectically constituted dimension in which a form of agency can be fostered. 'If force receives a dual power from the outside, the power to affect (other forces) and to be affected (by other forces), how could there not ensue a relationship between force and itself?' It is here, Deleuze suggests, that Foucault places the 'element of "resistance".[26] Deleuze concedes that the 'subject is always constituted, the product of a subjectivication'. But he maintains at the same time that the subject 'appears in a dimension that opposes all stratification or codification . . . [T]he relationship to the self *does not let itself be aligned* according to the concrete forms of power or be subsumed in an abstract diagrammatic function'.[27] Rather, the contrary. The self escapes into another, presumably 'third' dimension in which agency is enacted. In the words of Deleuze: 'It is as if the relationships of the outside folded to make a double [*doublure*] and allow a relationship to the self to arise that develops according to a new dimension'.[28]

Deleuze reverts to Foucault's analysis of the historical formation of the ancient Greek concept of *Enkrateia* to enunciate this fundamental dynamic further. According to Foucault, *Enkrateia* is 'a power exercised over oneself *in* the power one exercises over others'.[29] Deleuze adds that Foucault's understanding of *Enkrateia* presupposes the possibility of triumph over the subjugated self, for 'how could one claim to govern others if one could not govern oneself?'[30] From this perspective, Foucault must have accepted the viability of agency, the possibility to escape formalized forms of power that the ancient Greeks invented. 'Foucault's work was created by inventing a topology that actively puts the inside and outside in contact on the stratified formations of history', Deleuze explains further. 'It is up to the strata to produce layers that show and tell something new; but it is also up to the relationship of the outside to call the powers in place into question, and it is up to the relationship with the self to inspire new modes of subjectivisation'.[31] It is along this dialectical tabula rasa that the possibility 'to show and tell something new' can reveal itself. Fold a piece of paper and you will see. The crease is a surface effect of the 'inside' and the 'outside' and it holds together both. Multiply this piece of paper and the creases infinitesimally in order to simulate the complexity of human history and the power/resistance dialectics it has provoked, and you will get an impression of the structure that is imagined here. It is within that topological relationship between inside and outside, subject and object, self and other, resistance and power, in other words, where the contested space in which agency unfolds itself can be localized.

There is a second pathway along which we can traverse this power-resistance dialectic. It has been said that Foucault places resistance within power. That means that power and resistance are in a constant and 'violent' battle with each other. In that sense, the power of Orientalism would always also provoke resistance. Consequently, a history of Orientalism must always also be interrupted by a history of counter-discourses to it. There is no suggestion in Foucault's variant conceptualization of this dialectical struggle that power and resistance are somehow static or oppositional forces that retain their properties when they intermingle. Neither is there a clearly demarcated inside and outside to this dialectic, where we could neatly locate either power *or* resistance. Rather, as I have tried to demonstrate via Deleuze, resistance is a surface effect of a dialectic between indigenous forces and exogenous impingement. 'The relationship to self is homologous to the relationship with the outside and all the contents of the inside are in relation with the outside.'[32] Applied to the power-resistance dialectic under focus here, this means that Foucault's 'genealogies of power' are implicated in 'genealogies of resistance'.[33] Recent scholarship on this issue supports this view. It is quite literally 'axiomatic that where power goes in Foucault, there is resistance as well'.[34] If resistance goes along with power, and if '[p]ower is everywhere; not because it embraces everything, but because it comes from everywhere',[35] as Foucault adamantly maintains, then it must follow – quite logically – that resistance is contemporaneous with power. In short: If power is promiscuous, if the power of Orientalism is acutely penetrative as Said suggests, resistance to it must be as well.

So the charge, articulated by Said and others including Anthony Giddens, Jürgen Harbermas and Michael Walzer, that Foucault sides with the non-subjective aspects of power rather than with individual intentionality is problematic because it is based on the false premise that power and resistance are detachable or located in different dimensions.[36] The agency that unfolds itself in the dialectic between power and resistance is not a simple replication of the dialectic itself, neither is it a safe place, a Hegelian synthesis. Rather, it is an effect of power acting on resistance, which has swerved or departed from its original purpose to constrain the individual, to arrive in another dimension which opens up possibilities of agency that do not merely react to the original incentive of power, but effectively expand the boundaries of what is intentionally achievable. Agency reveals itself as a surface effect of a fundamental action–action dynamic. Foucault is very clear about this. 'When one defines the exercise of power as a mode of action upon the actions of others', he emphasizes,

> when one characterises these actions as the government of men by other men . . . one includes an important element: freedom. Power is exercised only over free subjects, and only insofar as they are 'free'. By this we mean individual or collective subjects who are faced with a field of possibilities in which several kinds of conduct, several ways of reacting and modes of behaviour are available . . . Consequently there is not a face-to-face confrontation of power and freedom as mutually exclusive facts (freedom disappearing everywhere power is exercised), but a much more complicated interplay. In this game, freedom may well appear as the condition for the exercise of power (at the same time its precondition, since freedom must exist for power to be exerted, and also its permanent support, since without the possibility of recalcitrance power would be equivalent to a physical determination).[37]

For this action–action dynamic to make sense, freedom, including the viability to resist, must come first. Deleuze interprets this to mean that 'a diagram of forces presents, alongside the singularities of power corresponding to its relationships, singularities of resistance, 'points, nodes, foci' that in turn act on the strata in order to make change possible.' He even goes one step further and argues that in Foucault the 'last word in the theory of power is that resistance comes first since it has a direct relationship with the outside. Thus a social field resists more than it strategizes and the thought of the outside is a thought of resistance (*The Will to Knowledge*).'[38] Consequently, a fundamental matrix is formed: Resistance precedes power ↔ resistance is a freedom that power acts upon ↔ resistance is a form of power. In other words, resistance is not only viable; it is a form of agency which necessarily exists as a part of the condition of humanity, viz. freedom. It is innate, slumbering within us only to be activated by incentives from the outside, a call for revolution, a movement for social justice, a rebellion for peace. It is in this sense that the possibility of power *must* imply the possibility of resistance. In the words of Foucault:

> The power relationship and freedom's refusal to submit cannot therefore be separated. The crucial problem of power is not that of voluntary servitude

(how could we seek to be slaves?). At the very heart of the power relationship, and constantly provoking it, are the recalcitrance of the will and the intransigence of freedom. Rather than speaking of an essential antagonism, it would be better to speak of an 'agonism' – of a relationship which is at the same time mutual incitement and struggle; less of a face-to-face confrontation that paralyzes both sides than a permanent provocation.[39]

In a well-argued article, Kevin Jon Heller attributes the widespread misinterpretation of Foucault's understanding of power to the inability of many scholars to divorce themselves from mainstream notions of power as uni-directional or inherently repressive.[40] This hierarchical effect of power seems to be what Said had in mind when he argues that Orientalism not only creates knowledge but 'reality' all the way down to the very constitution of the Oriental himself. Heller points out that for Foucault power could be both repressive and productive, that it 'is a *facility* not a *thing*'.[41] His argument can be linked to Gayatri Spivak's reading of Foucault's understanding of power and the problems of translating it into English. Spivak rightly points out that *pouvoir* in French not only (or even primarily) refers to 'repression' and 'submission' but that in its various conjugations it also refers to a form of 'can-do ness',[42] that it relates to verbs such as 'to enable' and 'to make possible', *vouz pouvez*, you can do it! From this perspective, power is no longer equated with repression. Rather power 'traverses and produces things, it induces pleasure, forms knowledge, produces discourse. It needs to be considered as a productive network that runs through the whole social body, much more than as a negative instance whose function is repression.'[43]

Foucault does not decisively answer the question whether or not such productive notions of power can be equated with resistance and what then the difference between resistance and power would be. But he does give us some clues about the battles at the root of the power-resistance dialectic. Given that Foucault believes that resistance precedes power, it must follow that power, at least in its 'first' appearance, is active, that it acts upon something pre-existing, viz. resistance, which is both necessary and sufficient for his theory of power to work. Resistance must be innate, there must exist a latent subliminal resistance drive that is dormant but which may be activated when power acts upon us; at least it is innate as an option. The parental command 'don't do this' which provokes an action to the action of the previous (sanctioned) action of the child comes to mind as an example. Resistance does not follow automatically, but it *is* an option. '[R]esistance or the possibility of resistance', it is argued in the recent secondary literature on this issue, 'constitutes the corner stone of the very definition of the "power relation", which is importantly *not* simply a relation of domination.' Rather, resistance 'comes first quite literally, resistance is what power works *on* and *through*'.[44] This does not mean that power is reactive (as much as it does not mean that resistance is reactive of course). It simply means that power and resistance are exactly coextensive. Again: where there is power, there *must be* resistance. Consequently, when Said used Foucault in order to express the discursive density of Orientalism, its total claim and wide-ranging penetration, he should have dispersed his argument with the period before and after the colonial interlude and the modes of resistance during its heydays. After all, the non-western world has had a history before, during and after colonialism.

It should be noted that resistance is not to be thought of as a 'state of nature', or a form of primordial authenticity. Rather, resistance is not realized without power acting upon it. Power 'actualises' resistance; 'its character *as* resistance derives from its opposition to some power relation'. This should not be considered a mere semantic necessity. Rather, 'it is a fact about the ontological constitution of resistance. Without power intervening upon me, I am simply doing, not resisting.'[45] Power activates the resistance drive. Again, this means that the power of Orientalism must provoke a powerful resistance discourse which needs to be captured analytically exactly because of the all-encompassing effects Said ascribes to the Orientalist regime of truth. It is this inevitability of the continuous provocation of resistance that explains the rather nonchalant attitude that Foucault seemed to have towards power, as if he wanted us to ignore it altogether, forcing us to focus on the viability of resistance instead (and what a liberating utopia that would be!).[46] Don't worry about power, he seemed to say. The more powerful a particular discourse, the more intricate the resistance to it: Where there is power, there must be resistance, power is not unidirectional, it cannot be monopolized, it is not a property, Orientalism cannot be all-encompassing, the Orient continuously resisted to be represented. Where there is reification of any powerful discourse, then, the power to narrate, to create reality, to construct meaning, to engineer Orientalism as a disciplinary regime, there must be – in this case quite automatically – 'de-reification', the power to counter-act, to create a dissident culture.

To break away from the textual evidence surveyed and to place Foucault more firmly within the intellectual currents of his period, one could add as a conclusion to this section that Foucault thought with reference to the major ontological and epistemological questions that captivated his generation and that continue to have an impact on critical theory until today: What is the structure of reality? How is culture socially constructed and maintained? How does the state and society enforce hegemony and reify oppression? And how can we imagine a counter-hegemonic regime, if at all? These questions were not only intensely debated in France, of course. They were a part of the intellectual *zeitgeist* enveloping Foucault.

It is surprising thus that transnational scholarly exchanges and theoretical cross-fertilization remained implicit. For instance, at the same time as Foucault pondered *The Order of Things* and the issue of agency and subjectivity more generally, Peter Berger and Stanley Pullberg published an influential essay on the same topic. In this essay, the authors presented answers to two principle ontological questions that in my opinion link up exactly with Foucault's concerns: 'How is it possible that subjectively intended meanings become objective facticities? Or . . . how is it possible that human activity (*Handeln*) should produce a world of things (*choses*).'[47] In order to address the two questions, Berger and Pullberg borrow from Marx and his concept of reification or *Verdinglichung* in German. 'By reification', they write, 'we mean the moment in the process of alienation in which the characteristic of thing-hood becomes the standard of objective reality.'[48] Objective reality is not to be understood as 'real' reality, but as a socially invented layer that envelops everything we do, giving our existence artificial meaning. This reified 'quasi-reality' is constantly under pressure from forces of 'de-reification', which could lead to the disintegration of social structures through resistance or fundamental challenges to established world-views. Where there is reification then, the power to narrate, to create reality, to construct meaning, to engineer History, there is de-reification, the power to counter-act, to challenge hegemony, to create a dissident counter-culture.

Berger was more explicit regarding that dialectic in *Sacred Canopy*, which was published in 1967. On the one side, he argues that reification is a form of agency, an ability to mould the world in accordance with our actions: 'The "stuff" out of which society and all its formations are made is human meanings externalized in human activity.' This is as much as to say that everything surrounding us is socially engineered. As a consequence, 'sociological understanding ought always to be humanising, that is, ought to refer back the imposing configurations of social structure to the living human beings who have created them.'[49] On the other side of this dialectic, the following happens: the dense structures (or cultures) of society thus created are intensely debilitating; they confine agency, for '[a]bove all, society manifests itself by its coercive power.'[50] Here we hear echoes of the pessimism ascribed to Foucault (and the 'negative dialectics' of the Frankfurt School, in particular Adorno, Horkheimer and Marcuse). Berger reinforces the seeming consensus amongst this generation of critical theorists that '[s]ociety directs, sanctions, controls, and punishes individual conduct. In its most powerful apotheosis . . . society may even destroy the individual.'[51] But the story does not end here. Resistance remains an option, even in the case of a totalitarian society. If a society threatens to negate and subsume the individual into a totality, a final galactic battle ensues where the 'whole of society' should be targeted as something 'to be destroyed. And then, we can only hope that it will never exist again.'[52] In short: If society is uncompromisingly totalitarian, resistance to it has to be – and will be – as well.

The purpose of this short contextual excursus is not to assimilate Foucault and Berger (and Pullberg) identically to each other. Obviously, Foucault was opposed to the term 'alienation', because for orthodox Marxists it implied the existence of a 'scientific reality' and an ideal society the contours of which they took the liberty to define. But I found the reification–de-reification nexus comparable to the action–action dynamic Foucault attaches to the power-resistance dialectic we discussed above. Ultimately, it does not conform to the common notion that Foucault subdues agency – that he subsumes the power to resist under totalitarian regimes of truth. Rather, instead of presenting easily delineated territories separating power and resistance, Foucault brought to the practice of challenging the interdependencies between truth and the invention of knowledge the patient criticism and real life experience of theoretical detail. I do not see how his generation of critical theorists could be dismissed for being too acquiescent in their scholarly tribulations or too apathetic in their political activism, especially once we compare them with today's dying breed of 'public intellectuals'.

Foucault and (sub)altern agency

Even if we allow for the previous section to counter accusations that the interest of Foucault 'in domination was critical but not finally as contestatory or as oppositional as on the surface it seems to be' as Said argues,[53] there must be something in the recurrent criticism that lends credence to such arguments against him, for even scholars sympathetic to his ideas regret that Foucault was quick to criticize Marxists for their 'loose theory' of class struggle, while 'his own conceptions of resistance, opposition and struggle remain virtually as enigmatic'.[54] It seems that indeterminacy is consciously inscribed in Foucault's theory of power and resistance exactly because of his conviction that the 'local intellectual' has to fight disciplinary power constellations not from an entrenched position or from a moral angle, but from the perspective of the 'genealogist' who is embroiled in a continuous fight against reified claims to 'truth' and 'reality'. 'I think to imagine another system', Foucault explicitly said, 'is to extend our participation in the present system'.[55] Here, the problem is not so much that Foucault attempts to approximate a 'non-position'. The problem is that his philosophy of resistance, much like the marginalization of modes of resistance to Orientalism in the scholarship of Said, is not placed on a firm empirical footing in order to be conceptually commensurate with his detailed accounts of disciplinary regimes of truth. I have pointed out this lack of empirical rigour with regard to other theories of power and resistance in the previous interregnum. With regard to Foucault, this is certainly the case up until 1978, when he started to refer to rather more concrete forms of resistance in his lectures at the Collège de France. It is no coincidence that he moved to extrapolate more explicit historical examples during this period. He was not only responding to voices that criticized the near-total absence of genealogies of resistance in his earlier writings, but also to political developments in which he invested as an intellectual. Consequently, one finds in these lectures reference to the 'dissident' movement of the Soviet Union, Poland and Czechoslovakia, which Foucault supported during that time and up until his death in 1984.[56] "'[D]issidence" in the East and the Soviet Union', he pointed out during his lecture on 1 March 1978, 'really does designate a complex form of resistance and refusal'.[57] During that lecture, Foucault referred to the Soviet novelist, playwright and exiled dissident Aleksandr Solzhenitsyn, whose *Gulag Archipelago* had a profound influence on his views on dissident activity, in order to contextualize his *discursus* on the resistance movement in the Communist east:

> [T]he political struggles that we put together under the name of dissidence, certainly have an essential, fundamental dimension that is refusal of this form of being conducted. 'We do not want this salvation, we do not wish to be saved by these people and by these means.' . . . It is Solzhenitsyn. 'We do not wish to obey these people. We do not want this system where even those who command have to obey out of terror. We do not want this pastoral system of obedience. We do not want this truth. We do not want to be held in this system of truth. We do not want to be held in this system of observation and endless examination that continually judges us, tells us what we are in the core of ourselves, healthy or sick, mad or not mad, and so on.' So we can say that this word dissidence really does cover a struggle.[58]

Resistance is aligned here more firmly with the action–action dynamic that was covered in the first part of this interregnum. (Pastoral) power (or conduct) acts upon the individual (or a community) actualizing specific forms of resistance (dissidence). If power is the 'conduct of conducts and a management of possibilities',[59] resistance is a form of 'counter-conduct':

> [M]aybe this word 'counter-conduct' enables us to avoid a certain substantification [or hero worship] allowed by the word 'dissidence.' . . . [B]y using the word counter-conduct, and so without having to give a sacred status to this or that person as a dissident, we can no doubt analyse the components in the way in which someone actually acts in the very general field of politics or in the very general field of power relations; it makes it possible to pick out the dimension or component of counter-conduct that may well be found in fact in delinquents, mad people, and patients.[60]

Foucault's struggle to come to terms with forms of resistance in these years unfolded in various, theoretically diffuse, yet politically immediate and pertinent ways. So it came at an opportune moment that in September 1978, he was commissioned by the Italian *Corriere della Serra* to embark on a journey to Iran in order to cover the revolution gripping the country. In the most recent appraisal of this episode of his life, his long-term companion Paule Veyne notes that Foucault was genuinely captivated by the events, that 'the strong personality of Khomeini fascinated him' and that 'deep down, he had been shaken by the heroism of the Iranian crowds as they stood up to the police and the army'.[61] Clearly impressed by what he saw, Foucault met with the leader of the revolution Ayatollah Khomeini who was in exile in Neauphle-le Châteu in France before he revisited Iran at the height of the revolutionary fervour in November 1978. The 'enthusiasm' for the revolution that Foucault displayed during this period may explain why he spent a considerable amount of energy and time reporting from Iran and trying to understand what was happening in the country during that winter of 1978–1979.[62]

The difference, however, was not only quantitative. Foucault's engagement with the revolution in Iran had distinct theoretical and empirical connotations as well. As indicated, it came during a period when he was developing a rather more elaborate approach to forms of resistance or 'counter-conducts'. From the perspective of Foucault, the unfolding revolution in Iran exemplified a particularly 'raw' event, the birth of an idea that may reveal a mechanism for resistance on a grand scale. 'There are more ideas on earth than intellectuals imagine', he wrote in *Corriere della sera* in November 1978. 'We have to be there at the birth of ideas, the bursting outward of their force.'[63] There is no doubt that Foucault thought that he was witnessing exactly that, what he termed a 'political spirituality' long lost in the west. Where else than in this 'the first great insurrection against the planetary system, the most mad and the most modern form of revolt'[64] could Foucault find empirical substance for his inquiries into new forms of power and counter-power which could constitute the beginnings of what one observer of his termed a 'vitalist theory of resistance'?[65]

It is too far-fetched to discern major flaws in Foucault's overall thinking from his writings on Iran – for instance what Afary and Anderson term his problematic 'anti-modern' and 'anti-Enlightenment' stance.[66] Foucault can be faulted for not engaging more deeply with the history of Iran and Islam, but it should be noted in the same breath that he repeatedly stressed his role as an outsider, a European, a westerner, a 'neophyte'[67] who is in a 'poor position to give advice to the Iranians',[68] someone who tried to understand those demonstrators who 'protested and were killed in Iran while shouting "Islamic government"'.[69] I do not think he tried to pose as an 'Iran expert' or 'Orientalist', as Afary and Anderson seem to imply.[70] Rather, he was genuinely trying to comprehend, as a self-conscious outsider with a Eurocentric upbringing, a new subjectivication of power with a genealogy that he mistook as taking 'nothing from Western philosophy, from its juridical and revolutionary foundations'.[71] Ultimately, his engagement with Iran did not go beyond a 'tentative application of his more theoretical ideas to a contemporary event in a non-Western society',[72] exactly because Foucault did not qualify some of his theoretical statements with an empirical and historical analysis of the Iranian situation. On that account, Said is right to indict him for his Eurocentrism which he found reflected in his ignorance towards alternative forms of non-western ideas, 'as if "history" itself took place only among a group of French and German thinkers'.[73] If there was a 'different way of thinking about social and political organisation', as Foucault claimed rather grandiosely, where was this new thinking genealogically located? What was the discursive function of the mosques in contemporary Iran? What was the difference and what the commonalities between the Islamic revolution that Foucault witnessed and other revolts in Iranian history, i.e. the Tobacco uprising in 1891, the Constitutional Movement in 1906–1911, the nationalization of the Anglo-Iranian Oil Company by Mohammad Mossadegh in 1951 and the subsequent MI6/CIA engineered coup d'état which reinstated the dictatorship of the Shah? What was Khomeini's concept of 'Islamic governance'? Addressing these questions would have set the signposts of a 'genealogy of resistance' to imperialism and the authoritarianism of the state in Iran, for it was those revolts that contributed to the perfection of anti-disciplinary counter-conducts that inscribed an infrastructure of resistance into the body politic of the country, and it was this pre-existing culture of resistance that was readily exploited by the revolutionaries supporting Khomeini as I will demonstrate in the next interregnum. To my mind, the only other time when Foucault talked about a topic without the necessary depth of empirical and historical knowledge to do so comprehensively was with regard to the paintings of Manet during a conference he organized in Tunis in 1971.[74]

And yet to conclude that his writings on Iran are without conceptual value stretches the criticism too far. In fact, an analysis of his articles on Iran reveals that Foucault viewed the events – unconsciously perhaps, certainly not explicitly – through the action–action dynamic that he attached to the relationship between power and resistance addressed in the first part of this discussion. There is almost a 'dialectical symmetry' from paragraph to paragraph between fascinating descriptions of resistance on the one side and strategies of power acting upon them on the other. Accordingly, in his first dispatch to *Corriere della sera* dated 28 September 1978, Foucault starts by describing the Iranian village of 'Tabas and forty villages' which had been 'annihilated' by a devastating earthquake. After a few introductory sentences, he quickly turns his prose to the way the villagers organized themselves 'under the direction of a cleric', how they 'planted a green flag' and how Islam was already 'facing' and opposing the Shah. 'Help your brothers, but nothing through the government, nothing for it', Foucault cites a message that Ayatollah Khomeini had given from exile in Iraq.[75] Foucault then moves his attention to the urban unrest and the demonstrations, before he analyses forms of disciplinary power, in this case those sections of the army and security forces that were mobilized in order to contain the rebellion. The fundamental matrix that I tried to explain in the first part of this discussion reveals itself: Resistance precedes power ↔ resistance is a freedom that power acts upon ↔ resistance is a form of power.

A similar pattern can be discerned from Foucault's second, third and fourth article written during October 1978. Once again, Foucault starts by describing modes of resistance, his conversations with oppositional activists, the political function of the Friday prayers, the commemoration of the 'martyrs', the imagery of Islam, Shi'ism and the role of Khomeini and intellectuals such as Shariati and their stance against the westernization of Iran espoused by the Shah. In a second dialectical step, Foucault focuses on the way power acts upon these diverse and transitory points of resistance, signposted by a short history of the modernization doctrine underlying the socio-economic policies of the Pahlavi dynasty (1925–1979), the corruption that went with it, the emphasis on Iran's Aryan, pre-Islamic heritage, the dependency on the United States, and the 'iron hand' of the Shah's intelligence service SAVAK. Here, it is striking that Foucault's emphasis on resistance increases in lieu with the success of the revolt. Hence, up until November, his articles strike a balance between modes of resistance and strategies of disciplinary power acting upon them, with a slight tilt towards the resources of the state, obviously because at that time its coercive power was still functional. The last article observing this balance was published in *Le Nouvel Observateur* in mid-October 1978.

In November, the discourse of Foucault changes in accordance with the success of the revolutionaries. In 'A Revolt with Bare Hands' published on 5 November, 'The Challenge to the Opposition', published on 7 November and 'The Mythical Leader of the Iranian Revolt', published on November 26, there is a pronounced emphasis on the unfolding revolutionary resistance, on the 'men and women who protest with banners and flowers in Iran',[76] on the regrouping of the opposition behind Ayatollah Khomeini,[77] his 'inflexible refusal to compromise',[78] and the 'collective will' holding the different strata of society together in opposition to the Shah.[79] In November, witnessing the slow disintegration of the state, Foucault seems increasingly convinced that Iranians are enacting 'a reality that is very near to them, since they themselves are its active agents'.[80] Thus, Foucault depicts them as engineers of a revolution that was moving 'from the strikes to the demonstrations, from the bazaars to the universities, from the leaflets to the sermons, through shopkeepers, workers, clerics, teachers, and students. For the moment', he adds at the same time, 'no party, no man, and no political ideology can boast that it represents this movement'.[81] From here, it is only one small step back to *The Will of Knowledge* and Foucault's suggestion that forms of resistance are not only 'a reaction or rebound, forming with respect to the basic domination an underside that is in the end always passive, doomed to perpetual defeat . . . [N]either are they a lure or a promise that is of necessity betrayed.' Rather most of the time 'one is dealing with mobile and transitory points of resistance'.[82]

And there is even more untapped substance in his writings on Iran. What emerges from November onwards is not only a more pronounced emphasis on the impingement of the revolutionary movement on the power of the Shah, Foucault seems also to remain faithful to his characteristic scepticism as a critical scholar, or what I have described as his anti-synthetic (contra-Hegelian) 'negative dialectics'.[83] Resistance precedes power, resistance is a freedom that power acts upon, but resistance also unfolds into a new form of power which commands its own 'regimes of truth'.[84] Foucault sees this coming. He already poses sceptical questions at the end of his articles in October 1978, that is, during the period when he was still striking a balance between descriptions of resistance and the counter-strategies of the state. Then in mid-November 1978, in a response to an Iranian woman in exile who was opposed to the Islamists who had gathered around Khomeini, Foucault refers to the 'elements that did not seem to [him] to be very reassuring'.[85] In his article on Khomeini published on 26 November, he is more defensive and points out that he 'cannot write the history of the future', that he is limiting himself to '*what is happening right now*, because these days nothing is finished, and the dice are still being rolled'.[86]

Notwithstanding this note of caution, Foucault affords a look into the future in his first article after the success of the revolution and Khomeini's return to Iran in January 1979. In this article, Foucault starts by presenting a 'summary' of events, how the Shah and his allies attempted to quell the revolt, how the struggle between state power and the resistance of the people revealed itself and how the situation has remained unresolved. Conscious that some of the energies of the revolution had already been channelled into the emerging 'Islamic government', Foucault also refers to the potential of the 'revolutionary model . . . to overturn the existing political situation in the Middle East and thus the global strategic equilibrium . . . [A]s an 'Islamic' movement', Foucault adds, 'it can set the entire region on fire'; it is a 'gigantic powder keg, at the level of hundreds of millions of men . . . The Jordan', he concludes dramatically, 'no longer flows very far from Iran'.[87]

With the benefit of hindsight, Foucault overestimated the potencies of the revolution while he underestimated the power of international society to counter anti-systemic movements. Yet it is striking how loyal Foucault remains to his power-resistance model in his writings on Iran. There is even an explicit reference to the phenomenon of the double (*doublure*) that we worked out in the first part of this discussion via Deleuze. From the perspective of Foucault, the Iranian revolutionaries are acting as a 'double'; they had one foot in the politics of the day and another in the intoxicating singularity of the revolutionary movement.[88] 'What has given the Iranian movement its intensity has been a double register', Foucault says. 'On the one hand, a collective will that has been strongly expressed politically and, on the other hand, the desire for a radical change in ordinary life.'[89] Islam promises to

> change their subjectivity . . . there was the desire to renew their existence by going back to a spiritual experience that they thought they could find within Shi'ite Islam itself . . . Let's say then, that Islam, in that year of 1978, was not the opium of the people precisely because it was the spirit of a world without a spirit.[90]

This is what the collective will, the utopia expressed by those Iranians, promises. But history strikes back with a vengeance: resistance unfolds into a new regime of truth. Let us remember that the relationship of the Iranian subject to the outside – history and other structures – folds to make a double. Thus, it allows a relationship to the self to arise that develops according to a new dimension in which agency can be enacted. This is the Islamic Republic which has not been aligned or codified according to the powers that be. But, at the same time, the post-revolutionary Iranian state is itself constituted: it is exactly a crease in the fabric of Iranian history that is held together by relationships to the utopia of the revolution and those pre- and post-revolutionary structures that have remained a part of the politico-cultural topology of Iran. The revolutionary event, the singularity of its intoxicating promise, was the force that made possible the crease at the top of which the Islamic Republic constituted itself, but it did not erase the historical fabric into which the new Iran was woven. 'Uprisings belong to history', Foucault writes after the return of Ayatollah Khomeini, 'but in a certain way, they escape it . . . [T]hey are thus "outside of history" and in history'.[91] In other words: Forms of resistance and political agency always retain a relationship to the outside (viz. history), a 'third dimension' that is neither entirely autonomous, nor entirely constituted by disciplinary power. In order to make that point clearer during his last interview on Iran, Foucault refers to Francois Furet's distinction between the 'totality of the process of economic and social and economic transformations', which relate to long-term structural factors that exist before and after an event such as a revolution, and the 'specificity of the Revolutionary event'.[92] In Iran then, Foucault found confirmation of the action–action dynamic that the continuous battle between power and resistance entails. Iranians may have tried to escape history, but history remained there. In their dialectical constitution as a 'double', Iranians may have overcome the regime of the Shah, but they remained caught up in its 'traditions, institutions that carry a charge of chauvinism, nationalism, exclusiveness'.[93] In his last article on the situation in Iran, written during a period when the new 'Islamicised regime of truth' was already established and when news about summary executions in Iran's prisons had reached the world, Foucault offered the following explanation:

> Because of the strategic positions that Islam occupies, because of the economic importance that the Muslim countries hold, and because of the movement's power to expand on two continents, it constitutes, in the region surrounding Iran, an important and complex reality. As a result, the imaginary content of the revolt did not dissipate in the broad daylight of the revolution. It was immediately transposed onto a political scene that seemed totally willing to receive it but was in fact of an entirely different nature. At this stage, the most important and the most atrocious mingle – the extraordinary hope of remaking Islam into a great living civilisation and various forms of virulent xenophobia, as well as the global stakes and the regional rivalries. And the problem of imperialisms. And the subjugation of women, and so on.[94]

The revolutionary event, encapsulated in the 'extraordinary hope of remaking Islam into a great living civilisation' was singular and unmediated; it engendered the crease in the history of Iran at the top of which the Islamic Republic positioned itself. Yet the new state does not exist in a vacuum. Its constitution unfolds within pre-existing relations to the outside of the revolutionary moment, including systems of imperialism, xenophobia, gender discrimination and so on. As Olivier Roy remarked: 'The government is the fruit of a history; the uprising is timeless; it is the rupture in the chain of causalities and determinations; consequently, it is the product neither of a history nor of a class strategy.' Rather it is 'phenomenon only'. From this perspective, then, 'Foucault rehabilitates the event, the phenomenon, as freedom, a rupture with determinisms, a rupture with history'.[95] A rupture yes, but it does not yield complete detachment. In Foucault's own words:

> The Iranian movement did not experience the 'law' of revolutions that would, some say, make the tyranny that already secretly inhabited them reappear underneath the blind enthusiasm of the masses. What constituted the most internal and the most intensely lived part of the uprising touched,

in an unmediated fashion, on an already overcrowded political chessboard, but such contact is not identity. The spirituality of those who were going to their deaths has no similarity whatsoever with the bloody government of a fundamentalist clergy. The Iranian clerics want to authenticate their regime through the significations that the uprising had. It is no different to discredit the fact of the uprising on the grounds that there is today a government of mullahs. In both cases, there is 'fear', fear of what just happened last fall in Iran, something of which the world had not seen an example for a long time.[96]

I do not think that Foucault's last comments on Iran are a belated admission of error forced upon him by the vitriol that his emphasis on the role of Islam and Khomeini provoked.[97] I think Foucault found his earlier scepticisms confirmed, both his theoretical scepticism about the viability of an absolutely new order and his notes of caution with regard to the Iranian case. After all, he dismissed the role of the clergy at quite an early stage. According to him, they were not a revolutionary force, 'even in the populist sense of the term'.[98] Rather they were products of the revolutionary momentum which was driven by the people from below: 'The men of religion are like so many photographic plates on which the anger and the aspiration of the community are marked'. Foucault was aware that once the clerics would position themselves as the purveyors of a new regime of truth in opposition to the people, they would lose that status. In the light of the mass demonstrations after the disputed re-election of President Ahmadinejad in the summer of 2009, some of which were targeted against the theocratic institutions of the Iranian state, Foucault showed foresight when he cautioned that if the clerics 'wanted to go against the current, they would lose this power, which essentially resides in the interplay of speaking and listening'.[99] From the perspective of many Iranians today, powerful segments of the clerical class have stopped listening to the demands of the people a long time ago. Hence their role is contracted to speaking to the converted.

The resistance of Foucault

'No, Foucault was not a structuralist thinker; nor was he the product of a certain line of "1968 thinking". Nor was he a relativist or a historicist.' This is how Paul Veyne, a former student and friend of Foucault, introduces the latest testimony on his life. 'He was something that, in this day and age, is rare, a *sceptic* thinker.'[100] But despite this engrained scepticism – one that brings us directly back to the beginning of this discussion – Foucault affirms the viability of resistance, agency, political action. This is what the Iran episode taught him above anything else. 'No one has the right to say, "Revolt for me, the final liberation of each man hinges on it". But I do not agree with those who would say, "It is useless to revolt, it will always be the same". One does not dictate to those who risk their lives in the face of power.' Rather one witnesses in silence the struggle between power and resistance which reveals itself ad infinitum: 'A delinquent puts his life on the line against abusive punishment, a madman cannot stand anymore being closed in and pushed down, or a people rejects a regime that oppresses it.' At the same time, '[t]his does not make the first one innocent, does not cure the second, and does not guarantee to the third results that were promised'. So there is no final judgement, no Hegelian synthesis, no end of history, no final victory. The dialectics remain negative:[101]

> No one is required to think that these confused voices sing better than others and speak the truth in its ultimate depth. It is enough that they exist and that they have against them all that strives to silence them, to make it meaningful to listen to them and to search for what they want to say. A question of morality? Perhaps. A question of reality, certainly. All the disillusionments of history will not change this. It is precisely because there are such voices that human time does not take the form of evolution, but that of 'history'.[102]

Power and resistance ad infinitum. Foucault is not interested in being the judge, he does not argue from an entrenched position, either moral or deterministically theoretical. He presents himself as an open-minded outsider equipped with an 'anti-strategic' ethics, '[r]espectful when a singularity arises and intransigent as soon as the state violates universals'.[103] Foucault was interested in the Iranian revolution because it affirmed his interest in resistance to established power constellations. He was sympathetic to the emergence and viability of 'subjugated knowledge', the agency of the (sub)altern, the oppressed,[104] for he was convinced that for Europe encounters with the non-European world would be entirely productive.[105] Ultimately, however, it is his great omission that he did not take the Iranian episode as a springboard to present a viable philosophy of resistance that would be commensurate with his writings on disciplinary regimes, both in terms of historical breadth and empirical detail. Said is right on this account. Foucault was not entirely willing to provide for enough space to the success of 'counter-discursive attempts' which have been useful in showing the 'misrepresentations of discursive power' and 'in Fanon's words, the violence done to psychically and politically repressed inferiors in the name of an advanced culture'.[106] For that Foucault stands accused until today, and perhaps rightly so. But a similar charge has been tabled against Said, whose background makes it even more emphatic and consequential. He too mentions only in passing the adversarial work of feminists and minority cultures. Those counter-discursive regimes that have lent a voice to the 'other' both here and over there in the non-western world remain fairly marginal to his scholarship. So really, the criticism should be extended to both Foucault and Said himself. As we have seen: In Iran yesterday and in Tunisia and Egypt today, the (sub)altern continues to shift overbearing regimes of truth, only to loosen a beautiful agency geared to the luring promise of a better tomorrow.

What Is Radicalism? Lessons from Contemporary Iranian History

My basic thesis is that today's humankind is generally incarcerated within several prisons, and naturally it becomes a true human being only if it can liberate itself from these deterministic conditions.

Ali Shariati

The flag is at full mast, never doubt that

Don't ever worry, my friend

We are a bunch of soldiers, there used to be more of us

Take my words seriously, I'm not one to joke around

Many of our friends are no longer with us

This new year our thoughts will be with you

I want the martyrs to know that if we are keeping it real

It is due to their blood which was spilt on the grounds for us

All the people keeping it real, know that our flag is flying high

If you are a real man then we are with you too

I pray for the world to be secure and peaceful

Amen

We have endured enough fire.

Lyrics of Iranian rapper Hich-Kas

Radicals or revolutionaries?

So far I have presented several approaches to power and resistance in close conjunction with empirical case studies mainly taken from the non-Western world. I will do the same in this chapter but with regard to a third and a fourth term that are interrelated to some of the concepts introduced so far, namely radicalism and revolution. The book is getting more conceptual along the way, but this chapter is less theoretically dense than the previous two and more historiographical, speaking to a different set of the human sciences. I intend to do what Foucault and Said did not: I will discuss how radical (sub)altern agency has been enacted, in this case in contemporary Iran. This interregnum demonstrates further that political agency, the ability to resist against all odds, was not decisively muted by the imperial machinery and its disciplinary cogs, including 'Orientalism'. In order to qualify this statement, I will delve into the dialectics of contemporary Iranian history, with particular emphasis on domestic politics in this interregnum, and Iranian–US relations in the next.

Let me start with a simple conceptual question: What does it mean to be 'radical'? In European political theory, radicalism has long been associated with leftist ideas and socialist theories. 'To be a "radical"', Anthony Giddens writes, 'was to have a certain view of the possibilities inherent in history – radicalism meant breaking away from the hold of the past'. Some radicals were immersed in the idea of revolution and many were fascinated by the possibility to bring about an entirely 'new' historical sequence. 'History was there to be seized hold of, to be moulded to human purposes', Giddens argues, 'such that the advantages which in previous eras seemed given by God, and the prerogative of the few, could be developed and organised for the benefit of all'.[1] This definition of radical politics as a revolt against the status quo is also emphasized by Fred Halliday. He focused on revolutions more specifically when he conceptualizes them as 'a break with the constraints of the past, the traditional or established society'. Revolutions made it possible to imagine 'a new society, even a new world, to be constructed. This emphasis upon breaking with the past, the creation of something new', he continues, 'was to become a prominent strain in the appeals and self-justification of revolutions'.[2]

Both Giddens and Halliday point to an important object of radical politics: the negation of the prevalent order. As such, radical politics and revolution are an outcome of a systematic resistance movement with transversal capability. When Lenin said that without theory there will be no revolutionary action, Ernesto Guevara stressed the indispensable need to explain the motives, ends and methods of the revolution in Cuba, and Marx imagined the final moment of the class struggle when everything would be decided in a momentous battle for the end of history, they alluded exactly to the necessity and possibility of systematic resistance to the status quo that would yield a transcendent order that was imagined in a largely secular sense, a Utopia that would be attainable here and now. Yet in their many pamphlets and writings, as much as in the scholarly treatment of radical politics and revolutionary action presented by Halliday and Giddens, it does not become entirely clear what the difference between 'radical politics' and 'revolution' would be. It appears that both radicals and revolutionaries attempt to overcome what they consider to be the injustices of the respective system, but that the radical would be satisfied with radical transformation (a revolt) while the revolutionary aims at overthrowing every political, socio-economic and cultural determination all the way down to the consciousness of the individual and all the way 'up' to the constitution of History. As Giddens puts it: 'Radicalism, taking things by the roots, meant not just bringing about change but controlling such change so as to drive history onwards.'[3] From this perspective, the radical subject retains some linkage and dependency with the prevalent order; there remains a degree of complicity with the determinations of history. The radical is a 'passive revolutionary', an agent of *transformismo* to use two of Gramsci's ideal-types.[4] Conversely, such relative interdependency with the status quo is wholly unacceptable, in theory and practice, to revolutionaries for whom the 'vision of revolutionary change is that of a world restructured and regenerated in all its aspects – social, political, economic, cultural, and familial'.[5] In this sense, one of the primary differences between revolutionary and radical politics, in their contemporary conceptualization, is the degree of the transformation envisaged and implemented. This is a nuanced difference between radical reform and a total break with the past, between agonistic and antagonistic politics, between a revolt and a mass movement, between a molar digression from the temporal order and the imagination of a parallel universe: RADICALISM ↔ revolt ↔ agonism ↔ riotous violence ↔ temporal trajectory (transformative); REVOLUTION ↔ mass movement ↔ antagonism ↔ structural violence ↔

temporal break (utopian).[6] So radicalism is 'second' to revolution in the typology of demands for political change. Its most prominent manifestation is a revolt. It is followed by 'reform' which Halliday defines as 'change that is more cautious or limited, and "evolution", suggesting change that does not involve a radical break with the past'.[7] As indicated, all of these political struggles fall within the purview of resistance.

In the following paragraphs, I will discuss the two types of politics espoused by radicals and revolutionaries with two principle digressions: empirical and theoretical. I will take the contemporary emergence of radical and revolutionary politics in Iran as my empirical departure point, partially in order to further contribute to a comparative conceptualization of theories of power and resistance. Both historiographers and critical theorists largely have ignored the Iranian case despite the international tremors that Iranian politics continue to provoke. And yet, the unrest after the controversial re-election of President Mahmoud Ahmadinejad in the summer of 2009 and the crackdown on the oppositional 'Green Movement' that continues at the time of writing reveal the salience and obduracy of radical political subjectivity in Iran. Thus, delving into the dialectics between state and society in the country promises to unhinge a wealth of theoretical insights. In many ways, Iranians have never really ceased to believe in 'making history' and many theoreticians of politics and comparative historiography have failed to ask why.[8] In order to address this shortcoming, and to position the Iranian case more firmly in those fields, I will discuss how the contemporary radical subject in Iran emerged out of the dialectics between state and society in the late nineteenth century. I will sketch, moreover, how out of the depth of the political disillusionment with the Pahlavi monarchy, political radicalism turned to revolutionary action yielding the Islamic Republic in 1979. Throughout the following paragraphs, I will attempt to identify, at once cautiously and tangentially, aspects of the Iranian case that merit theoretical deduction.

A (short) history of radicalism in Iran

The contemporary 'radical subject' is very different from earlier ideal-types of Iranian politics in that its political activism is systematic, institutional (theo-)nationalistic and ideological. This is largely due to the historical syntax out of which the radical subject emerged. Radical politics developed only gradually within Iranian society, in the many institutional and organizational loci that increasingly were networked and politicized at least from the late nineteenth century onwards. A variety of agonistic political discourses were perfected by oppositional clerics, intellectuals (another 'new' subject), students, philosophers, teachers and workers who were positioning themselves both against the arbitrariness of the state and the structural violence of imperialism, at first in its British and Russian manifestation and later in its 'American' form.

More specifically, the contemporary radical subject in Iran emerges out of the dialectics of the first mass upheaval of Iranian history engendered by the 'tobacco revolt' of 1891. We are transferred back to a period when Iranian politics was seriously affected by the interplay of the imperial interests of Russia and Britain. In 1891, the Qajar monarch Naser al-Din Shah (1831–1896) granted an exclusive monopoly for the sale and export of tobacco to Major Talbot, a British citizen. The Shah had to cancel the monopoly not only because of Russian opposition, but primarily due to the nationwide protests and an ensuing boycott of tobacco products. For the first time in contemporary Iranian history, different strata of society cooperated in order to bring about and sustain a radical 'counter-regime' that was intrusive enough to affect the politics of the state. The emerging discourse thus signified was transversal, uttered by a range of artists, clerics, intellectuals, military personnel, merchants and Islamic 'revivalists'.

Already in the nineteenth century those agents of political change in Iran had access to a privileged political and cultural infrastructure that was chaperoned by the Qajar dynasty, in particular Naser al-Din Shah. In order to buttress their religious legitimacy, the Qajar monarchs invested in the building of mosques, tombs and shrines dedicated to the descendants of the twelve Shi'i imams called *imamzadeh*. They also expanded places of mourning for the killing of the twelfth Imam of the Shi'i and the grandson of the prophet Muhammad, Hussein ibn Talib, called *tekyieh* and secular educational institutions including art schools. The latter produced an art movement in Iran that was not – perhaps for the first time in Iranian history – entirely dependent on the patronage of the elites in the country, in particular the royal court. It was the favourable conditions under Naser al-Din Shah and the emergence of a relatively affluent middle class in the late nineteenth century, for instance, which allowed Mohammad Ghaffari (or Kamal al-Molk

1847–1940) to study at the Dar al-Fonun and to return to Iran from exile in Iraq after the success of the constitutional revolt in 1906. Upon his return to Iran, this doyen of contemporary Persian art established his own prestigious art school which produced some of the foremost artists of the country.[9] At the same time, the burgeoning religious institutions such as the mosques were increasingly used by society to discuss social, political and economic issues and sometimes to arbitrate between feuding neighbours. The most prominent allusion to the mosques as places of political activity came from Ayatollah Khomeini in the build-up to the revolution of 1979 when he repeatedly urged Iranians to 'organise meetings in mosques and public places' in order to 'defend the Qur'an and Islamic justice'.[10] As we will see in greater detail in the following paragraphs, Khomeini and his followers took advantage of a readily available religious infrastructure that was geared to Shi'i norms and symbols at least since the Safavid dynasty (1502–1736) which established Shi'ism as one of the main national narratives in Iran.[11]

As an institutional ideal-type that multiplied social networks within Iranian society, the communicative power of the mosque complemented a range of tea- and coffee houses (*chai-khuneh* or *ghave-khuneh*) that proliferated in Iran's major cities from the late nineteenth century onwards and which provided an equally opportune social context to exchange ideas and dissolve disputes within the community. These new sites of communication, blended in with more traditional forms of socialization, such as poetry nights (*shab-e sher*), and reconstituted spaces of political and social activism with ancient roots such as the 'houses of strength' (*zurkhaneh*), a place of immense physical and mental exercise, and houses of joy (*safa khaneh*), where scholars, poets and artists would gather to deliberate about the politics of the day. The house of joy in Isfahan, later renamed the Constitution House, for instance, served as a place for inter-faith dialogue among the Muslims, Jews and Christians of the city during the constitutional revolt between 1905 and 1911 and thereafter. At least from the late nineteenth century onwards, then, the relationship of the individual and the state changed; the political subject, individualized as he appears, has privileged access to new institutional sites that exist in relative autonomy of the state. A whole new micro-world with exciting opportunities opened up to Iranians of that generation and they made ample use of them in the decades to come.

The developments had a profound political implication: The category 'society' was distanced from the category 'state' whose claim to exercise 'sovereign' power without accountability was suddenly questioned. Now some members of the *ulema* (Muslim clergy), the Islamic revivalists and nationalists created fields of political activism that were separated from the formal power of the monarchy. It is in this way that in the tobacco revolt of 1891, the *fatwa* (religious verdict) of 'Grand Ayatollah' Shirazi forbidding his followers to use any tobacco-based product merged with the 'anti-imperial' pamphlets of Jamal al-din al-Afghani and the speeches and secret memoranda of 'nationalist' officers who called for resistance against any economic concessions that would galvanize foreign influence in Iran. Similarly, the mosques were increasingly reorganized to serve as places of political activism and resistance providing sanctuary to protesters. They did not function merely as places of worship and social activity. Rather, they increasingly became sites of communicative, mass-ideological transmission as indicated. For the first time in contemporary Iranian history, diverse strata of society were equipped with both a national 'micro-geography' to organize their political agenda and the structural (religious and non-religious) legitimation to that end. The contemporary radical subject emerges out of this modified dialectic between state and society in the country. From now on, resistance is not merely scattered, the radical subject utters not just a whisper in the cacophony of Iranian politics. From now on, the radical subject speaks with a voice that is simultaneously peremptory in its ideological ellipses and emphatic in its sublating demands.

Ervand Abrahamian, Homa Katouzian and Nikki Keddie have chronicled the contemporary history of Iran most comprehensively, and they rightly interpret 1891 as a precursor to the 'Constitutional Revolution' of 1905–1911.[12] However, the term revolution to designate these events has been applied without much theoretical reflection. It was not the revolutionary subject that was dominant during this period. In Persian, the Arabic term *inqilab* which is derived from *qleb* meaning 'to overturn' or 'to knock over', attains its ultimate revolutionary politico-cultural significance in the discourse of the Marxist-Leninist, the communist *Tudeh* party and, more significantly for the trajectory of the revolution in 1979, in the influential writings of Jalal Al-e Ahmad, Ali Shariati and the clerical revisionists supporting Ayatollah Khomeini.

The revolutionary subject in Iran is a hybrid creature constituted by the tapestry of overlapping Utopian-romantic ideas espoused by both the Islamic and leftist revolutionaries. This revolutionary subject had stopped to negotiate and called for a new social and political status quo at least from the 1950s onwards. Yet the radical subject, who was at the centre of the constitutional revolt, was satisfied with an amendment to the political order. The radical constitutionalists did not call for a wholesale overthrow of the political and social system (neither did they command the discursive capabilities to do so). The events leading up to the establishment of a constitutional monarchy in 1906 centred on very specific grievances: in Mashhad bread rioters agitated against high food prices; in Tehran women demonstrators protested against worsening social conditions; senior clerics deprecated the 'trade' of Iranian women who were forced into 'sexual slavery' because of deteriorating economic conditions; *bazaaris* (merchants) contested the high taxes that were levied in order to bankroll the lavish life style of the monarch and his court; and students of the Dar al-Fonun began to translate constitutional and republican forms of governance into the political situation encompassing Iran. Consequently, the outcome of the revolt was a radical, not a revolutionary, transformation of the political order in the country: On 5 August 1906, Muzaffar al-Din Shah, the fifth monarch of the Qajar dynasty, agreed to institute nationwide elections. According to the new constitution, the Shah's oath of office had to be made before the newly established National Assembly; and he had to accept both the ministers and officials proposed by it and the bills signed into law by its elected members. At the same time, the Shah would be the head of the executive, commander-in-chief of the armed forces, and would retain significant legislative and executive rights.[13] The *majles-e melli* was born, and the discourse of democracy and republicanism emerged. However, the monarch remained a significant institution of the political system, and in 1907 Iran was divided into Russian and British 'spheres of influence', and the country subsequently descended into a virtual civil war until the coup d'état of Reza Khan on 21 February 1921. The latter eventually established the Pahlavi dynasty (1925) and the mandate of absolute monarchic authority was reconstituted, this time not around God but around a novel, modernistic mythology that proved to be by far more susceptible to this-worldly contention.

The political culture enveloping and delivering the constitutional revolt, which I can dissect only rather sketchily here, equipped the radical subject with extraordinarily diverse institutional and discursive powers. The new moment in Iranian society was an expansion of the geography of politics. This expansion can be discerned from two interdependent factors: first, the emergence and re-imagination of a whole new vocabulary constituting the political discourse. Terms denoting the new phenomenon of the 'masses' such as *tudeh* and *khalgh*; terms conscribing the idea of democracy, constitutionalism and the exigencies of the nation-state model such as *jomhuri* (republic), *mashrute* (constitutional), *melliyat* (nationality), *demokrasi* (democracy) and *vatan* (homeland); terms differentiating the newly established political field and the party competition exercised therein such as *chap* (left), *rast* (right), *melli-gera* (nationalist) or *sosialist* (socialist); and terms that were re-signified in order to construct a radical discourse of Islam that would depart from the quietist tradition of the orthodox Shi'i clergy. It is within this latter field that the Ayatollah establishes his (no women Ayatollahs yet) significance. From this point onwards, those senior oppositional *mujtahids* who sided with the demands of the people were referred to as *Ayat Allah*, a sign of God, a discursive challenge to the religious authority of the Shah who was traditionally referred to as *ill-Allah* or the 'Shadow of God' and at times as *Ayatollah* as well. In this way, the dialectics of the constitutional movement produced an important factor of the Islamicized revolution of 1979. Since the constitutionalists emphasized, in the name of equality, that no aristocratic or religious titles should be used anymore, the *Ayatollah* turned into an exclusively clerical ideal-type. It is true, as Fakhreddin Azimi recently argued, that the 'constitutional demystification of monarchy meant that the Shahs could no longer claim to be shadows of God on earth, fully entitled to their patrimonial fiefdom'.[14] But it seems equally true to argue that God cast another shadow: from now on, God exited the domain of the palace and wandered back into the praying rooms of the mosque. Here He (this was a very gender-specific god) increasingly deified what was considered to be the ultimate form of political authority by an increasing number of Iranians and Shi'i-Muslims more generally.

Second, this political discourse now was professionally dispersed by a set of new institutional ideal-types: places of education such as the Dar al-Fonun which was established under the patronage of Amir Kabir in 1851 and which was turned into the University of Tehran in January 1935. Dar al-Fonun, whose faculty was dominated by European academics under the Qajars, further facilitated the translation of canonical European books in the fields of human sciences and literature, including the works of Darwin, Voltaire, Dumas, Fenelon, Descartes and Verne. A whole new archive informing an 'Iranian' dialectic with 'European' modernity was engineered during this period. Yet far from educating the 'native' population into apathy, the European presence enmeshed itself in the newly devised 'Iranian' narrative, provoked its own 'native' form of resistance. Various political organizations, a whole range of *anjumans* (associations), stratified in accordance with 'sub-national' affiliations (Armenians, Azeris, Lurs, Kurds, etc.) or, interdependently, religious preference (Muslim, Zoroastrian, Jewish, Christian, Baha'i), institutionalized their political agendas and transmitted them through the pages of a burgeoning local press and publications such as *Asr-e Now* (New Age), *Nasim-e Shomal* (The Northern Breeze), *Esteghlal* (Independence), *Eghbal* (Progress) or *Sur-e Israfil* (Israfil's Trumpet), the latter written mainly by the famed lexicographer Ali-Akbar Dehkhoda.[15] A second rather more contested factor has to be added here: that is, the role of institutionalized discourses of Islam in the radical politics of this period. As Hamid Enayat noted: 'The religio-political tracts of the time denote an attitude which, while returning to the compromise of the Safavid period, is as anxious to prevent the monarchy from lapsing into despotism and corruption.'[16] Enayat points to the writings of Mullah Mohammad Kazim Khorasani and Mohammad Hussein Naini to support his argument, and to the emergence of a 'pre-constitutionalist mentality' in the chief doctrines of the *usuli* school of Shi'i-Islam with its emphasis on the necessity of *ijtihad* and critical reasoning which had become increasingly influential in Shi'i jurisprudence since the emergence of Mohammad Baqir Wahid Behbehani (1704–1791).[17] The *usuli* discourse equipped progressive members of the *ulema* with the critical devices to accommodate and further the constitutional demands for democratic legislation and public accountability of the state, both in the build-up and in the aftermath of the constitutional revolt.[18]

The point of adding this latter factor is not to unearth the signposts of a 'truer' history of the constitutional movement. I am not interested in fighting

History with History here. Yet it must be added that, in the name of a critical attitude toward the way History is written in general and the political economy of 'Iranian Studies' in particular, the fortunes of Islamo-centric, nationalist or socialist representations of this pivotal period do not ebb and flow in accordance with their truth value, but too often instead with political allegiance and/or the hegemonic political culture of the day. It is such guided cultural constellations and the discursive regimes of truth that they inform which set the conditions for the production of a 'truer' history of Iran.[19] Hence, Ahmad Kasravi, who managed to chronicle the history of the constitutional movement in sublime prose and from a staunchly anti-clerical perspective, has been central to the nationalist narrative and its adherents, while the writings and pro-constitutional activities of clerics such as Naini are rather more pronounced in 'Islamist' representations of Iranian history. It is no coincidence, of course, that the 'Islamist paradigm' proliferated in many quarters especially after the establishment of the Islamic Republic in 1979.[20] Ultimately, if there is one thing that the contemporary dialectics of power and resistance in Iran taught us, it is that it is impossible to hermetically shut down the idea of the country in either a purely Islamic habitat or a sanitized 'national-Persian' environment. The transnational and multicultural realities of the history of Iran are indicative of a post-modern condition that continuously escapes any form of ideational fascism.

Battles over the official history of Iran too often are parochial and ideologically tainted and shall not concern me beyond their value for a critical reading of the way discourse/power/knowledge constellations determine how an Iran is represented. What has been more central to my reading of Iran thus far is to show that, at least from the latter half of the nineteenth century onwards, the radical subject revolted in the name of nationalist fervour, anti-imperial passion, socialist rationality and/or Islamic reasoning. Of course, these are all my ideal-typical 'categories' that do not exhaust the range of causes that challenged the political status quo during that period.

What can be discerned from such developments, at least since the latter half of the nineteenth century, is a steady growth and transversal networking of the sites – institutional and individual – of political discourse in Iran. The radical subject was endowed with a whole new space to function and to propagate against the state. Out of the fierce nationalism and constitutionalism of this moment, many voices were raised, feminine and male, in condemnation of Iran's subservience to imperial powers and the abandonment of the constitution of 1906 by the Pahlavis, in the accent of an elite class that was adamant to constrain the power of the monarchy. At least from the latter part of the 1940s onwards, the target was Mohammad Reza Shah, who acceded to the Peacock Throne in 1941 after the British forced his father, Reza Khan, into exile on the pretext that he wanted to collude with Nazi Germany.

Here, the poetry of Nima Yushij (1896–1960) is an important signpost in the development of resistance art in Iran and a central marker in the consolidation of the humanistic tradition in the country. His poems such as *Morghe-Gham* (The Bird of Sorrow) and *Ay Adamha* (Oh Humans), published in 1938 and 1941 respectively, are an expression of the troubled history of Iran in the early twentieth century, the sorrow of the people and the despair of the intellectuals. Nima Yushij is the metaphorical and aesthetic nodal point of resistance art in modern Iran, and at the same time an individual voice and a channel for the grievances of the people of his period and thereafter. In his poems, the worldliness and universal aspects of Iranian art are expressed in the rhythmic beauty of *sher-e now* (new poetry). In addition, they brought forward a political dimension that revealed his class consciousness as Mehdi Akhavan-Saless writes in one of his reviews of Nima's work.[21] Nima Yushij enmeshed the individualized subject in Iran into a wider narrative that is at once stratified in accordance with class and universalized in synchrony with humanistic values. In *The Amen Bird*, this dialectic between the individualized social subject and his environment is expressed through the metaphor of the 'amen bird', which is introduced from the outset of the poem as an interlocutor for the emotions of the people:

> Drenched in pain, the amen bird is left wandering
>
> He has gone to the other side of this era of injustice. Having returned, no longer does he yearn for water and seeds.

The bird charters and expresses the pain of the people and it holds the key for their salvation:

> That penetrating gaze (the concealed ear of our suffering world) looks at
>
> The oppressed people.
>
> With every amen that the friendly bird utters,
>
> He brings together the people

Lessening their crushing pain.

. . .

The Bird says:

'May all the chains that have shackled the people's feet be broken.'

The people say:

'May the chains be broken.'

The bird says:

'May the despairing masses be the masters of their own fate

. . .

May they leave their ruined state

For their prosperity to

Pay for their crimes.'

The bird says:

'May this destruction be a due reward

For those who thrived on injustice.'

'Shall it be thus!' (cry, the distressed people)

'Shall it be thus, amen!'

. . .

'A punishment for their ugly deeds

Which murdered noble souls

And disdained compassion.'

'Amen!'

'This is a just reward

For their shameful deeds

Which only opened a path for the traders who sought gains,

And by which only a trace was left from us on the swamp's throne.'

'Amen! Amen!'[22]

Beyond this immensely powerful underbelly of resistance within Iranian society, the primary driving force of the opposition to the Shah's rule in the period 1949–1953 was not only Mohammad Mossadegh, the Swiss educated 'aristocrat' who died a great and almost 'prototypical' nationalist. The expansion of the discursive geography of politics brought with it the emergence of politically functional individuals who were introjected by a range of counter-hegemonic ideas.[23] There emerged a mass psychology that was geared towards achieving the Utopia of full independence and to constraining the authoritarianism of the state. The radical subject thinks and acts within a political counter-culture that is entirely sophisticated both in terms of its ideological vigour and its internationalist outlook. The radical subject has privileged access to socialist, Marxist-Leninist, social-democratic, nationalist and 'Islamist' discourses, all of which created their own fulminating momentum merging with the demand for radical change. The radical subject joined a variety of different groups: those espousing violence as a political strategy such as the *Fedaiyan-e Islam* (Devotees of Islam) who were responsible for a range of terrorist atrocities in Tehran and beyond; the Communist Tudeh Party which was established in 1941 and which turned increasingly pro-Soviet in the latter 1940s, bowing to the irresistible ideological pressures and financial incentives of Stalinism;[24] clerics such as Ayatollah Seyyed Abol-Qassem Kashani who was sympathetic to the nationalists' cause; and at the helm of the revolt Mohammad Mossadegh and his National Front party (*Jebhe-Melli*). Mossadegh managed to turn the prevalent mood for radical action into a popular movement that would bring about the nationalization of the Anglo-Iranian Oil Company in 1951, two years before he was ousted by a MI6/CIA engineered coup d'état which would reinstate the dictatorship of the Shah.

Mosssadegh is a singularly important figure in history, not merely because he managed to nationalize the Iranian oil economy or because of his democratic credentials. Mossadegh demonstrated that it was possible to overthrow, on the one side, the institution of the monarchy in Iran, and, on the other, to resist the 'superpowers' of the day. Henceforth, the new counter-culture in Iran is no longer organized around questions such as: How can we negotiate with the state? How can we pressure it to accept a particular agenda? How can we confine its authoritarianism? How can we bargain with it? How can we play the superpowers off against each other? Since Mossadegh, the dialectic between Iranian society and the state is no longer organized around the agonistic politics, semi-ordered revolts and 'realistic' calculations of the radical subject. It is premised on revolution, on a total break of the prevalent system, both within Iran and beyond – from now on Utopia is not only thought, from now on it is enacted.

Licentious power versus revolutionary libido

For the revolutionary subject, death is a beginning, justice is transcendental and martyrdom is *Erlebnis,* an ineffable concession to the cause. The revolutionary subject craves climactic events; it functions according to what I term a 'libidinous bio-ontology'. The revolutionary subject is adamant to demonstrate political prowess, the ability to channel passion into political action. The revolutionary subject relentlessly tries to elicit as many 'ineffable' events as possible in order to establish a superior counter-discourse which would be linked, with the help of an intellectual vanguard, into a strident, ideologically charged counter-culture simulating the viability of a temporal break with everything that 'is'. This is what Marx called the 'sixth great power', which would overwhelm, quite inevitably, every other power in its way. In *Labour of Dionysus,* Michael Hardt and Antonio Negri allude to this transformative dynamic that drives the revolutionary subject. According to them: 'It is as if the world is unmade and reconstructed on the basis of a set of thoughts, actions, and intuitions established on the individual and collective singularity that organize it through its desire and its power.'[25] This desire and power of the revolutionary subject is organized and infused by the Utopia that everything is possible. Time and being are conceived of as limitless, and the revolutionary subject is placed at the edge of that possibility, with a clear view of what is to come in the future. The revolutionary subject employs a distinctly modern, positivistic syntax that is almost impervious to disappointment and taking as its primary battle ground the official writing of history and the national narratives thus spun.

Charles Kurzman has recently termed the revolution in Iran 'unthinkable', a coincidence of several factors that were unpredictable and that delivered the revolution almost as a *bonne chance* of history.[26] However, Kurzman does not take into account that Iranians began to 'think' the revolution at least since the late 1950s. Indeed, in the most influential writings of Iran's prototypical revolutionary intellectuals, such as Jalal Al-e Ahmad and Ali Shariati, Iranian history in particular and Islam in general were rewritten to function as building blocks for a viable and uncompromising ideology that was quite overtly and explicitly revolutionary. So for the former, the thirteenth-century astronomer and philosopher Nasir ad-Din Tusi (1201–1274) becomes the prototypical 'aggressive intellectual' (*rowshanfekr-e mohajem*), 'who made history' after obliterating the prevalent order seeking to 'destroy the contemporary governmental institutions in order to erect something better in their place'.[27] For the latter, we find a comparable signification of revolutionary change which is likened to a golden age of justice, a classless society, social equality, and the final victory of the oppressed masses against their oppressors. According to Shariati, there was no choice toward that end since the victory of the revolution was historically determined. This would make it mandatory for the vanguard to 'object to the status quo and to negate the ruling systems and values'.[28] With Al-e Ahmad and Shariati, then, an entirely new ontology for Iran is imagined and increasingly enacted.

This newly imagined Iran was not provincial, as some scholars have argued. The revolutionary subject in Iran was not confined to a nativist habitat, even if it indulged in the Utopia of 'authenticity'.[29] In the writings of intellectuals such as Al-e Ahmad and Shariati we hear echoes of – and see direct reference to – Che Guevera, Marx, Sartre, Marcuse, Fanon and others. After all, this radical culture of resistance was also inscribed in the very linguistic infrastructure of Iran's capital Tehran after the revolution where major streets, boulevards and squares were named 'Bobby Sands', 'Ghandi', 'Africa' and 'Palestine'.[30]

Despite the obvious tilt to Islam as a liberation theology, it is in Shariati's work especially that east meets west on an immensely innovative critical spectrum, and where the potentialities of a seemingly contradictory 'Islamo-socialist' discourse are exploited in order to channel what was considered to be the emancipating message of Islam and socialism to receptive constituencies within Iranian society. This internationalist cross-fertilization was not limited only to the intellectual/theoretical realm. For instance, the nascent Iranian armed movements of the 1960s drew their inspiration from theories of guerrilla warfare developed in Cuba, Nicaragua, Vietnam, Palestine and China. '[A]long with centres for study of present and future zones of operations, intensive popular work must be undertaken to explain the motives of the revolution, its ends', Che Guevera suggests in his manual for guerrilla warfare that was translated and widely distributed in Iran in the 1960s. It is imperative, according to Guevara, 'to spread the incontrovertible truth that victory of the enemy against the people is finally impossible. *Whoever does not feel this undoubted truth cannot be a guerrilla fighter.*'[31] In Iran such 'bio-ontological' re-education toward the revolutionary subject gained momentum out of the disillusionment with the political order after the enforced downfall of Mossadegh in 1953, and more exponentially in the late 1950s. From now on, the revolutionary subject plots to reverse History *in toto*. From now on, the revolutionary subject in Iran takes on a dual combat: resisting the 'bipolar' world order, dominated by the Soviet Union and the United States on the one side and combating the monarchy of the Shah on the other.

So at least from the 1950s onwards, something quite bio-ontological occurs in Iranian politics. On the one side, politically conscious Iranians become the target of more systematic, certainly more consequential, revolutionary agitation. On the other side, *zoon politikon*, the 'political animal', becomes the target of a formal, systematic and overbearingly paternalistic form of state-power which is entirely 'licentious'. The power of the state, that the revolutionary subject not only is attempting to resist but also to conquer, turns to a perversely excessive form of ideational self-assertion. 'Identity' becomes the major issue in the representation of Iran's national narrative and in the making of the legitimacy of the state. Now we enter the world of 'genetic' manipulation: licentious power forcefully induces, on the 'macro-level' of the state, the factor of race into the idea of what the Iranian nation 'is'. In the political biology propagated by the Pahlavis, Iranians were first and foremost 'Aryan', quite Indo-European due to the Persian language and very much distinct from the Semitic Arabs and 'their' Islamic history. Accordingly, Shah Mohammad Reza Pahlavi was to be referred to as *Aryamehr* or 'Light of the Aryans'. At the height of his megalomania, exemplified by his Napoleon-esque self-coronation in 1967 and the extravagant festivities at Persepolis in 1971, the Shah changed the Islamic solar hijra calendar into an imperial one. Suddenly, Iran was in the year 2535 based on the presumed date of the foundation of the Achaemenid dynasty. In lieu with the effort to Iranianize the Persian language, which had already been pursued by his father Reza Khan, the Pahlavi state also sponsored systematic efforts to substitute Arabic terms with Persian ones. The situation in Iran was assessed, with increasing worry for the stability of the Pahlavi regime, in an intelligence report by the CIA, dated May 1972, and declassified in June 2006:

> The Shah sees himself in the role of a latter-day Cyrus the Great who will restore to Iran at least a portion of its old glory as a power to be reckoned with in [sic] its own part of the world. His coronation in 1966, 25 years after he

assumed the throne, and the grandiose celebration of the 2,500th anniversary of the founding of the Monarchy were the Shah's way of publicly affirming his belief in the validity of royal rule. Although he frequently insists on the possibility of a true constitutional monarchy in Iran, his actions suggest that he does not foresee it in his time. A noncharismatic leader, he has taken on many of the trappings of totalitarianism; scarcely a town of any size does not have its Avenue Pahlavi and it is a mean city, indeed, that does not have a traffic circle dominated by a statue of the Shah or his father. Massive rallies are held, complete with giant portraits of the Shah and banners bearing quotations by him, and no politician ventures a suggestion without carefully pointing out that it fits within the framework approved by the Shah . . . The Shah is the master of what has been called the 'Pahlavism'.[32]

The ideational architecture of 'Pahlavism' was crafted around the symbolism of monarchic rule and the metaphysics of modern nationalism consisting of romantic myths about the authenticity of the Persian language and the Iranian civilization. Their impact on the making of a modern 'identity' of Iran devoid of an intrinsically 'Islamic' component comes out in an article which the Shah placed in *Life* magazine in May 1963: 'Geographically Iran is situated at the crossroads of the East and the West; it is where Asia and Europe meet', the Shah asserts. 'On one side thrived the old civilisations of China and India; on the other those of Egypt, Babylon, Greece, Rome, and, later on, the modern Western World.' His country was not a part of any civilization per se, but 'Iran welded her own civilisation from all those many sources'. This distinctly Iranian civilization holds a universal religion and universal art which 'have left their traces all over the world'. But this universal religion that the Shah refers to is not conceptualized as Islamic. Rather, he heralds the pre-Islamic era, 'the old Iranian religion of Mithra' and the 'teachings of the mystic prophet Mani'.[33] So Islam did not have much of a role in the making of an Iran during this period. A discourse of Islam only re-enters the re-imagination of what it means to be Iranian in the counter-culture of the 1960s and 1970s and after the Islamicized revolution of 1979.

There were more dramatic developments for the dialectic between state and society. On the micro-level, the *vision* of Shah Mohammad Reza Pahlavi about the past (Aryan), present (transitionary) and future (*tamadon-e bozorg* or the great civilization) was enhanced by a sophisticated *supervisionary* regime that extended the licentious power of the state upon the very body of its object of desire, that is, Iranian society. In 1957, the Shah established a new intelligence agency called SAVAK which employed thousands of operatives and informants across the country and beyond. SAVAK, which was created under the tutelage of the FBI and the Israeli Mossad, introduced, for the first time in Iranian history, professional techniques of torture in the expanding number of prison cells in the country. Other institutions such as the Imperial Inspectorate and the J2 Bureau, which functioned as the intelligence branch of the imperial army, joined the supervisionary network. The budget for the military – meant to be one of the pillars of the Shah's rule and hence closely supervised by him – expanded from US$60 million in 1954 to US$7.2 billion in 1977 (at 1973 prices and exchange rates).[34] In the later 1970s, the military budget of Iran was one of the largest in the world – per Gross National Product. Much of this expansion of the security bureaucracy was possible because of increasing oil revenues, which skyrocketed after the OPEC boycott of 1973.[35]

At least from the early twentieth century onwards, and later on abetted and catalyzed by the modernization doctrines of the Pahlavis themselves, the state in Iran was confronted with three novel social tendencies: First, the urbanization of Iranian society, the physical concentration of persons in towns which the growth of the population of the country facilitated; second, the social and political expansion of the geography of politics that caught more and more people within its space; and third, the emergence of new politically savvy ideal-types in society such as the *rowshanfekr* (intellectual), *kargar* (the worker), the *zan-e mobarez* (resisting woman) and the oppositional Ayatollah. All of these actors now were endowed with enough institutional space and discursive leverage to impinge on the territory of the sovereign.

This impingement on the sovereignty of the state that the expansion of the geography of politics brought about dramatized the problems of management and surveillance of an increasing number of persons. The state reacted by instituting a range of novel disciplinary strategies, techniques of power and knowledge that made it possible for its bureaucracy to organize the population and to make it visible, to attempt to turn society into an object of formal power (e.g. judicial and administrative), especially after the Shah was reinstalled in 1953. A particularly prominent example in this regard is the so-called White Revolution launched by the Shah ten years later. It not only led to land reform, but also to unprecedented levels of industrialization and social change (women's rights, including the right to vote and growth of the educational sector). It was not merely an ideological device to pre-empt the revolutionary rhetoric of the burgeoning Left in the country. The White Revolution simultaneously territorialized Iranian society and made it visible to the 'gaze' and the disciplinary apparatus of the state. As part of land reform, which was the main pillar of the proposed changes, a professional census was taken of Iranians and they were mapped in accordance with the newly devised 'provinces'. This made possible, for the first time in Iranian history, the authoritative, 'scientific' language of the second census of the country published in 1966 which established that 'Iran had a population of 25,323,064 distributed over an area of 628,000 square miles'.[36] From now on everything and everyone within this newly delineated anatomy – the Iranian body politic – was affected by the state, at least formally: families who wanted to apply for birth certificates to enable their children to go to school or to marry; people who had to apply for a passport in order to travel abroad; farmers who had to qualify for government subsidies to finance the fertilization of their crops; students who applied for government scholarships, and so on.

But despite this modernization of the disciplinary apparatus of the state, it would be wrong to assume that the licentious form of power, despite its 'rational', 'scientific' pretensions and despite the FBI/Mossad torture handbooks, is equal, in status and efficiency, to the omnipresent, yet 'clandestine' power that Michel Foucault describes. In *Discipline and Punish*, Foucault describes such 'panoptical power' as unspectacular, capillary, almost invisible. It strikes from afar, it is not immediately identifiable: 'If it is still necessary for the law to reach and manipulate the body of the convict', Foucault writes, 'it will be at a distance, in the proper way, according to strict rules, and with a much "higher" aim'. Consequently, the executioner was relieved of his task by a whole army of technicians such as 'warders, doctors, chaplains, psychiatrists, psychologists, educationalists'. By their very immediate presence close to the prisoner these professional enforcers of the law 'sing the praises that the law needs: they reassure it that the body and pain are not the ultimate objects of its punitive action'.[37] No Iranian polity, including the Islamic Republic which reintroduced the spectacle of public executions, really has been successful in instituting a micro-strategic disciplinary regime that would be as 'omniscient' as the panoptical model that Foucault ponders. That is not because the state in Iran is somehow 'primitive', but exactly because modern power, at its tangents, retains a degree of unmitigated aggressiveness towards the political enemy that is not at all 'measured' and 'capillary' as Foucault imagined. A few examples illustrate the point: On 4 May 1970, members of the Ohio National Guard entered the campus of Kent State University in the United States killing four unarmed anti-war students and injuring nine others, one of whom remains paralyzed. On 2 June 1967, Benno Ohnesorg was killed by a plainclothes German policeman during a protest against the state visit of Shah Mohammed Reza Pahlavi.[38] And during the miners strike between 1984 and 1985, the Thatcher government in Britain was directly and indirectly responsible for the arrest of thousands of protesters, the jailing of hundreds of others, the injury of tens of thousands and the killing of two miners who died on the picket lines and eight more who died in related events. And of course there is the sadistic sexual violence unleashed on the inmates of the Iraqi Abu Ghraib prison complex as a part of the international rendition regime that the George W. Bush administration supervised. Modern state power was never as timid as Foucault believed. When the interests of the power elite are at stake, democracies will kill, if necessary with frightening arbitrariness.[39]

Perhaps I am describing what Susan Buck-Morss terms a 'wild zone of power' which she conceptualizes as 'a zone in which power is above the law and thus, at least potentially, a terrain of terror'.[40] As she rightly observes, this zone never really can be total; it never really can subsume all segments and particles of society. So both in the panoptical model of Foucault and beyond the wild zone of power of Buck-Morss, the possibility of escape, dissidence and an arena for rebellion – however contracted and minute – retain the promise for political transformation. Where there is power, there is resistance, Foucault was right to claim, and the points of resistance are not only 'a reaction or rebound, forming with respect to the basic domination an underside that is in the end always passive, doomed to perpetual defeat . . . [N]either are they a lure or a promise that is of necessity betrayed.' Rather, most of the time 'one is dealing with mobile and transitory points of resistance'.[41]

This power-resistance dialectic is an important part of the explanation as to why the radical subject has not been subdued until today, in Iran (and elsewhere). While the Shah launched the White Revolution and professionalized the disciplinary apparatus of his increasingly oppressive state, the opposition managed to extend the geography of revolutionary politics, the transitory points of resistance to the arbitrariness of the formal power of the monarch. From the late 1950s onwards, all strata of Iranian society became a target of ideological agitation. This is exemplified by the range of new associations that were involved in mobilizing the masses, now more visibly than before from an explicitly 'Islamic' disposition, for instance the Islamic Association of Engineers (*anjuman-e Islami-ye mohandesin*), the Islamic Association of Teachers (*anjuman-e Islami-ye mo'allemin*) or the Monthly Religious Association (*anjuman-e mahanih-ye dini*). In addition, and in order to pick up a thought I expressed at the beginning of this interregnum, intellectuals, artists, poets, even sportsmen cultivated their ideas and the social networks to sustain them in institutional ideal-types such as mosques and coffee/tea houses. Perhaps the most famous example for the former is the HosseiniehErshad in Tehran which was finished in 1967 and which hosted the fiery revolutionary lectures of Ali Shariati and Ayatollah Morteza Motahari that drew thousands of listeners, before the mosque was closed by the Shah in 1972.[42]

An appropriate example for the coffee houses, where entertainment and politics mingled more frivolously, is Cafe Naderi founded around 1927 by the Armenian immigrant Khachik Madikiyans. In the late 1960s and early 1970s Cafe Naderi became a hub for intellectuals, poets and artists who organized exhibitions and public talks in the ample space that the two halls within the grand building provided. It was in these transversal, multi-modal communicative spaces where discussions about the poetry of Simin Behbehani (b. 1927), Forugh Farrokhzad (1935–1967), Sohrab Sepehri (1928–1980) and Ahmad Shamlu (1925–2000), the writings of Simin Daneshvar (1921–2012) and Houshang Golshiri (1938–2000) and the 'new wave' movies of Dariush Mehrjui (b. 1939) reverberated. The art of these luminaries of Iran's modernist intellectual movement acted as aestheticized transmission points for the grievances of the people which were always also of a political nature.

Yet the Shah and his supporters remained unfazed. In the 1960s, the White Revolution continued to be the grand bargain of the monarchy. Determined to push his policies through, he held a mock referendum on the White Revolution and announced its 'victory' in January 1963. Ayatollah Khomeini reacted with a strongly worded declaration denouncing the Shah's domestic and foreign policies. In the same month, the Shah ordered the army into Qom, the religious centre of Iran and the place where Khomeini lived, taught and studied. Army units stormed the seminaries which had become a hub for revolutionary agitation and, in another signpost of the 'discursive war' characteristic of this period, the Shah denounced the clergy as 'black reactionaries' (*irtijai-e siyah*). The confrontation culminated in Khomeini's speech at the Feiziyeh seminary on the afternoon of Ashura (3 June 1963), which is commemorated by Shi'i Muslims as a day of mourning for the martyrdom of Hussein (the grandson of Prophet Mohammed), his family and his followers who were killed by the forces of the Umayyad caliph Yazid at the Battle of Karbala in the year 61 of the Islamic calendar (680 AD). 'O Mr. Shah, dear Mr. Shah, abandon these improper acts', Khomeini advised with the full force of Shi'i symbolism behind him.

> I don't want people to offer thanks should your masters decide that you must leave. I don't want you to become like your father. When America [the United States], the Soviet Union and England attacked us [during the Second World War] people were happy that Pahlavi [the Shah's father, Reza Shah] went. Listen to my advice, listen to the clergy's advice, not to that of Israel. That would not help you. You wretched, miserable man, forty-five years of your life have passed. Isn't it time for you to think and reflect a little, to ponder about where all this is leading you, to learn a lesson from the experience of your father? . . . You don't know whether the situation will change one day nor whether those who surround you will remain your friends. They are the friends of the dollar. They have no religion, no loyalty. They have hung all the responsibility around your neck. O miserable man![43]

Two days after delivering this speech, Khomeini was arrested and incarcerated, sparking the historic uprising of 15 Khordad 1342 (June 1963). Unrepentant, Khomeini continued resisting the Shah especially after the monarch pushed through the Iranian parliament what came to be known as the 'Bill of Capitulation' in the jargon of the revolutionaries, granting US military personnel diplomatic immunity on Iranian territory. As a consequence of his intransigent opposition, Khomeini was exiled, first to Turkey, then to Iraq and finally to France before he returned to lead the final stage of the revolution in 1979 and the creation of the Islamic Republic.

The conceptual point underlying the preceding snapshot of Iranian history can be summed up with an analogy in reverse: if Bentham's Panopticon is Foucault's ultimate architectural and organizational example for the invisible, omnipresent 'carceral' complex that contributes to controlling (European) society, Evin, Iran's first professionally designed modern prison, is an example for the way the state has failed to produce politically apathetic and socially submissive objects. Foucault witnessed for himself how the Pahlavi state failed to discipline society, when he travelled to Iran during the revolution, and when he wondered how Iranians produced 'a movement strong enough to overthrow an apparently well-armed regime while being close to old dreams that the West had known in times past, when people attempted to inscribe the figures of spirituality on political ground'.[44] It is very likely that the excesses of the revolution prevented Foucault from engaging with the Islamic Republic in a more conceptual manner. Yet if Foucault would have theorized the confines of modern power in Iran, if he would have expanded the empirical scope of his scholarly corpus beyond Europe, he may have taken more seriously his own proposition that resistance is inherent to power. Modern panoptical power, whether in its Iranian or western variance, can never really be all-encompassing. Political subjects continue to express agency; they continue to think political change and to put revolts into practice.[45]

Thus, the absence of an all-encompassing disciplinary regime in Iran that would educate society into submission can be isolated as one of the reasons for the very success of the revolutionary subject at least from the late 1950s onwards. It is no coincidence that all of the major figures of the revolution – Khomeini, Montazeri, Taleghani, Khamenei, Rafsanjani, Motahari, Bazargan, Bani-Sadr and Shariati – had a prison experience in pre-revolutionary Iran at some stage of their lives. Neither the political bio-ontology espoused by the Pahlavis nor the modern prison system 'disciplined' these individuals; rather, the contrary. If they entered the prison as notorious radicals, they exited as angry revolutionaries. It is difficult, if not impossible, to establish a threshold according to which radicalism turns into revolutionary action, but (a) the inability of the Shah to socialize society with the bio-ontology of Pahlavism, (b) the expansion of the geography of politics in the country and (c) the creation of a functional revolutionary counter-discourse within that space, can be isolated as major factors in the moulding and success of the revolutionary subject.

The extraordinary devotion to a new order of things was inscribed in the names of the burgeoning militant parties, for instance the *Fedaiyan-e Khalgh* (devotees of the masses) which employed urban guerrilla warfare tactics against the state in the 1970s, the *Mujahedin-e khalgh* (warriors of the masses) which mixed socialist ideology with Islamist imagery, and the discourse of the aforementioned intellectuals such as Jalal Al-e Ahmad and Ali Shariati who deprecated the Shah's cultural and political subservience to the west and who called for a return to Iran's 'true identity' which increasingly was imagined in Islamic rather than in 'Aryan', terms.[46] To sum this up: the 'wild zone of power' carved out by the Pahlavi state remained 'licentiously modern'; it did not perfect a panoptical disciplinary regime that would be truly totalitarian and omnipresent.

Iran's zoon politikon today

What is radical can be measured only against what is considered to be normal in a given society. What is considered to be normal in a given society is seriously affected, if not entirely determined, by the cultural texture which sets the normative guidelines according to which society is supposed to function and deliberate. The state, due to its administrative tentacles which follow us into our very living room and its ideological power which assaults our very cognition, is a central agent of the normative consensus that is meant to keep radicals at bay, exactly because radicals are coded to question the status quo. It must follow quite logically that any increase in the number of political prisoners in a country is not indicative of the ability of the state apparatus to subdue the combatant population. On the contrary, it is a measure of opposition, defiance and resistance.

I have argued that the state apparatus of the Shah introduced the modern prison system to the country in the 1970s. This was not merely an institutional development. With the modern prison there came modern interrogation techniques, a whole culture of incarceration and physical violence that was increasingly professionalized. To that end, interrogators were sent to the

United States and Israel so that they could learn the trait of 'scientific torture' that would not kill unnecessarily, but would discipline, through nail extraction, sexual violence, water boarding, stress positions, sleep deprivation and/or mock executions.[47] This was merely one of the central excesses of western modernity in Iran. The overheating economy, the colossal socio-economic upheavals, cultural uprooting and alienation that the 'develop*mental*' ideology of the Pahlavis brought about were others. No wonder then that the country's revolutionary intellectuals expressed their antagonism to the west in so vivid and at times utterly melancholic terms. They encountered western modernity at first through the political-economic violence of imperialism and then through the psychological violence of the develop*mental* state. Both were rejected.

But the revolution in Iran also points to the impossibility of total change as indicated in the last interregnum. Power and resistance, once reversed, remain power and resistance. Revolutions, as we know them, do not merge them into one, because they have not nullified *either* resistance *or* power. So after the Islamic revolution of 1979, the power of the Islamic Republic, which had been used to fuel the resistance to the Shah, remained as licentious as the power of the Pahlavi state, if less pretentiously 'modern' in its respect for universal declarations of human rights and prohibitions against torture. If the Pahlavi state punished in the name of a royal prerogative, a monarcho-formal jurisdiction that rationalized the brutality of the state, the Islamic Republic punishes in the name of a deity, exercising licentious power that is mandated by God. A central pathology ensues. The state turns God into an accomplice and the punished is relieved of his right to pray for mercy. The *mohareb* (enemy of Islam) and *mofset fel arz* (corrupters on earth) enter the politico-judicial discourse as the archetypal enemies of the state. Both offences are punishable by death. From once being a callous method to exert the sovereignty of the king, punishment is now imagined as a moral necessity to safeguard humanity from itself.

I do not have the luxury here to present a comprehensive analysis of the judicial discourse after the revolution. Suffice it to say that in terms of disciplinary surveillance and the securitization of state and society, the Islamic Republic is by far more professional (namely modern) than the Pahlavi state ever was. This is partially due to the mandate that the state usurped and the sovereignty that it appropriated which Khomeini, quite from the outset, did not restrict to worldly matters. If the French Revolution in 1789 promised a new order for mankind and communism rendered the end of history inevitable, the Islamic revolution thrust itself into the transcendental space beyond mankind and History, the very space that used to be the sole prerogative of God. The humble outfit of the Iranian nation-state was not merely elevated to the level of ontological transcendence, but it was heaved higher, in close proximity to the otherworldly. In this sense, the Islamic revolution in Iran also promised to bring about the first metaphysical revolution in the history of humankind. To that end, the constitution, adopted by a plebiscite in 1979, institutionalized the sovereignty of the *velayat-e faqih*, the Supreme Jurisprudent who represents the highest institution of the political system in Iran. The *faqih's* mandate is both transcendental, privileged in relation to God, and transnational, mandated to rally the *umma* (Islamic nation) and the *mostazafan* (oppressed) masses of the world against the oppressors. No wonder then that Iran's 'enemies of the state' are not only considered counter-revolutionaries but also *mohareb*, that is, enemies of God on earth. They are considered to be enemies of *the* state that is positioned at the nexus of the here and now and the millenarian promise of a Utopian tomorrow.

This hubristic extension of the sovereignty of the ruling elites in Iran, a sort of Islamic reincarnation of the Hegelian *Geist* that was meant to descend upon nation-states in nineteenth-century Europe, is safeguarded by a range of this-worldly institutions that have been created after the revolution in order to discipline Iranian society into accepting the ideology of the state. Thereafter, SAVAK was substituted by the Intelligence Ministry, the army units of the Shah's Imperial Guard merged into the *Sepah-e Pasdaran-e Enqelabi* (Revolutionary Guards Corps) which joined the national army and the military wings of the *Baseej-e Mostazafan* (Mobilisation of the Oppressed) to constitute the defence forces of the country which were placed under the command of the *velayat-e faqih*, that is, at first Ayatollah Khomeini and, since his death in 1989, Ali Khamenei. In recent years, the *Pasdaran* has become a major economic player creating, for the first time in Iranian history, a sophisticated military-industrial complex with political clout. Moreover, today almost every major street in Iran has its own military compound, police station, *Baseej* headquarter or Islamic 'committee building' attached to the Intelligence Ministry; and at the time of writing, major streets in Tehran, Shiraz and Isfahan are being equipped with CCTV cameras. Before the revolution Iranian police drove two-door hatchbacks, today they are equipped with E-class Mercedes and BMW motorbikes.

This 'transversal power' of the Iranian state is one of the major reasons why the mass demonstrations after the disputed election of Mahmoud Ahmadinejad in 2009 failed to seriously challenge the state. In my opinion, it was not the brute force of the Ahmadinejad government that confined the so-called Green Movement, debilitating as state power in Iran surely is, but the diffuse, multi-structural power that the Iranian state and its underbelly disseminate. Whereas in 1979 a relatively unified society in a revolutionary mood was pitted against a centralized one-man state, in 2009 the Iranian state was not a totalitarian monolith that was pitted against a revolutionary society. Whereas in 1979 the bad guy (the Shah) was easily identifiable to all revolutionaries, in today's Iran such immediate identification is not easily possible. Who was the villain in the unfolding drama? President Ahmadinejad? Those who demonstrated in support of him would beg to differ. Ayatollah Ali Khamenei? I would argue that he commands even stronger loyalties within the country and beyond. The Revolutionary Guard or the Baseej? Mohsen Rezai, one of the presidential candidates and opponents of Mahmoud Ahmadinejad who contested the election results, used to be the head of the former institution. The state as a whole? What about the range of *bonyads* or foundations that form its social and ideological underbelly and which have enhanced social mobility in Iran? These *bonyads* are responsible for the welfare of millions of Iranians who live below the poverty line. In the final analysis, the support for the Green Movement came primarily from a particular section of the middle classes in Iran, and the thrust of the movement remained confined to this 'horizontal habitat' and failed to transverse to other constituencies, exactly because there was no systematic support from the poorer strata of Iranian society, the bazaaris and the workers who were at the forefront of the revolution of 1979.

The picture becomes even more complicated when we take into consideration that some institutions of the state such as the parliament, via its Speaker Ali Larijani, called for an investigation of the violence perpetrated by members of the Baseej and the police forces in a raid of student dormitories of Tehran University. 'What does it mean that in the middle of the night students are attacked in their dormitory?' Larijani asked.

The fact that he said that 'the Interior Ministry . . . should answer for it' and that he stated that the 'Parliament is seriously following the issue' does not indicate that the Iranian parliament has been pursuing the human rights violations in the country of course. The human rights abuses in Iran remain largely unaccounted for by the Iranian state. But criticisms from within the system indicate that the majority-minority situation as much as the good-versus-bad verdict in today's Iran is by far blurrier than in 1979 when the system was centralized and represented by the Shah and his coterie. There is simply no single 'headquarters for human rights abuses' that could be easily stormed.

There was a second major difference to 1979. In that summer of 2009, the opposition was fighting the establishment with the establishment. One of the representatives of the Green Movement, Mir Hossein Mousavi himself, was the prime minister of Iran during the first decade of the revolution, that is, during a period when the current supreme leader, Ayatollah Khamenei, was president. Mohammad Khatami, one of the main supporters of Mousavi, was president between 1997 and 2005. Ayatollah Hashemi Rafsanjani, another political ally, is the head of the Assembly of Experts and a former president of the Islamic Republic. They are the engineers of the Islamic revolution and would never devour their own project. The dispute was about the future path of the Islamic Republic, the meaning of the revolution, and not about overthrowing the whole system. The resistance remained, to return to our typology at the beginning of this chapter, indicative of a reform movement rather than a revolution. It did not ameliorate all strata of society and it failed to create decisive transversal movements beyond the spectacle of demonstration. This was very different to the situation of Iran in the late 1970s as we have seen. As Mousavi himself said in his fifth letter during the protests in June 2009: 'We are not up against our sacred regime and its legal structures; this structure guards our Independence, Freedom, and Islamic Republic.'[48]

And yet, the Islamic Republic, as with any other contemporary state, does not like to take chances. Conscious of the technological challenges that the internet poses to the disciplinary power of the state, the Iranian government has put the World Wide Web under surveillance as well. In December 2001, the Supreme Council of Cultural Revolution set up an inter-agency organization called the 'Committee in Charge of Determining Unauthorised Sites', which is responsible for centralizing and formalizing the criteria according to which websites are filtered. The Committee comprised members of the ministries of Islamic Guidance, Intelligence and Communication. Additional layers of regulation have been added since then. Under one of the most central censorship legislations, voted into law by the conservative-dominated parliament in 2006, it is the owner of commercial Internet Service Providers (ISPs) who would be charged if their clients break the Cyber Crimes Bill. Political agitation and pornography are particularly high on the list of censorship priorities. At the same time, all major Iranian ministries and other institutions tied into the state apparatus have their own, rather sophisticated internet presence including on Facebook and Twitter. Recently, even the notoriously clandestine Intelligence Ministry has offered its own website, complete with an 'about us' section.[49]

Yet despite all of these formal levers of policing and surveillance, state power in Iran remains dysfunctional. The 'wild zone of power' exists, but the radical subject continues to operate at its tangents. The disillusionment and lost causes that have punctured radical activism so disastrously in much of the late capitalist world seem like marginal impediments when compared with the continuation of radical politics in Iran, not entirely different, in audacity and vigour, from other contemporary manifestations of radical politics in the non-western world. Much of this has to do with the dialectics between state and society in contemporary Iranian history, as I have explained. The revolution of 1979 added an additional factor to this interaction: the revolutionary libido that was absorbed by the state and re-channelled onto the populace created the very social and political conditions for the re-enactment of radical politics today. On the one side, in political terms, the revolution granted Iranians the absolute right to rise up and question authority, exactly because the oppressed–oppressor dialectic espoused by Khomeini suggests and creates the conditions for an ongoing interrogation of the state and – given that the state is mandated to interpret the law of God – the realm of God itself. Yet, once this Utopia of a just and transcendental state was ideologically appropriated, it set the high standard according to which the Islamic Republic is measured and judged. As I have argued, we are not talking about merely an ideological Utopia that was central to the French, Russian, and Chinese revolution here. This is a 'divine' Utopia encapsulated in the millenarian promise that the Twelfth Imam of the Shi'i will return to create the just rule of God on earth. Today, this interpretation of the Islamic Republic is espoused by the former President Mahmoud Ahmadinejad and leading functionaries of the Revolutionary Guards among others. They have attempted to monopolize the custodianship of the divine Utopia and reserve it for a tight clique. This nucleus of Iran's current power elite is by far less inclusive than the 'Khomeinist' factions during the first decade of the revolution when Khomeini successfully forged cross-political alliances. Moreover, the rather closed interpretation of the Shi'i mythology and the revolutionary heritage adhered to by the Ahmadinejad administration and its supporters are rejected largely by the old conservatives and the reformists. The opposition, which is galvanized by Iran's radical civil society, continues to argue that the revolution has failed to live up to its expectations, certainly in realizing a rather more democratic and just political order which was thought to be possible under the banner of Islam. Consequently, a counter-discourse has emerged that is confronting the ideologized Islam of the guardians of the disciplinary state with a transformative, 'secularized Islam' defended by cumbersome reformists.[50]

On the other side, social policies such as the wide-ranging literacy campaign implemented immediately after the revolution and the massive expansion of the higher education sector after the revolution and especially in the 1990s, further expanded what I have called the geography of politics in Iran. In 1980, there were merely 175,000 students and 15,000 lecturers spread around 20 cities in the country. In 2012, there were four million higher education students and over 110,000 lecturers in 120 cities. Every little provincial town in Iran has a branch of the Islamic Azad University. Similarly, Iran in 2010 ranked higher (seventieth) in the United Nation's Human Development index than Brazil (seventy-third), Venezuela (seventy-fifth) and Turkey (eight-third) and the country has secured a place among the technological innovators in the region, primarily due to the systematic investments in a functioning research and development infrastructure.[51] According to the Royal Society, the number of scientific publications in Iran increased from 736 in 1996 to 13,238 in 2008, the fastest such growth in the world.[52] In addition, the number of internet users rose dramatically by 13,000 per cent, from 250,000 users at the turn of the century.[53] In 2012, Iran announced that it will establish a nanotechnology centre and allocated 4 per cent of GDP to research and development as part of a comprehensive plan for science. As a result of these policies, Iran has become a force in stem-cell research and satellite technology. In 2011, the country successfully launched the Rassad satellite and sent its first bio-capsule of living creatures into space in February of the same year using the *Kavoshgar-3* (Explorer 3) carrier. In January 2012, Iran sent a monkey into space; by 2019, Iran plans to send its first astronauts. The geography of knowledge production in Iran and its concomitant impact on state–society relations is by far more complex and politically diverse than even a decade ago.

Indeed, one central reason why women's rights activists are at the fore-front of political dissent in the country is their central position in Iran's highly educated middle class.[54] As such, the radical subject, which today speaks in an emphatically feminine voice, has become an integral part of the 'pluralistic momentum' in the country.[55] After all, it is the very body of Iranian women onto which the disciplinary apparatus of the state has exercised its power, turning it into a major site of war in contemporary Iran. The attempt of Reza Khan to unveil Iranian women by decree in 1924 resonates with Ayatollah Khomeini's enforcement of the veil in one significant way: it divided Iranian women into 'good' and 'bad' in accordance with the hegemonic ideational system espoused by the state. Hence, a reverse logic of resistance ensued: During the reign of the Pahlavis, every veiled woman was suspect, which turned the veil from a cultural expression into a political symbol. As Fanon wrote in his essay 'Algeria Unveiled', the efforts of the French colonizers to unveil Algerian women in the name of their brutal *mission civilisatrice*, turned Algerian women at once into a symbol of insurrectionary resistance and an object of paranoid surveillance and control. In revolutionary Iran as well, secular women espoused the veil as a symbol of defiance (and not necessarily a symbol of religious piety). Conversely, in the period after 1979, light veiling has become an act of resistance and bad hejab is punished by the morality police under Iran's criminal code. Both before and after the revolution, then, the body of Iranian women, indeed their very sexuality, has become an object of paranoid obsession for the patriarchal state. In order to pick up the theoretical formula worked out in the last interregnum: state power acted precisely against the liberty of women which is innate to their existence as human beings. Ironically, Ayatollah Khomeini repeatedly alluded to this 'god given right of liberty and freedom' that Islam guarantees in his speeches in the build-up to the revolution, but ultimately he did not break with the patriarchal norms of Iranian society.[56] Comparable to the decree of Reza Khan, this failure to de-politicize the issue of veiling in the country yielded its own forms of dissent. The bio-insurrectionary resistance of Iranian women, which has been coterminous with the disciplinary power applied to them, has been one of the most decisive driving forces of change and reform in contemporary Iran, in many ways until today.[57]

It is this pluralistic momentum – diffuse, scattered, molar, eclectic, yet full of political impact – which is both the effect of and the arena for Iran's burgeoning civil society and the radical democratic politics that it engenders. I offer this in cautious conclusion of the two central topics of this interregnum: First, as a part of the genealogy of the radical subject in Iran, who today is neither apathetic, subdued by a feeling of political paralysis, nor unduly euphoric, intoxicated by a sense of an impending triumph over its right-wing competitors. And second, in support of my disquisition on the centrality of the Iranian experience to a truly comparative and critical theory of contemporary power and resistance and the histories of defeat and triumphalism that they provoke. After all, what is the purpose of critical theory if not to reposition nationalized histories in a global context?

Discourse and Power: The Paradoxical Case of the Iranian–American Conjunction

The supreme art of war is to subdue the enemy without fighting.

Sun Tzu

Words and Violence

There has been a fundamental theoretical premise underlying this book that I would like to consolidate at this stage of the study. At the most basic level, I have been writing about dialectics, interactions between power and resistance, self and other, state and society, Islam and the west and so on. My dialectical notion has been 'negative', that is, the interrelationships between the concepts do not ebb away in a grand Hegelian synthesis where dissonance is resolved. For Hegel dichotomies were reconcilable. In that sense his dialectics were 'positive'. A negative dialectic suggests that interactions open up a skewed and traumatic field in which differences do not amalgamate to form a unity. Negative dialectics atomize the properties of the concepts in a centripetal process, but they do not turn them into a unit where the original properties are synthesized. Theodor Adorno likened the late style of Beethoven to such 'negativity' and Edward Said picked up this notion of dissonance in his last book published posthumously:

> Beethoven's late works remain unreconciled, not co-opted by a higher synthesis: they do not fit any scheme, and they cannot be reconciled or resolved since their irresolution and unsynthesized fragmentariness are constitutive, neither ornamental nor symbolic of something else.

Beethoven's late compositions are in fact about 'lost totality', and are therefore catastrophic.[1]

This is a useful starting point to discuss the methodological significance of negative dialectics further. Negative dialectics imply that there will always be a space beyond; that the Hegelian quest for an end to history, which was always also an expression of his Eurocentric theorization, has revealed itself as a dangerous fallacy. The reference of Adorno and Said to the late style of Beethoven is very pertinent here, for toward the end of his life Beethoven was adamant to rupture and resist the legacy of his own oeuvre which he increasingly deemed too synergetic.[2] There is political value in this artistic self-deconstruction, for in politics and history too there is no end note, no aria that heralds finitude. In the previous interregnums I have shown, theoretically and empirically, that power and resistance act upon each other ad infinitum. Power can never really entirely subsume resistance and the other way around. I have alluded to a similar irresolvable 'conjunctive dissonance' when I discussed how the liberal notion that resistance begets authentic autonomy was rejected by Fanon and Sartre. We have established that the violence of the colonizer always also embroils and entangles him. Colonizer and colonized are trapped in the same system of violence. Both enact their roles on the same stage and they create a common narrative littered with mutual memories of death and destruction. The liberal pretension that violence can ever be unidirectional, that subjectivity could be entirely autonomous from culture and the system in which we are embedded, is revealed as a dangerous fallacy. There is always blowback, especially in a relationship characterized by enmity as any feuding couple can confirm.

In order to bring this important theoretical premise closer to the empirical case in this chapter, allow me to start with the assumption that Iran's self-declared resistance to US power does not beget detachment or 'manifest independence' as the revolutionaries imagined. Since the revolution of 1979, Iran and the United States have been engaged in a discursive war of attrition that was meant to ostracize the other side and to accentuate the supremacy of the respective self. Discourse, that is, syntactically and ideologically structured word formations that are arranged systematically have truly productive powers in world politics. They can build trust or they can legitimate war. In the case of relations between Iran and the United States in the last three decades, the right words have not been chosen. This is one of the central reasons why the two countries continue to be adversaries, for any reconciliation has to start with a peaceful dialogue. There were short periods when the leaders in both countries struck the right tone, for instance in 1998 when the former Iranian president Mohammad Khatami spoke of his 'respect for the American nation [and] their great civilisation'[3] or when President Obama referred to the 'common humanity' that binds both nations together in a message on the occasion of the Iranian new year in 2009.[4]

Alas, Khatami and Obama's words were exceptions to the rule and both presidencies did not coincide with each other. But as I will argue further in the following: even the vitriolic recriminations that have been standard currency at least since US embassy personnel were taken hostage in Tehran in 1979 have not yielded detachment. Rather the contrary. Today, 'America' and Iran inhabit a common discursive field that is densely narrated and entirely interdependent. Not a day passes without some reference to the United States in the political discourse of the Islamic Republic. A comparable obsession can be discerned from the mainstream discourse on Iran in the United States. In particular, the right wing on both sides thrives within a context of mutual antagonism. The 'bad Mullah-global arrogance' narrative functions very well to that end. But if these protagonists of a clash between the two countries imagined that, by demonizing the other side, they would achieve some kind of detachment, they are wrong. Processes of 'othering' do not result in autonomy; 'us' and 'them' continue to inhabit a common, dialectically constituted discursive field. Complete or manifest independence could only be achieved if Iranians and 'Americans' would stop referring to each other. Surely, this is not the case. Hence, Iran and the United States continue to be conjoined, today perhaps more than ever. To show how this conjunction reveals itself politically is one of the main purposes of this interregnum.

I have started with the statement that Iranian–American relations have been beset by mistrust and occasional outbreaks of vitriol and violence for the past three decades now. In order to substantiate that statement, I will map, theoretically and empirically, the 'discursive field' in which relations between Iran and the United States reveal themselves. I am interested in representations of Iran and the United States, and how the fundamental friend–enemy distinction which is meant to set the two countries politically apart has come about. I take as a starting point, with critical theorists of international relations, that discourse has a real and present impact on policy and that a lot of what is happening in world politics can be adequately contextualized with an appreciation of the linkages between 'utterance' and 'action'.[5]

What do I mean by the term 'discursive field'? I have explained in detail elsewhere how politico-cultural inventions affect and condition the way we perceive our surrounding social worlds.[6] Perceptions in world politics are particularly compromised and manipulated because the ontological fabric of the international system is professionally constructed. Discourse, at a more basic-level language, is central to this process of wilful interference. The articulation of words represents the most sophisticated form of self-externalization in society; it is the first step towards defining ourselves and others and to understanding our status within a world that has been pre-created and whose historical fabric is beyond our control. This is what Karl Marx meant when he famously observed: 'Men [women] make their own history . . . not under circumstances they themselves have chosen but under the given and inherited circumstances with which they are directly confronted.'[7] Structure, expressed and embedded in history, is everywhere for Marx and penetrates our consciousness. Discourse narrates history; it is a fundamental building block – always also political (and thus violent) – in our efforts to invent cultural realities. 'The facts which our senses present to us are socially preformed in two ways', writes Horkheimer, 'through the historical character of the object perceived and through the historical character of the perceiving organ'.[8] He adds the important caveat that '[b]oth are not simply natural; they are shaped by human activity . . . The perceived fact is therefore co-determined by human ideas and concepts, even before its conscious theoretical elaboration by the knowing individual.'[9] It should follow from this that any interaction in the social world, including relations between Iran and the United States, does not reveal itself within a detached or neutral habitat. Rather, international relations, including relations between Iran and the United States, are entirely constituted and conditioned by norms, institutions and other cultural artefacts which are socially engineered and thus subject to human manipulation.

We can derive an important methodological premise from the short discussion above. Whenever we encounter what Foucault terms a 'discursive formation', whenever 'between objects, types of statement, concepts, or thematic choices, one can define a regularity (an order, correlations, positions and functionings, transformations)', we are compelled to delve into the dynamics of this field, into the rapturous and tumultuous forces that are actively preoccupied with the production and transformation of reality and the subjectivication of knowledge.[10] So, for instance, the 'reality' that Iran is a 'terrorist' state is one subject that has emerged out of the discursive field of Iranian–American relations. The 'fact' that the United States is a 'neo-imperial' force, indeed that its government represents the very re-incarnation of satanic evil, is yet another.

On the linkages between discourse and the construction of cultural realities, of which world politics in general and foreign policies in particular would be a part, there are more lessons to be learned from an essay by Walter Benjamin published originally in 1921 and titled 'Critique of Violence'. In this essay, Benjamin asks if the non-violent resolution of conflict is possible.[11] His response is yes: 'Nonviolent agreement is possible wherever a civilised outlook allows the use of unalloyed means of agreement . . . Courtesy, sympathy, peacableness, trust . . . are their subjective preconditions.' Benjamin puts primary importance on language as a mediating and ameliorating force, central to the build-up of these subjective preconditions. According to him, there exists 'a sphere of human agreement that is nonviolent to the extent that it is wholly inaccessible to violence: the proper sphere of "understanding", language'.[12]

That language can be a source of mediation, empathy and inter-cultural dialogue has become central to communicative theories of politics, most famously expressed by Jürgen Habermas (1984). On the level of the functions of language for not only 'achieving understanding' (*Verständigung*) but also 'empathetic understanding' (*Verstehen*), Habermas recaptures Benjamin's point that language is central to processes of reconciliation. In this regard, Habermas remains within a tradition that takes understanding of the 'other' as one of its main goals. This ambition has been rightly termed the 'rationalising' core of Habermas's communicative action theory, which is said to 'inform a view in which establishing consensus is the program both for living within that social world and for building bridges to other social worlds'.[13] Benhabib adds that in Habermas's conceptualization of communicative action reaching out to such other social worlds requires taking 'a stance in relation to the reasons which agents in those cultures would consider "good" or "appropriate" to justify certain claims'.[14] From this perspective, in language, instead of setting boundaries between ourselves and others, we are urged to engage in rational discourse, which by itself presupposes recognition of the other whilst leading to an unprincipled exchange, the aim of which would be to find a mutually acceptable, smallest denominator that would mitigate conflict. According to Thomas Risse:

> Arguing implies that actors try to challenge the validity claims inherent in any causal or normative statement and to seek a communicative consensus about their understanding of a situation as well as justifications for the principles and norms guiding their action. Argumentative rationality also implies that the participants in a discourse are open to being persuaded by the better argument and that relationships of power and social hierarchies recede in the background. *Argumentative and deliberative behaviour is as goal oriented as strategic interaction, but the goal is not to attain one's fixed preferences, but to seek a reasoned consensus.* Actors' interests, preferences, and the perceptions of the situation are no longer fixed, but subject to discursive challenges. Where argumentative rationality prevails, actors do not to seek to maximize or to satisfy their given interests and preferences, but to challenge and to justify the validity claims inherent in them – and they are prepared to change their views of the world or even their interests in light of the better argument.[15]

But what about interfering factors that do not allow for an exchange that yields a 'reasoned consensus' as Risse foresees? What if discourse reveals itself within a field of violence and suspicion such as in international politics? What if language itself is inscribed with pain and terror? What if it prescribes murder? What if our words are untrustworthy?

Foucault points to such epistemic violence which he finds inscribed in language and expressed through the disciplinary powers of institutions and larger constellations he calls 'regimes of truth'. According to him, each society is endowed with such a regime which defines not only 'the types of discourse it accepts and makes function as true', but also the very 'mechanisms and instances that enable one to distinguish true and false statements'.[16] Foucault suggests that violence is inscribed in discourse and that it may not yield understanding of the other, but his or her condemnation. The discursive field enveloping Iranian–American relations serves as an example here. What US and Iranian political elites are reacting to is not the immediate reality of the other side, but representations of that reality which are filtered through thick layers of normative and institutional structures. What makes the relationship between Iranians and Americans conflict-ridden is not some innate antagonism between the two peoples, not even the hostage crisis in 1980 or the CIA (and MI6) engineered coup d'état which deposed Iran's first democratically elected prime minister – Mohammad Mossadegh – in 1953. What has hampered relations between the two countries, the true impediments of reconciliation, are invented myths about the other side which have not been entirely dispelled either politically or even intellectually.

Within such a discursive field, one which is pierced by violent narratives reified by those powerful stakeholders who have a particular interest in war and confrontation, communicating rationally in a Habermasian sense has resembled a Sisyphean act. Former president Mohammad Khatami (1997–2005), who reached out to the United States via his 'dialogue amongst civilisations' initiative, and US President Barack Obama at the beginning of his presidency had/have it so difficult not because they are not genuinely interested in facilitating trust-building measures between the two countries, but because they are operating within a discursive field that is permeated by memories of violence and populated by powerful social agents who are entirely antagonistic to the other side. Hence, repeatedly, the 'rational majority' have only managed to roll the rock up halfway to the top of the mountain, only to see it roll back down again (in the case of Khatami, crushing him and his reformist movement along the way). Consequently, in order to address why there has not been a major rapprochement between the two states yet, some understanding about those sources of mistrust is necessary. Of course, the signposts presented cannot be fully explained within the confines of this interregnum. I will not be able to dissect the institutional sites that give stakeholders in Iranian–American relations the status of 'authorities'. Neither do I claim to delve into the wider politico-cultural system that accommodates the politics of enmity between the two countries. All I can do is to point to a few narratives that are indicative of the signs and symbols that populate what I have called, rather sketchily, the *discursive field* enveloping Iranian–American relations, and to give some understanding of the syntactical settings of that field. What I am bringing into focus, ultimately, is the movement 'within' the hyphen that seems to set Iranian–American relations politically apart.

Pahlavi Iran, Aryan myths and the Indo-European bond

It was Edward Said who argued most forcefully that, after the Islamic revolution in 1979 and the subsequent occupation of the US Embassy in Tehran on the 22 October, Iran and Iranians became a major source of anxiety and anger within the United States: 'An important ally, it lost its imperial regime, its army, its value in American global calculations during a year of tumultuous revolutionary upheaval virtually unprecedented on so huge a scale since October 1917.'[17] The international focus on Iran intensified further after the end of the Cold War. From the perspective of Said, Iran, and along with it Islam, has come to represent America's major foreign devil. It is considered to be a terrorist state because it backs groups like Hezbollah in South Lebanon.'[18] Said may be too obsequious to his Orientalist paradigm here, but he is right to point out that reactions to events such as the occupation of the US embassy cannot be divorced from a larger discursive constellation that represented post-revolutionary Iran as an entirely fanatical, irrational and evil entity.

This emerging narrative of the 'mad Mullahs' that Bill Beeman ponders lodged its force into a discursive field, the ideational attributes of which were radically transformed after the revolution in 1979.[19] Before the revolution, political elites in the United States dealt with an image of Iran that was rather amenable to Orientalist notions of the country as historically friendly and generally closer to the western canon than the 'Semitic Arabs'. Iran was Persian, Aryan, whiter than the Arabs surrounding them and seemed to be, on the ideological surface, more like 'us'. The Shah himself was mystified as an occasionally autocratic but enlightened leader, who was on the path of transforming Iran into a modern (viz. western) country. A correspondence from the US Embassy in Tehran from 1951 – that is, two years before he was ousted by Mossadegh and subsequently reinstated by the CIA/MI6 – is indicative of official attitudes towards the Shah during that period. In this memo, the Shah is described as 'confused, frustrated suspicious, proud and stubborn, a young man who lives in the shadow of his father'.[20] At the same time, he was deemed to have 'great personal courage, many Western ideals, and a sincere, though often wavering, desire to raise and preserve the country'. Nine years before the revolution in 1979, the Shah was described as 'completely self-assured' and 'confident that he is leading the country in the right direction'.[21] US officials also found him to be 'well-informed' and they were convinced by his 'ability to keep abreast of developments around the world' and by his 'agile mind'. Richard Nixon, in a private conversation with Alexander Haig and Douglas MacArthur II on 8 April 1971, was equally impressed. 'Iran's the only thing there', he said. 'By God, if we can go with them, if we can have them strong, and they're in the centre of it, and a friend of the United States.' Nixon also seemed to be impressed by the ability of the Shah 'to run, basically, let's face it, a virtual dictatorship in a benign way . . . Because, look, when you talk about having a democracy of our type in that part of the world, good God, it wouldn't work, would it?' 'No Sir', MacArthur replied. 'They don't even know – they don't know what it is. You know what happened in the Congo?' MacArthur asked, 'Belgium gave them a constitution, wonderful buildings, all the nice trappings, but these people had never practiced it at all'.[22] Those endorsements of the Iranian monarch were topped by the now famous proclamation of former president Jimmy Carter on New Year's Eve in 1977. Raising his champagne glass, Carter toasted the Shah at a lavish state dinner in Tehran calling him 'an island of stability in one of the more troubled regions of the world'. A year later the Shah was in exile.

This representation of the Shah as an enlightened and visionary, if periodically indecisive yet pleasingly pro-western, leader is reminiscent of comparable attitudes towards the former Egyptian president Hosni Mubarak as indicated. But due to the country's oil reserves and its strategic location in the Persian Gulf, Iran has always been a rather more contested and misrepresented topic than any other country in West Asia including Israel. So it should not come as a surprise that the endorsement of the Shah as a compliantly pro-western leader was reified in the mainstream scholarly discourse about his rule. Roger Savory, for instance, writing in 1972 in the *International Journal of Middle East Studies*, the flagship journal of the field in North America, accentuated the 'warmth and spontaneity of the Shah's welcome by the people when he returned to Iran on 22 August 1953'.[23] Whereas the Shah is complimented for his progressive social reforms, the nationalists, the Left and their intellectual avant-garde were considered naive, blind, unrealistic and utopian. Moreover, their opposition was inexcusable 'since it should have been obvious to them that Muhammad Riza Shah was not, and could not become, the same type of despot as his father'.[24] 'Much has been written recently about the politics of cynicism and pessimism in Iran', Savory observes further, 'and, in my opinion, much of the political unrealism of the Persian intellectual from 1907 onwards stems from a cynical and pessimistic outlook . . . Is it too far-fetched to suggest', he adds in typical Orientalist parlance, 'that this attitude has its roots deep in two traditional channels of Persian thought: first, Persian mysticism, and, second, Shi'ite martyrology?'[25]

Here we find why and to what purpose Said defined Orientalism 'as a discourse . . . by which European culture was able to manage – and even produce – the Orient . . . politically, sociologically, militarily, ideologically, scientifically, and imaginatively during the post-Enlightenment period'.[26] Although Orientalism asserts factual validity, even a scientific status, Said points out that it is the product of ideological fiction, with no real linkage to the cultures and peoples it claims to explain. As indicated in the fourth interregnum, it follows for Said that Orientalism has muted the Orient. The subject (the Orient) is not represented in the discourse of Orientalism, it does not speak; it is entirely *spoken for*, constituted all the way down to her identity by the 'Orientalist brotherhood' of scholars whose modern lineage Said traces back to the writings of Silvestre de Sacy, Ernest Renan and Edward William Lane and the Napoleonic expedition to Egypt between 1798 and 1801 more generally.[27]

Aside from proving that the ideologues of the Pahlavi state in Iran and the Pahlavi monarchs themselves were somehow products of European Orientalism, Said's argument that representations of the other can be entirely constituted by a discipline such as 'Orientalism' is difficult to hold. As I have argued in the fourth interregnum, Orientalisms of any kind are dialectical formations. There is both an outflow of representations of self and other and an inflow; subject and object may be entirely reversible, they interpenetrate each other, they are hybrid. Let me give an example. When in 1971 Nixon says that Iran 'at least has got some degree of civilisation' in contrast to 'those Africans' who according to him 'are only about 50 to 75 years from out of the trees'.[28] When he considers Iran to be not 'of either world, really', that is, neither Arab (Muslim) or western (Christian), when he considers Iran a bit whiter, a bit more civilized, he is not only articulating an Orientalist bias with particularly racist connotations, he is also reacting to the self-designation of the Shah himself, who was adamant to legitimate his alliance with the west via processes of bio-ontological engineering. To be more precise, it was a particular function and goal of the discourse of the Pahlavi monarchs to represent themselves as Aryan, different from the Arab-Semitic other and thus closer to the 'Indo-European' family of western nations. This strategy was deemed to be functional in order to solidify Iran's relation with the west (and Israel) ideationally. At the same time, it served to legitimate this alliance to suspicious domestic constituencies who protested against Iran's dependence on foreign countries, and here especially on successive US governments.

I have already indicated in the previous interregnum that the Aryan and Indo-European narrative was institutionalized by Reza Shah, the founder of the short-lived Pahlavi dynasty who was ousted by the British in 1941 in favour of his son Mohammad Reza who was only 21 years old when he ascended to the throne in the same year. Ervand Abrahamian notes how, during the reign of the first Pahlavi monarch, organizations such as *Farhangestan* (Cultural Academy), the Department of Public Guidance, the National Heritage Society, the Geography Commission, the journal *Iran-e Bastan* (Ancient Iran) and the government media via newspapers such as *Ettela'at* (Information) and *Journal de Teheran* 'all waged a concerted campaign both to glorify ancient Iran and to purify the language of foreign words . . . especially Arab ones, [which] were replaced with either brand new or old Persian vocabulary'.[29] The most consequential step towards institutionalizing the Aryan myth came in 1934 when Reza Shah decreed that the country's name should be changed from Persia to Iran in all international correspondence and cartographic designations. Abrahamian stresses further that in order to invoke 'the glories and birthplace of the ancient Aryans', the National Heritage Society went even as far as to build a rival 'Aryan' mausoleum next to the religious pilgrimage site in Mashhad which is dedicated to Imam Reza, the seventh descendant of the Prophet Muhammad and the eighth imam of the *Ithna Asharia* (Twelver Shi'a) branch of Shi'ism which is followed by the vast majority of Iranians. Adopting methods developed in the science of phrenology, members of the Society dug up 'bodies to inter in these mausoleums [and] meticulously measured skulls to "prove" to the whole world that these national figures had been "true Aryans"'.[30] Official textbooks published during the period thickened the bio-ontological reengineering of the meaning of Iran by expressing a distinctly Irano-centric politics of identity with racist undertones: 'History now practically belongs to the narrative of the people of the white race', one textbook asserted. 'The white race has several branches the most important of which is the Aryan one.'[31]

When during the Pahlavi dynasty Iranian scholars and the state itself adopted a 'scientific' discourse that was meant to 'prove' the purity of the Aryan race, they were not only reacting to the Orientalist theses expressed, amongst others, by Count de Gobineau and Ernest Renan, who argued that Persians are racially superior to the Arabs and other 'Semitic races' because of their 'Indo-European' heritage. True, forerunners of the Aryan myth in Iran, cultural luminaries such as Mirza Fath Ali Akhundzadeh and Mirza Agha Khan Kermani internalised Orientalist notions of racial purity and introduced these ideas to the intellectual life of late-nineteenth-century Persia.[32] But there was also an 'Occidentalist' breeding ground for such narratives to gain currency amongst the intelligentsia of the country, a whole range of nationalist myths which have survived throughout the centuries and which have been repeatedly tapped into in order to define, somewhat metaphysically, the national narrative in Iran. The Pahlavi monarchs were fascinated by the imperial history of pre-Islamic Persia, and found its historical vigour conducive to legitimate their rule. To that end, they invoked the myth that their dynasty was somehow related to Xerxes, Cyrus and Darius, the legendary kings of the Achaemenid Empire. Thus, as indicated in the previous chapter, Mohammad Reza Shah adopted the official title *Aryamehr* or 'Light of the Aryans', celebrated 2,500 years of Iranian monarchy in a lavish festival in Persepolis in 1971 where he invoked the legacy of the legendary Persian king Cyrus and subsequently abandoned the Islamic solar hijra calendar in favour of an imperial one, suddenly catapulting Iran into the year 2535 (based on the presumed date of the foundation of the Achaemenid dynasty) going beyond both the confines of Muslim history and western modernity. In the imagination of the Shah, this was the beginning of a new era for Iran, an era that was meant to set the country apart from its Islamic heritage by fast-forwarding it to the gates of a 'great civilization' (*tamadon-e bozorg*).

The subject that emerges out of the Shah's bio-ontological discourse is the Aryan Persian, Indo-European, heir to a lost civilization but willing to catch up along an imagined western temporality (or historical spectrum). The Shah repeatedly stressed that the culture of Iran was 'more akin to that of the west'. The country was deemed 'an early home of the Aryans from whom most

Americans and Europeans are descended'. Racially, Iranians were considered to be 'quite separate from the Semitic stock of the Arabs'. As such, Iran was deemed to be the 'oldest culture that was racially and linguistically linked to the west'. After all, Persian 'belongs to the Indo-European family which includes English, German, and other major Western tongues [sic]'.[33] Elsewhere the Shah stated that Iran was an 'Asian Aryan power whose mentality and philosophy are close to those of the European states, above all France'.[34] Along with that emphasis on Iran's western heritage went an imperial narrative: 'If you Europeans think yourselves superior, we have no complexes', the Shah emphasized in an interview with Oriana Fallaci. 'Don't ever forget that whatever you have, we [pre-Islamic, Aryan Iran] taught you three thousand years ago.'[35]

This Persian-Aryan subject that emerges out of the identity politics of pre-revolutionary Iran has a tolerated presence in mainstream western high culture via the discourse of Orientalism. It tingles with the imaginations of Zarathustra, Scheherazade, Sinbad, Ali Baba, the tales of *One Thousand and One Nights*: The Shah ↔ the west ↔ Aryanism ↔ Indo-European-ness ↔ Orientalist blowback. A new subject now emerges out of the turmoil of the Islamic revolution in 1978/79. Now we are confronted with the revolutionary Iranian, somewhat darker, Arab, certainly more Muslim and third worldly, and more radical in the unsettling sense of the term. Suddenly, the discursive field signifying Iranian–American relations is populated by different representations of the other: Ayatollah Khomeini ↔ the Orient ↔ Islam ↔ the third world ↔ revolution ↔ terrorism. The reading of Iran changes. At the beginning of the revolution, the 'Persian psyche' is thought to be dominated by 'an overriding egoism'. 'The practical effects' of this egotistical trait 'is an almost total Persian preoccupation with self and leaves little room for understanding points of view other than one's own'. Indeed, Iranians were thought to have an intrinsically irrational psyche attributable to the influence of Islam which suddenly appears as a topic after the revolution, as if Iranians living under the Shah were truly non-Muslim Frenchmen as the Shah seemed to think. 'Coupled with these psychological limitations is a general incomprehension of causality. Islam, with its emphasis on the omnipotence of god, appears to account at least in major part for this phenomenon.' For US decision-makers, it was surprising that the superior civilization standards of the west did not have an effect on those seemingly westernized Iranians who were also part of the revolutionary movement (there is reference to Foreign Minister Ibrahim Yazdi in this section of the document). The limitations of the 'Persian psyche' were just too grave: 'Even those Iranians educated in the western style and perhaps with long experience outside Iran itself frequently have difficulty grasping the inter-relationship of events.'[36]

Such views about Iran were not only limited to the revolutionary period or decision-making circles in the United States. For best-selling author Mark Bowden, for instance, the 'capture of the U.S. Embassy in Tehran was a glimpse of something new and bewildering. It was the first battle in America's war against militant Islam, a conflict that would eventually engage much of the world.'[37] These lines were published in 2006, that is, in the middle of the 'war on terror' which was adopted as the main strategic plank of the George W. Bush administration after the terrorist attacks on the country in September 2001. Bowden is clearly echoing the pronounced view of US neoconservatives that Iran, Iraq, al-Qaeda, Hezbollah, Hamas, etc. are all part of the same problem: the global Islamic threat. 'Iran's revolution wasn't just a localised power struggle; it had tapped a subterranean ocean of Islamist outrage.'[38] Such views on Iran as a fanatical entity can also be discerned from Hollywood movies such as *Not without My Daughter* starring Sally Field and the blockbuster *300*. How archaic and alien does it seem to us today that Pahlavi Iran was considered to be of 'either world' and a courted member of the international, viz. western, community of nations, despite the dictatorship of the Shah, despite his human rights abominations, despite his nuclear energy programme, despite his support to bombing/insurgent/guerrilla campaigns in neighbouring countries.

Revolutionary Iran and the question of terrorism

I have argued that in 1979 a massive rupture occurred within the discursive field enveloping relations between Iran and the United States. This space, where representations of Iran and the United States reveal themselves and interact with each other, is created dialectically. In other words, there is both an inflow and outflow of signs and symbols, defined in terms of social constructions of self and other, subject and object, which are entirely interpenetrated and thus interdependent phenomena, but which claim, nevertheless, 'factual' validity as something distinct. The authorship of the signs and symbols that penetrated this field so vigorously, the idea of Iran as revolutionary, anti-imperial, Islamic, the vanguard in the fight of the 'oppressed' multitudes against the 'arrogant' forces, lay with Iranians themselves. My point is that the revolution equipped Iranians with the irresistible power to express their own narrative which was enunciated, nonetheless, primarily in relation to, and in vigorous cross-fertilization with, the concept of the west The revolution may have created a form of latent independence. Undoubtedly, the decisions of the Iranian state are not determined by external actors anymore. But at the same time, the constant reference to *amrika* as an ideological and strategic competitor has created a discursive dependency that has invited the United States back in, not at least as a 'taboo theme park' for the neo-bourgeois youth in the urban centres. As such, America continues to be an ideational reference point for the Iranian state *and* society. Certainly, Iran is receptive to the idea of America, whether that construct appears as a mortal enemy or a potential partner.

That was not the intention of the revolutionaries. The social engineering of Iran's post-revolutionary identity discourse was precipitated and seriously affected by the writings of activist intellectuals whose ideas were widely disseminated among the anti-Shah intelligentsia, especially in the late 1960s and 1970s. Two narratives, *gharbzadegi* (or west-toxification) and *bazgasht be khish* (return to the self), were particularly hegemonic. The former was the title of a highly influential book authored by Jalal Al-e Ahmad. In this book, Al-e Ahmad likens the increasing dependence of Iran on western notions of modernity to a disease he terms *gharbzadegi*. If left untreated, *gharbzadegi* would lead to the demise of Iran's cultural, political and economic independence, because society was made susceptible to penetration by the west. 'Today', writes Al-e Ahmad, 'the fate of those two old rivals is, as you see, this: one has become a lowly groundskeeper and the other the owner of the ballpark'.[39] In order to escape this fate, Al-e Ahmad argued, Iran had to be turned into the vanguard in the fight of the oppressed east against the imperialist west, and if necessary through revolutionary action.

Ali Shariati was equally adamant to challenge the policies of the Shah and his real and perceived dependence on the politics of the United States. The narrative of *bazgasht be khishtan* picked up Al-e Ahmad's theme accentuating cultural authenticity, and the wider anti-colonial struggle at the head of which Iran should position itself, not at least in order to find a way back to the country's 'true' self which Shariati defined in socialist and Islamic terms. In an intellectual tour de force, Shariati turned Jesus, Abraham, Muhammad, and above all Imam Hussein (grandson of the Prophet Muhammad) and his mother Fatimah, into revolutionary heroes who were positioned at the helm of a new movement for global justice and equality. In his many speeches and written tracts, Shariati emphasized that Islam in general and Shi'i Islam in particular demands revolting against unjust rulers. At the centre of Shariati's oeuvre we find Imam Hussein, who is represented as the ultimate *homo Islamicus*, a martyr in the cause of justice who fought the 'tyranny' of the Ummayad caliph Yazid and who sacrificed his life and that of his family at the Battle of Karbala in 680 AD. 'Look at Husayn!' Shariati demands in 1970.

> He is an unarmed, powerless and lonely man. But he is still responsible for the *jihad* . . . He who has no arms and no means has come with all of his existence, his family, his dearest companions so that his *Shahadat* [bearing witness to God, martyrdom] and that of his whole family will bear witness to the fact that he carried out his responsibility at a time when truth was defenceless and unarmed . . . It is in this way that the dying of a human being guarantees the life of a nation. His *Shahadat* is a means whereby faith can remain. It bears witness to the fact that great crimes, deception, oppression and tyranny rule. It proves that truth is being denied. It reveals the existence of values which are destroyed and forgotten. It is a red protest against a black sovereignty. It is a shout of anger in the silence which has cut off tongues.[40]

The narratives of *gharbzadegi* and *bazgasht be khishtan* simulate a bifurcated syntactical order: justice ↔ oppressed (*mostazafan*) ↔ Muslim ↔ Islam ↔ revolution ↔ resistance *versus* imperialism ↔ oppressors (*mostakbaran*) ↔ superpowers ↔ the west ↔ the United States. In the writings and speeches of Ayatollah Khomeini, the dichotomies prescribed by this syntactical order find their explicit political articulation. The great utopia of universal justice, central to the former side of the dichotomy, could be turned into reality by the *vali-e faqih*, the supreme jurisprudent who would position himself at the helm of a global movement of resistance carried by the 'oppressed' masses of the world. With Ayatollah Khomeini, Islam not only becomes a desirable object of history, it is turned into a revolutionary, anti-imperial ideology with a universal claim. During the same period that the Shah proclaimed Iran's new civilization based on the country's pre-Islamic heritage, and at the same time as mainstream scholars in the United States were explaining the benevolence of his rule, a different meaning of Iran was being *formula*ted: a discourse that produced revolutionary Islam and its radical subject. On the necessity to establish the ideal Islamic polity in order to ward off imperial intrusions, Ayatollah Khomeini was explicit: '[T]he imperialists and the tyrannical self-seeking rulers have divided the Islamic homeland', he lectured in exile in Najaf (Iraq) in 1970.

> They have separated the various segments of the Islamic *umma* from each other and artificially created separate nations. There once existed the great Ottoman State, and that, too, the imperialists divided . . . In order to assure the unity of the Islamic *umma*, in order to liberate the Islamic homeland from occupation and penetration by the imperialists and their puppet governments, it is imperative that we establish a government. In order to attain the unity and freedom of the Muslim peoples, we must overthrow the oppressive governments installed by the imperialists and bring into existence an Islamic government of justice that will be in the service of the people. The formation of such a government will serve to preserve the disciplined unity of the Muslims; just as Fatimat az-Zahra (upon whom be peace) said in her address: 'The Imamate exists for the sake of preserving order among the Muslims and replacing their disunity with unity'.[41]

Of course, I can only provide a mere microcosm of what was happening below the surface of the official discourse sponsored by the Shah's state apparatus in the 1960s and 1970s. The identity discourse of Iran was being populated by new symbols and signs. Suddenly, the same people who were represented as heirs to the pre-Islamic Persian empires, as Aryan, Indo-European, even French and largely non-Muslim by the Pahlavis, appeared as primarily Islamic, anti-imperialistic, revolutionary and supportive of the struggles of the third worlds. The occupation of the US embassy in 1979 was the practical epitome of this discourse. It was not merely planned in response to the admittance of the Shah to the United States for medical treatment which was interpreted as the beginning of yet another plot to reinstate his rule in Iran. The self-proclaimed 'students following the line of Imam Khomeini' were driven by ideas, coded by the powerful revolutionary narratives, some of which I have sketched above. As Masoumeh Ebtekar, one of the female students who was involved in the occupation of the US Embassy, writes in her account of the events: 'My sense of women's rights and responsibilities derived much from the Iranian context, from Dr. Shariati's book *Fatima is Fatima*, in which he describes the Muslim woman and her role in the world of today with a mixture of eloquence and penetrating insight.'[42] Note that Fatimah, conceptualized as the ultimate female vanguard of the new order, reappears here. She travelled from seventh-century Arabia to claim a presence in the writings of Shariati and Khomeini (see above) and in the very consciousness of the revolutionaries. More strategically, the students deemed the occupation of the US Embassy a necessary step towards achieving Iran's full independence from the international system, even if that meant that Iran would be labelled a pariah or rogue state by its most potent guardians. In other words, the choice to try to detach Iran from that system which was deemed corrupt and geared towards the imperial interests of the superpowers was self-consciously made by the more radical forces that gathered around Ayatollah Khomeini. As Ebtekar writes: '[T]he Islamic Revolution in Iran transformed a once devoted ally of the west into a "rogue state" that insisted on taking orders from none other than God.'[43]

The message of an author and the reception of her oeuvre are different matters. The subject that emerged out of the revolutionary narratives weaved into Iran before and after the revolution was not welcomed as the new vanguard who would rescue humanity from its 'fallen present'. The revolutionary Muslim subject that confronts us now came to us full of residues of the past, carrying the heavy baggage of Orientalism with all its historical suspicion towards the so-called Muslim other. The occupation of the US Embassy and other signposts of escalation, such as Ayatollah Khomeini's *fatwa* calling for the killing of Salman Rushdie in 1989, in effect reified that pre-existing image of Muslims as violent, archaic and fanatical in the imagination of many stakeholders dealing with the region. A revolution (during the Cold War) – a concept associated with communism, Fidel Castro, un-American 'leftists' and the Soviet other – in the name of Islam – a concept associated with the Arabs and Turks, the fiercest competitors with the idea of the west and its Christian residue – has found it very difficult indeed to move beyond the canonized archives of western Orientalism, even after the Iranian revolutionaries re-evaluated the project to export their Islamic-republican model after the end of the Iran–Iraq war and the death of Ayatollah Khomeini in 1989. So the terror label stuck, not because its point of origin lay in the abominations of Iran's radical politics, not because of the violence unleashed by the revolution per se, but because it confronted US foreign policies and their beneficiaries – primarily the Israeli state – through a radically transversal discourse that threatened to alter the political composition of a region that has been considered vital to US national interests because of its oil resources. In other words, Iran and its allies were not a military threat to the status quo; they did not purport to change the political composition of the region through military conquest. But they were a *discursive* threat which made it necessary to fight them with a potent counter-discourse: This is when the terror narrative emerges.

To those who would immediately interject by saying that Iran was associated with terror because the country supported a range of movements – Palestinian, Lebanese, Iraqi, Afghani, etc. – and organizations such as Fatah, HAMAS, Hezbollah that use political violence in order to further their political aims, allow me to respond that 'terrorism' as a noun and 'terroristic' as an adjective are the terminological surface effect of discursive representations: they are concepts that emerge out of a particular politico-cultural configuration which commands its own signifying powers out of which the terror label and its derivatives are distilled. I am not saying that killing civilians is not immoral and taboo of course; it is and it should be. I am saying that, in the reality invented for us, it is not that moral taboo that represents a country or movement as terroristic but the discourse which signifies the fundamental categories of 'friend and foe', 'terrorists and freedom fighter'. The normative difference between these categories cannot be measured and defined in terms of the type of political violence unleashed, but by its representation in the political and media discourse of a particular period.

Let me give you a few empirical examples with regard to the discursive field under scrutiny here. In the early 1970s, the Shah, via his intelligence organization SAVAK, the CIA and the Israeli MOSSAD, sponsored a sustained 'covert war' of Iraqi-Kurdish factions under the leadership of Mustafa Barzani against the Ba'thist leadership in Iraq which led to bombings of oil installations in Kirkuk and other infrastructural facilities with civilian use and subsequently to a full-fledged insurgency. Among us, we may deem the methods employed by the Kurdish movement 'terroristic'. But this was certainly not the official view in Washington (or Britain, Iran and Israel). A White House Memorandum authored by Henry Kissinger and dated 5 October 1972 refers to 'Mustafa Barzani's Kurdish resistance movement'.[44] In the same memo it is indicated, that CIA Director Richard Helms reported the delivery of 'money and arms . . . to Barzani via the Iranians without a hitch. More money and arms are in the pipeline', it is stated. 'Barzani received the first two monthly cash payments of each for July and August . . . By the end of October, the Iranians will have received for onward shipment to the Kurds 222,000 pounds of arms and ammunitions from Agency stocks and 142,000 pound *[sic]* from [Retracted].'[45] Note also that since its inception in 1979, the Iraqi government was put on the US State Department's list of state sponsors of terrorism. The country was taken off that list in 1982 in the middle of the Iran–Iraq war and at a time when the Reagan administration was aware of Saddam Hussein's directives to use chemical weapons against advancing Iranian army units and Iraqi civilians who resisted his regime.[46] Iraq was put on that list again after its invasion of Kuwait in 1990. Ultimately then, the allocation of the terror label shifted with the particular political context in which it was employed.

Moreover, other declassified documents from the 1970s show that the label terrorist was readily applied to student activists protesting the dictatorship of the Shah. A US State Department telegram of August 1972, for instance, observes: 'Terrorist activities in Iran seem to be increasing instead of usual summer subsidence due to vacation for students, perhaps indicating better organisation and broadening of appeal to non-student groups.'[47] In the same memo, it is indicated that there 'have been 28 confirmed explosions (11 of which directed against US presence), ten shootouts and several other incidents including unsuccessful attempt to kidnap daughter of Court Minister Alam, and plot to sabotage Isfahan steel mill'.[48] The fact that these terrorists seemed to use similar measures as the Kurdish movement that the Nixon administration supported during the very same period was not the measure according to which the terror label was allocated here. Rather, it was the fact that the students were acting against a leader who was considered to be an ally of the United States that turned them into terrorists. So in the discursive field I am dissecting here, the term terror and all its derivatives do not have any normative or analytical value beyond their signification within a particular politico-cultural constellation. Not because it is me who is blurring their meaning for the sake of my argument, but because politicians have twisted and turned them for their own purposes since the birth of the term during the reign of terror in the aftermath of the French Revolution.

The Iranian–American syntax

Let me return to the beginning of this essay and recapture the issue of trust now within such an untrustworthy discursive field. The subject that emerges out of the turmoil of the revolution and the subsequent devastating war between Iran and Iraq (1980–1988) does not speak to the American side in order to mitigate conflict, but to accentuate difference. Revolutionary Iran was adamant to define the Islamic Republic in strict juxtaposition to the west in general and the United States in particular. This discourse has suggested, as I mentioned, a bifurcated syntactical order within which the fundamental boundary between subject and object, self and other, has been cemented with layers and layers of narrated inventions, all of which were meant to solidify the fundamental difference between the two states. In other words, the political independence of Iran has been achieved via a discursive dependency. By defining Iran's new 'self' in relation to the American 'other', the discourse of the Islamic Republic has become entirely dependent on invented images of the United States in particular and the concept of the west more generally. Thus an oppressive syntactical dependency has been created which demands that Iran takes the United States and the west permanently into account at each and every twist and turn of the country's official political discourse: *Marg bar amrika* (death to America), *marg bar engelis* (death to England), *marg bar israel* (death to Israel); calling for the death of America, Israel and Britain guarantees their syntactical existence in the here and now.

Thus, the west has a rather pronounced presence in Islamic Iran, particularly amongst the right wing. When the Iranian state confronts pro-democracy demonstrators with the charge that they are following the orders of the 'global arrogance', they are confirming that the United States continues to have a presence in Iran, in this case as an instigator of opposition to the state. The Iranian right wing, far more than the reformists, is politically dependent on the United States, for it is they who invite the country into the domestic politics of Iran especially during times of crisis. So the United States or, to be more precise, an invented image called 'Amrika' or the global arrogance is entirely functional for right-wing politics in Iran especially as an enemy image that is useful to quell domestic dissent or to outdo political competitors. By blaming the United States for every major incident in the country, a form of dependency on that American other is reified. It is due to this reliance of the right wing on the narrative of the global arrogance that Iranian independence has remained 'latent' and has not progressed to become 'manifest'. Manifest independence requires a broader consensus and acceptance of Iran's policies within society and a more robust cultural anchoring of the country's position in international affairs.

I am emphasizing not only that a discursive field is always social, but also that that sociality could be violent, neutral, intimate, or friendly; it could be charged with negative or positive energy, but it always remains the loci within which shifts from enemy to friend or ally to foe can be signified. Let me point out that I am accentuating the effects of discourse, our language towards the other, as the main source of trust-building measures. I am re-emphasizing this because Iran and the United States did occasionally reach out to each other out of expediency without changing their language towards the other side. When the 'great satan' and the 'mad mullahs' colluded via Israel in what became to be known as the Iran-Contra-Affair in 1986, they remained just that: staunch antagonists who made a deal not in order to engender trust, but as a means to achieve divergent strategic interests. In the case of the Iranian leadership, the deal was necessary in order to secure the supply of arms and weaponry during a period when the chemical weapons attacks by Saddam Hussein's troops were beginning to demoralize the Iranian army. The Israeli government of Shimon Peres, on the other side, acted on the premise 'that moderate elements in Iran can come to power if these factions demonstrate their credibility in defending Iran against Iraq and in deterring Soviet intervention. To achieve the strategic goal of a more moderate Iranian government', it is stated in a White House memorandum authored by then US National Security Advisor John Poindexter, 'the Israelis are prepared to unilaterally commence selling military material to Western-oriented Iranian factions . . . It is their belief that by so doing they can achieve a heretofore unobtainable penetration of the

Iranian governing hierarchy.'[49] In response to this memo, President Reagan authorized assisting individuals and groups 'sympathetic to U.S. Government interests . . . for the purpose of: 1) establishing a more moderate government in Iran, 2) obtaining from them significant intelligence . . . and 3) furthering the release of the American hostages held in Beirut'.[50]

It should become clear that in this clandestine transaction none of the stakeholders were interested in pursuing strategic trust-building measures, which would have involved, at minimum, the acknowledgement of the trustworthiness of the other side.[51] The first major step towards that direction after the revolution in Iran was made by former president Mohammad Khatami (1997–2005) via the 'dialogue amongst civilisations' initiative which did not yield, however, the results he and his supporters envisaged. Rather the contrary, as Iran was named a part of the 'axis of evil' and a major target in the global war on terror pronounced by the administration of George W. Bush in the aftermath of the terror attacks on the country in September 2001. Thus far, this narrative–counter-narrative dialectic has not delivered a pacified discursive field in which a strategic leap towards trust can be signified.

Discursive fields are never immutable or unchangeable; they are impure, creolized phenomena, porous and polluted spaces that are open for interpretive penetration. Their relative ontological salience does not emanate from the a-historical codification of the objects that engage each other therein, but from the fact that none of them can be explained solely by their own properties. In this sense, discursive fields are social phenomena; representations of self and other are entirely interdependent. Iranians and Americans may have parodied seemingly divergent identities aimed at setting each other apart, but their performative acts achieved the opposite. By allocating to the other side a prominent discursive presence, the interdependence between the two countries increased. Before the revolution, Iran and the United States were entangled in a social relationship that was beset by trust; after the revolution, they were immersed in a social relationship beset by active distrust. The latter constellation required far more laborious political construction efforts, because: (a) the intentions of the other side were largely obscured, not immediately visible (there was no easily accessible intelligence in CIA parlance), and (b) the enemy image (mad mullah, great satan) had to be constructed within a discursive field that was suddenly ruptured by the Islamic revolution.

Premise (a) can be immediately linked to Sun Tzu's ancient note of caution: 'Know the enemy and know yourself; in a hundred battles you will never be in peril'[52] or to the popular proverb that you should 'keep your friends close, but your enemies closer', which re-appears in Francis Ford Coppola's movie adaptation of Mario Puzo's novel *The Godfather*. In other words, after the revolution, Iran and the United States had to take each other permanently into account; they had to open up spaces for the other side in their official discourse because, in the absence of diplomatic relations, both sides suffered from a pronounced sense of insecurity about each other's intentions. Indeed, a quick perusal of the main strategic speeches of successive US presidents indicates that the presence of Iran in the syntax of US foreign policy proclamations has progressively increased to the extent that today President Obama mentions the country whenever he addresses three central international issues (the first and third of which are global): the topic of nuclear disarmament and the Non Proliferation Treaty (NPT), international relations in West Asia and US relations with the Muslim world.

Premise (b) refers to the process via which the unknown enemy has to become the socially engineered invention par excellence because he has to be made visible. Turning him into a 'real and tangible enemy' requires ongoing performative processes, the ultimate aim of which would be to reveal his hidden face. An incredible amount of Kantian *Einbildungskraft* (power of imagination) is needed here in order to turn him into something easily recognizable. If the enemy image is conducive to the politics of the day, the expressions of his face have to be drawn threateningly enough to mobilize the libidinous anger of the nation that would, ideally, stare at him with outrage and in readiness to take up arms. Of course, once this image is created, it is difficult to be re-manipulated; indeed the whole process of enemy-making threatens to become a self-fulfilling prophecy.

Dialectical Conjunctions

Political elites deceive themselves whenever they believe that they can monopolize the signification of a particular discursive field without taking the other side into account. No hegemony is all-encompassing, no discourse can be co-opted fully by a particular agent, no discursive field is indifferent to temporal change. In a situation that is intensely social, where the bonds between country A and country B are not easily dissoluble, violence towards the other will always involve some blowback. The psychological (i.e. strategic) impact of violence between family members is more intimate than a pub brawl, the violence between Iran and the United States causes more strategic and cognitive scars (on both sides) than the violence between say the United States and Tanzania or Iran and Austria. It is in this sense that the United States and Iran share a 'common fate', their actions in world politics remain linked, despite efforts to the contrary. Of course, that statement does not mean that the strategic goals of the two countries are compatible, as they are not. Neither do I think it likely that Iran would act as a yay-saying junior partner to US foreign policies. What that statement implies is that today Iran and the United States inhabit a discursive field in which their respective identities are linked. The practical outcome of this conjunction is not only a common memory of violence, distrust and confrontation, quite comparable to a recently divorced couple, but also the hundreds of thousands of Iranian Americans who are a part of that discursive field and who engineer it on a daily basis.

This paradoxical Iranian–American conjunction also creates ironic technological exchanges: In April 2012, Iran successfully downed the bat-wing RQ-170 Sentinel drone, one of the most sophisticated unmanned spying aircraft in the possession of the Pentagon. At the time of writing, Iranian engineers are busy cracking the codes and dissecting the technology of the drone, parts of which are said to appear in Iranian-built models soon.[53] In June 2009, the Iranian nuclear programme was targeted by a cyber-attack. The so-called Stuxnet worm destroyed 1,000 of the country's 5,000 gas centrifuges, but it failed to have a serious impact on the country's nuclear enrichment programme.[54] Immediately after the attack, Iran established a Cyber Command headquarter under the leadership of Brigadier General Gholamreza Jalali, one of the figureheads of the Islamic Revolution Guards Corps who is also Director of Iran's Passive Defence Organisation.[55] The organization has established its own cyber-army that specializes in cracking the code of the various worms and viruses aimed at sabotaging Iran's nuclear energy programme. The cyber-war against Iran has proven to be a form of enhanced US-Iranian technology transfer with unintended consequences: In July 2012, cyber-security experts at Kaspersky Lab and Seculert found out that the computer systems of major Israeli companies that are a part of the water, computer and electricity infrastructure of the country were infected by malware. Some of the computer codes used in this particular strain were written in Persian and the domain names were registered in Iran.[56] Similarly, in November 2012, the US company Chevron complained that its computers were infected by Stuxnet.[57] In the cyber-world as well, Iran and the United States (and its allies) cannot escape interdependencies of structures, networks and systems.

At the beginning of this chapter, we presumed that the hyphen separating the term Iranian–American is a sign of unbridgeable difference. Certainly, after the Iranian revolution in 1979, there have been immense efforts on both sides to convince us that Iran and the United States are essentially different entities, that there is an inherent epistemological difference between these two ideas. But upon closer inspection, the hyphen reveals itself as a conjunction, a grammatical particle, a via media that indicates that in the word formation Iranian–American nothing is detachable, autonomous, at liberty. We are confronted with a particular form of what Gilles Deleuze termed 'disjunctive synthesis',[58] the interdependence of exclusive concepts, Iran (Iranian, mad mullahs, etc.) on the one side, America (American, great satan, etc.) on the other. Ultimately, within the discursive field at which we are looking, each of these terms is intensely interdependent; they not only signify a common discursive field, but also a conjoined cognitive region.

It is time that we catch up with this political paradox – with the violently interdependent, latently empathetic potentialities of word formations. Uttering trust towards the other, after all, calls for the triumph of the conjunction 'and' over the predicate 'is'; the former restricts exclusions, the latter pronounces them. There are many 'ands' between Iran and the United States that could be developed, not only historical conjunctions such as the heroic death of Howard Baskerville (1885–1909) who fought in Tabriz for Iranian democracy, but the linkages created by the life of millions of Iranian Americans who enact the meaning of being Iranian and American on a continuous basis.[59] Their daily lives create cultural and political impulses which disturb the concept of homogenous national ideas and inevitable ideational differences. These days we cannot really afford to indulge in the hideous dream of national purity anymore. Iran and the United States are cognitive neighbours. A rational approach to this paradoxical conjunction would translate the real and present interconnections between the two countries into a neighbourhood policy accentuating mutual respect, reconciliation and peace.

Neighbourhood Policies: *Muqawamah* or the Meaning of Power and Resistance Today

Most of the dead had choked on flying dirt and other debris. Their bodies, intact, preserved their final gestures: a raised arm called for help, an old man pulled on pants. Twelve-year-old Hussein Hashem lay curled in the fetal position, his mouth seeming to have vomited earth.

The late Anthony Shadid reporting the aftermath
of the Israeli bombing of Qana (southern Lebanon) in 2006

Conjunctions in theory and in practice

I started the present study with a discussion of the ruptures that the Arab revolts have provoked in their primary arenas, Tunisia and Egypt, as well as in fields of secondary representations such as the western media and mainstream culture more generally. So solid has been the consensus on the difference between Islam and the west, Orient and Occident, east and west, and so strong has been the ideological commitment to the idea of a retroactive and apathetic 'Middle East', that no note was taken about forms of resistance within Arab and Muslim societies until they finally erupted with such vehement force between 2010 and 2011. The *zeitgeist* of the war on terror demanded emphasis on al-Qaeda, Islamist terrorism and the wars in Iraq and Afghanistan. With the revolts in the name of democracy and social justice, this image of so called 'Middle Easterners' as incubators of a recurrent 'clash of civilisations' between Islam and the west has been disturbed. Within a very short period of time much of the conventional knowledge on the region that was premised on the ultimate difference of the Muslim other seems trivial. Indeed, the compelling impact of the revolts on Europe and North America has been that the other has finally emerged as neighbour, that the idea that Muslims, Arabs, Iranians, or Pakistanis are ultimately different has been questioned. This comes as a major surprise to the right wing here and there. Their narratives, which are constructed around a syntax simulating irreconcilable religious and civilizational schisms, have been subdued, at least for a very short moment.

In the previous interregnum, I have argued that relations between the United States and Iran reveal themselves in a densely populated social field which requires an effective neighbourhood policy between the two countries to foster diplomatic engagement. Comparable to all major terms that constitute the methodical grid underlying this book, the concept of neighbour in theory (and therefore also in praxis, for theory begets our constructed reality) refers to an interconnection, a dialectical arena where norms, institutions, narratives, national myths and/or belief systems engage themselves. In the following paragraphs, I would like to conceptualize neighbourhood policies further with a particular emphasis on the Israeli–Palestinian conflict. It seems inevitable for a study on power and resistance that is empirically situated in West Asia and North Africa such as the present one to not ignore one of the most emotive and entrenched conflicts in the world. The absence of a sound neighbourhood policy between Israelis and Palestinians, after all, is a festering wound on the ideational surface of the region and cannot be ignored or set aside with a clear conscience by anyone dealing with the contemporary politics of the area. The issue of Palestine transcends, probably like no other. While there is no claim in the following to provide an exhaustive genealogy of the Israeli–Palestinian conundrum, which is not the topic of this study, I will pick up a central source of the conflict and reveal its irrationality: The idea of distinction that lies at the heart of the Israeli state until today.[1]

The Palestinian neighbour: Monstrosity or Friend?

When I suggested that the revolts in Tunisia and Egypt have opened up the opportunity to appreciate the other as 'neighbour', I am not talking about the neighbour in Emmanuel Levinas' influential interpretation of the term. For Levinas, and his contemporary interlocutor Slavoj Žižek, the neighbour can always also be turned into a primordial enemy.[2] The prescription of Jesus to 'Love thy neighbour' (Leviticus 19:18), central to contemporary Judeo-Christian theology that Žižek and Levinas articulate, is not taken to be a principled disposition, a constructive starting point for engagement, but affection towards the neighbour is deemed dependent on her intentions. If she encroaches on the carefully cloistered territory of the self, in this case if the Palestinian neighbour is too audacious in her demands for political independence from Israel, she must be ostracized as the ultimate other. In Žižek this latent hostility is apparent in his rather paranoiac attitudes towards the potentially evil intentions of individuals in general and in particular those closest to us. From his perspective, the neighbour always also could reveal herself as a 'monstrosity', a menacing Freudian Thing (*das Ding*), the manifestation of evil: 'One should hear in this term all the connotations of horror fiction: the neighbour is the (Evil) Thing which potentially lurks beneath every homely human face. Just think about Stephen King's *Shining*', Žižek suggests, 'in which the father, a modest failed writer, gradually turns into a killing beast who, with an evil grin, goes on to slaughter his entire family'.[3] From this perspective, a successful neighbourhood policy is stunted by existential paranoia about the potential cruelty of the other and her ability to hurt us in an immediate and unmitigated manner.

Levinas, on the other side, revealed a problematic blind spot in his theory of empathy towards the neighbour when he defended the Israeli massacre in the Sabra and Shatila refugee camps in Beirut in 1982. In an interview covering those events, he made it clear that the neighbour 'is not *necessarily* kin', but that he can be under particular circumstances, which do not however apply to the Palestinians.[4] While it is possible to be 'for the other' which implies being 'for the neighbour', Levinas emphasizes that reciprocity can and must be severed when the neighbour reveals himself as enemy:[5]

> If your neighbour attacks another neighbour or treats him unjustly, what can you do? Then alterity takes on another character, in alterity we can find an enemy, or at least then we are faced with the problem of knowing who is right and who is wrong, who is just and who is unjust. There are people who are wrong.[6]

Levinas' conception of the neighbour as potential enemy is reflective of Enlightenment thought which produced the idea of European modernity and its 'significant others'. Enlightenment thought accelerated what the social anthropologist Jack Goody called the 'theft of history',[7] which severed Europe's links to the Arab-Muslim Orient despite the common Abrahamic territory and Aristotelian heritage that both traverse (and, in the case of the state of Israel, the very physical territory onto which it is expanding). Ultimately, European modernity was a great self-cleansing exercise. In particular, Arabs and Muslims were deemed exterior to the western universe. Islam was ghettoized, the neighbour was banished to the 'favalas' of history, which made it possible to imagine the mirage of western superiority and exclusivity in the first place. At the core of the idea of western modernity, then, is a myth: the invention that Islam and the west, Orient and Occident, we and they, are dichotomous entities.[8]

The theft of history is an important component in the fortification of the 'clash regime' which has floated rather decisively into the political void left behind by the Cold War and its underlying us versus them mentality.[9] As such, the marginalization of the other in 'our' archives undergirds the solid historical, cultural and philosophical foundations of the unremitting thesis that we have to fight the neighbour. Almost undisturbed by her presence, and socialized within purified historical archives, the subject of western modernity imagines a historical, cultural and philosophical calling that fluctuates between outright racism and more subtle claims to hegemony that are coded in a metaphysical language. Levinas' ideas fall into the latter category; his is a metaphysics of difference; for him, otherness cannot be overcome: The closer the Palestinian neighbour gets, the more fortified Israel has to construct its identity, the more the Israeli 'self' has to be cloistered. In concrete terms, the neighbour as a potential monstrosity means that Israel emerges as the threatened victim amid a hostile environment populated by Arabs and Muslims which appear conjoined as a gigantic anti-Israeli conspiracy by the Palestinian other. This is how Palestinians can emerge as a burden to the traumatized Israeli soul:

> For Israel, the land is either what is at stake, or the point of impasse. This impasse is what is referred to in their expression: *en brera* meaning 'there is no choice!' It is the position of an armed and dominant State, one of the great military powers of the Mediterranean basin facing the unarmed Palestinian

people whose very existence Israel refuses to recognise! But is that the true state of affairs? Is not Israel, in its very real strength, also one of the most fragile and vulnerable things in the world, poised in the midst of unopposed nations, who are rich in natural allies and surrounded by their lands? Land, land, land, as far as the eye can see.[10]

Despite the many nuances in designations of self and other, for Levinas the unity of the fused in-group is signified by its ethical burden to rescue humanity from its fallen present, if necessary by destroying any common danger to civilisation from the 'outside'. In other words, the totalization of the group objectifies itself, if it has to, in the destruction and murder of the neighbour. There is nothing inherently prideful or chivalrous in this task. Rather it is a burden achieved through blood and labour. For instance, when Levinas refers to 'my Muslim friend, my unhated enemy of the Six-Day-War', he acknowledges the fight against the Palestinian collective not out of hatred but out of necessity.[11] For Levinas, 'Zionism is a movement to acknowledge Jewish suffering and reduce it. It is politics constituted to reach out to the afflicted, to the hurt, to the abandoned',[12] even if that means fighting them to sustain the unity of the state of Israel. Such romantic belief in the possibility of complete ontological detachment, in this case from a people 'who call themselves Palestinians, who are surrounded by the great Arab people of which they are a part',[13] is symptomatic of the deceptive exuberance inherited from enlightenment positivism and its belief in total causal efficacy. The intractability of the question of Palestine would be less pronounced if the discourses legitimating the Zionist project would have been filled with less causal violence. To put this in less theoretical language: The idea that Israel is a unique oasis in the midst of an arid land of otherness populated by Arabs, Muslims and Palestinians allows Levinas to equip his people with a distinctly millenarian mission and to fortify them behind a barb-wired wall in order to ward off the Arab-Muslim coterie which is thought to threaten this polis from the outside.

Earlier comments by Levinas reveal that the neighbour as enemy is not only thought in relation to the Palestinians, but within a wider dichotomous contest between the Judeo-Christian civilization and the rest that Gil Anidjar traces so convincingly in his genealogy of the enemy.[14] This attitude is exemplified in a comment on the conflict between Maoist China and the Soviet Union in 1960.

According to Levinas, Russia was battling a 'yellow peril [which] is not racial, it is spiritual'. If Russia was 'to abandon the West' it may 'drown itself in an Asiatic civilisation', the 'yellow' other which 'does not involve inferior values; it involves a radical strangeness, a stranger to the weight of its past, from where there does not filter any familiar voice or inflection, a lunar or Martian past'.[15] China emerges here as obscure, different and essentially separate, the Oriental other is banished to another, barren universe with strangely Martian characteristics.[16] In a similar vein, Levinas repeatedly defended the unity of the Jewish-Christian civilization during the Second World War, which he juxtaposed to European barbarism.[17] In the 1960s, he identified the 'underdeveloped Afro-Asiatic masses' as a major problem for the 'sacred history' inscribed in the western Judeo-Christian tradition:[18] 'Humanity consists of the Bible and the Greeks', he famously stated, 'all the rest – all the exotic – is dance.'[19] As such, Levinas' self–other dialectic reveals itself as biased and almost exclusive to inventions of the self which are represented in distinctly metaphysical terms.[20]

I have arrived at a point where I can argue that the neighbour that Levinas imagines is dispensable. In its real appearance, his self–other dialectic is neither reconciliatory nor emancipatory, but ambiguous and divisive. It adds up to a patronizing call to protect the Palestinians as the other, if only they would stop resisting Israel's overwhelming spiritual and material power. Stripped of its metaphysical veneer, his empathy for the neighbour succumbs to his passion for millenarian Zionism which he sought to identify with his own interpretation of redemptive Judaism. From this perspective, Israel is more than a mere nation, it is a metaphysical utopia; it is literally 'out of this world'. Consequently, Israelis have to go beyond providing 'a shelter for those without a country, and beyond the sometimes astonishing, sometimes doubtful, accomplishments of the State of Israel'. Israel has to act as a carapace for a new kind of prophetic politics. In Levinas' words: 'Since 1948, there it is, surrounded by enemies and still being called into question, yet it is also engaged in events, in order to think through – to build and rebuild – a State that should embody a prophetic morality and the idea of its peace.'[21]

In Levinas, the Israeli self is centred. It is the logos not only of the prophecy of the Jewish God, but the nodal point for a new kind of politics around which the state of Israel would be built. Palestinians are turned into dependent variables. Israel is constant, steeped in Judaic time which encompasses this world and the hereafter. Zionism, after all, 'repeatedly turns toward cosmic and historical time', since it articulates both a metaphysical and historical claim, as Jacqueline Rose rightly stressed.[22] Palestinian nationalism never really developed such a transcendental conception of the self. There is no Palestinian god that could be drawn into a cosmic conflict, which is why mainstream (secular) Palestinian nationalism could never really compete with Zionism as an ideology and metaphysical system. So unique, purified and immunized from the undue influence of the neighbour does Israel appear in Levinas, that one must almost be relieved that there are no calls for the Palestinian neighbour to be annihilated. So trans-territorial and meta-spatial is the conception of Israel, that one must almost be grateful that Palestinians are merely confined beyond the expanding borderlines of the Israeli polis.

Zionist space politics and the fate of the other

Borders are central to a people claiming territory. Delineation, space, difference, segregation, drawing lines in the sand: at base this is what the Israeli–Palestinian conflict has been all about from the outset. I see Zionism, above anything else, as an ideology of space, comparable to any other strand of modernist nationalisms but with a particularly intrusive and meticulous 'architecture of occupation' as Eyal Weizman puts it.[23] Zionist space politics has expanded in two directions. First, it has taken an ideational direction which preceded the making of the state and required inventing the idea of Israel in strict juxtaposition to the Arab and Muslim inhabitants of the area. This ideational invention of the national myths that constitute Israel today necessitated dichotomies between self and other, Jew and Arab, Israeli and Palestinian.

The idea of fortified borders enabled the early Zionists to pursue the delineation of Israel on the ground – that is, the creation of the state, its sovereignty, legitimacy and expanding borders. In other words, the idea of distinction and segregation preceded the creation of Israel and has fed into a politics of space that has not accommodated the Palestinian other. As long as there is no common Palestinian–Israeli narrative, the material segregation of Palestinians will continue. The hyphen separating Israel–Palestine is not realized as a disjunctive synthesis but as an antagonistic disjuncture, which is why until today Israeli power and Palestinian resistance have not merged to constitute a common territory where engagement could be possible. Ultimately, it is due to this ardent adherence to such modern ideas of difference and sanitisation that Israel's progression into a post-modern state of hybridity has been stunted.

If my statement that the idea of Israel as we know it today has required ideational segregation (which could then be translated into material borders) is correct, I should be able to find plenty of support in the policies and statements of Israeli leaders before the establishment of the state in 1948. The idea of the 'iron wall' that was conceptualized by Vladimir Zeev Jabotinsky (1880–1940) – one of the most influential early leaders of the Zionist movement – is an obvious starting point, for it is this idea that has acted as a metaphor for a militaristic state which would be powerful enough to hold off Arab resistance to the colonization of Palestine until today.[24] If Levinas acknowledged the right of existence of the neighbour, Jabotinsky and his followers did not envisage such compromise. For them the colonization of the territory claimed by the Zionists had to be continued and developed 'only under the protection of a force independent of the local population – an iron wall which the native population cannot break through'.[25] According to Jabotinsky, who set up the New Zionist Organisation in 1935, 'every indigenous people will resist alien settlers as long as they see any hope of ridding themselves of the danger of foreign settlement'.[26] In other words: Jabotinsky saw the resistance of Palestinians coming and advocated cloistering Israel behind an iron wall in order to delineate the dream of Eretz Israel. The Israeli state had to resort to hard power politics because the Arabs in Palestine were bound to revolt against the colonization of their territory: 'That is what the Arabs in Palestine are doing', Jabotinsky warned, 'as long as there remains a solitary spark of hope that they will be able to prevent the transformation of "Palestine" into the "Land of Israel"'.[27]

The idea of an Israeli self with no real connections to the native population of Palestine was central to revisionist Zionism and was carried forward by successive Israeli prime ministers. Comparable to the flirtations of the early Zionists with the ideology of Nazi Germany, the Revisionists were partially inspired by the fascist doctrines of Benito Mussolini in Italy. For instance, Abba Ahimeir (1897–1962), one of the early leaders of the Revisionist movement, praised the superiority of European fascism over communism and democracy in a series of articles published in 1928 and called for a messianic inscription of an 'eternal Jewish soul' into the doctrines of Zionism.[28] The second prominent leader of the Revisionist movement, Uri Tzevi Greenberg (1897–1981), was equally absorbed by the racialized politics of difference that were so prominent in Europe at the beginning of the twentieth century. For Greenberg, there was a biologically determined difference between Jews and non-Jews that made any form of compromise impossible. The Israeli nation-state had to be conquered through a campaign of violence and it had to be equipped with the crushing power of arms.[29] The former Israeli prime minister Yitzak Shamir is widely seen as the last of the Revisionist leaders in Israel. Shamir was one of the founders of the 'Stern Gang' which was responsible for several terrorist attacks against the British, including the bombing of the King David Hotel in 1946 and the Deir Yassin massacre in 1948.[30] He also condoned the assassination of the Swedish UN diplomat Count Folke Bernadotte in 1948 who was serving as a mediator in Palestine.[31] Shamir famously stated that 'neither Jewish morality nor Jewish tradition can be used to disallow terror as a means of war' and that terror was an appropriate 'part of the political war' that Israel was waging.[32] This emphasis on violence echoes the views of Menachem Begin, another Israeli prime minister who was socialized into the politics of terror advocated by the Irgun and the Haganah, the two main paramilitary forces of the Zionist movement. While for Begin the early Zionists were not engaged in terror per se, but in a 'revolutionary war of liberation', he too charged the Israeli narrative with immense violence when he proclaimed with unmistakeable pride the birth of 'the fighting Jew'.[33] These attitudes on political violence and power were typically modern, charged with the causal vulgarity that European modernity engendered including racist depictions of the Arabs who Begin describes as not 'particularly courageous' and generally not willing 'to read much'.[34]

From the outset, the founding myths of the Israeli state were dependent on such territorialization and centring of the Israeli self. Berl Katznelson, the major theorist of Labour Zionism, declared as early as in 1929 that the 'Zionist enterprise is an enterprise of conquest' and that 'it is by no chance that I use military terms when speaking of settlement'.[35] Moreover, we find in the writings and speeches of Jabotinsky the residues of the racial theories dominant in Europe during that period and which were used so devastatingly by the Nazis against Europe's Jews (and homosexuals, gypsies and other strata of society deemed degenerate) after Hitler's takeover of power in Germany in 1933:

> Territory, language, religion, common history do not form the substance of a nation, they are only its attributes . . . The substance of a nation, the first and last fortress of the uniqueness of its form, is found in its specific physical character, in the 'recipe' of its racial composition . . . all said and done, when all sorts of coverings due to history, climate, the natural environment, external influences are removed, the nation is reduced to its racial hard core.[36]

From this perspective, the cloistered territory carved out for the idea of Israel is racially defined. Such bio-political re-engineering strategies were meant to naturalize segregation scientifically and render difference unbridgeable. Within the confines of the identity politics of Zionism, segregation is thought absolute, coded, irreversible, organic. Zeev Sternhell goes as far as to term these founding myths of the Israeli state as nationalist-socialist triggered by a messianic obsession to populate 'the promised land'.[37] By using the term nationalist-socialist, Sternhell makes an implicit reference to the theories that informed the cod-science of the Nazis in Germany. Although I shall not stretch that reference too far, the comparison is not without analytical merit and supports my depiction of Zionism as a typically divisive modernist ideology. Indeed, some of its most prominent theorists, for instance the ultra-nationalist Heinrich Graetz and Moses Hess, experimented with race theory in the latter part of the nineteenth century to present a pseudo-scientific legitimation for an authentically Jewish homeland. Others, such as Arthur Ruppin, kept working relationships with eugenicist theorists in Germany including the infamous Hans Friedrich Karl Günther (called *Rassegünther* or race Günther) who developed the race theories of Eugen Fischer at the University of Freiburg and who became a highly decorated functionary of Hitler's NSDAP.[38] The common motivator of these Zionist experimentations with race theory was the emphasis on racial difference. As Nathan Birnbaum, who invented the term Zionism in 1890, emphasized:

> You cannot explain a people's particular mental and emotional distinction except by means of the natural studies. 'Race is all', said our great fellow national Lord Beaconsfield [Benjamin Disraeli]. The distinction of the

people stems from the distinction of the race. The variety of races accounts for the great diversity of nations. It is because of the differences between the races that the German of the Slav thinks differently from the Jew. It is this difference which explained why the German created the Song of the Nibelungen and the Jew, the Bible.[39]

The key words in this paragraph are 'distinction' and 'difference'. Together they appear (in variations) six times, thereby simulating the myth of a distinct Jewish race. Birnbaum and his colleagues wrote during a period when race theories were deemed scientific, so their emphasis on primordial racial differences between Jew and non-Jew were quite emblematic. The *zeitgeist* of the period lent itself to such genetic engineering and the invention of the idea of a Jewish race. Racism appeared here as space politics, by other means turning the embrace of the neighbour into an impossibility. Henceforth, 'the "victorious" Jews would live surrounded by an entirely hostile Arab population, secluded inside ever-threatened borders, absorbed with physical self-defense', as Hannah Arendt anticipated as early as in 1948: '[S]ocial experiments would have to be discarded as impractical luxuries; political thought would centre around military strategy; economic development would be determined exclusively by the need of war.'[40] Arendt was correct: Today, the state of Israel has one of the highest military expenditures per capita of GDP (6.5 per cent) in the world.[41] The limitations of political thought that she alluded to are equally apparent: In recent years, dissenting Israeli voices, even senior academics, have been harassed into exile.[42]

The modern premises of segregation and difference continue to be strictly adhered to by contemporary Israeli leaders. In particular, the current Israeli Prime Minister Benjamin Netanyahu has adopted many of the prescriptions of the early engineers of Zionism. He interprets the idea of the iron wall to refer to a form of 'deterrence, to have them smash against your defences or against your offenses'.[43] Moreover, Netanyahu agrees that the power of the Israeli state has to be primarily militaristic, as Jabotinsky suggested.[44] The segregation wall is the most obvious contemporary example of that politics of spatialization which is meant to fortify a fleeting national identity under threat by post-national politics and processes of globalization[45] On the most primitive level, the wall creates facts on the ground, an ad hoc sovereignty and a convenient way to encroach on Palestinian territory and to disrupt any prospects of contingency of a future Palestinian state. As such, the segregation wall is the material realisation of the idea that Jabotinsky expressed at the beginning of the twentieth century. Behind the wall, on the Israeli side, the policies of geographical segregation are complemented by a discriminatory legal regime. A law passed by the Knesset in August 2003 that prevents Palestinian spouses of Israeli citizens from living in Israel is a prominent example. According to this law, married Palestinian-Israeli couples are forced to leave Israel or to live separately. The law is exclusive to Palestinian-Israeli couples – that is, if any person other than a Palestinian marries an Israeli citizen, he or she will be entitled to Israeli citizenship. Such policies of seclusion are meant to disrupt and puncture any movement toward a common Israeli-Palestinian narrative. As indicated, this conjoined territory could only be artificially segregated with the myth of a distinct Israeli nation and, in material terms, by barb-wired walls and a discriminatory legal regime.

It should be reemphasized by means of concluding this section that in the philosophy of Levinas, and this is certainly true for the founders of the state of Israel and the early Zionist thinkers that we have perused so far, the politics of space symbolizes more than a competition over geographic delimitation. Israel is more than a national space and the battle with the Arabs represents more than a conventional clash. For Levinas, the 'struggle has always been, in one sense, like the uprising in the Warsaw ghetto where there is no hiding place and where each step back has implications for the whole struggle'.[46] This trauma of shelter, from the racism of the Nazis, which revealed itself in spatial segregation, the ghettoes and the concentration camps, this whole idea of segregation impinges on the conception of Israel and partially explains the failed neighbourhood policy of the Israeli state. For a people whose immanence in humanity has been under such existential threat, acknowledging the immanence of the Palestinian neighbour who criss-crosses the very body of what is claimed as Israel is that much more difficult. 'Zionism arises on the back of European anti-Semitism, on the one hand, and the pogroms of Eastern Europe on the other', Jacqueline Rose expresses that sentiment. According to her, 'as well as being fueled [sic] by the birth of nineteenth-century nationalism, the drive to Jewish self-determination must be understood as the response to that history'.[47]

The Israeli–Palestinian dialectic and our composite future

The weight of evidence that has been unearthed by Israel's 'new historians' shows that the dream of what David Ben-Gurion and the early Zionists called 'ingathering', the colonization of Israel, could only be realized through the cleansing, ethnic and historical, of the complex interdependencies between the Jewish self and the Arab/Muslim/Palestinian other.[48] Ilan Pappe has demonstrated through archival research that at least 'thirty-one confirmed massacres – beginning with the massacre in Tirat Haifa on 11 December 1947 and ending with Khirbat Ilin in the Hebron area on 19 January 1949' occurred during the *Nakba* (or catastrophe), a term used by Palestinians to depict the period immediately before and after the establishment of the Israeli state in May 1948.[49] Pappe notes further that 'the aim of the Zionist project has always been to construct and then defend a "white" (Western) fortress in a "black" (Arab) world' which he likens to the 'thick walls' surrounding the 'impenetrable castles' of the medieval Crusaders in Jerusalem and the 'siege mentality' of the 'white settlers in South Africa during the heyday of Apartheid rule.'[50]

There is prominent empirical evidence for this view of Israel as the beacon of civilization embroiled in a cosmic clash with the barbarian Arabs and Muslims that Pappe points out. Benny Morris, the first Israeli historian to acknowledge the ethnic cleansing of Palestine, for instance, justified the policy to uproot the Palestinians on the grounds that there is a clash of civilizations between Islam and the west of which Israel would be a part.[51] In an interview with the Israeli daily *Ha'aretz* in 2004, Morris compared the west with 'the Roman Empire of the fourth, fifth and sixth centuries: The barbarians are attacking it and they may also destroy it'. Responding to the question of whether the Muslims are barbarians, Morris replied that the 'Arab world as it is today is barbarian . . . The phenomenon of the mass Muslim penetration into the West and their settlement there is creating a dangerous internal threat. A similar process took place in Rome. They let the barbarians in and they toppled the empire from within.'[52]

In this interview, Morris clearly displays the fear of impingement that is characteristic of Zionist ideology and other forms of ultra-nationalism that developed out of the sanitized laboratories of western modernity. Enclosure of the self and the fencing in of the other is characteristic of the logic underlying such ideologies of difference.[53] But Morris goes beyond the mere denunciation of the Palestinian neighbour. To Morris's mind, Palestinian society is sick, it is 'in the state of being a serial killer'.[54] Speaking in the aftermath of several terrorist attacks in Israeli cities perpetrated by Palestinian militants, Morris suggested that therefore 'something like a cage has to be built for them'.[55] This may sound 'terrible' and 'cruel', but from his perspective 'there is no choice. There is a wild animal there that has to be locked up in one way or another'.[56] The inevitable dialectics of death that we discussed with Sartre, the view that death, even murder, cannot divorce victim and perpetrator, that it creates bonds and a common memory steeped in the powerful symbolism of blood, are not even considered. Detachment is imagined to be possible through a process of self-cleansing, if necessary through violence. It does not come as a surprise, then, that the greatest threat to this iron wall approach that Morris explicitly affirms is the hybrid subject that the Israeli–Palestinian narrative created, namely 'the Israeli Arab' that Morris deems the 'emissary of the enemy that is among us'.[57] They are castigated as a potential 'fifth column . . . . So that if Israel again finds itself in a situation of existential threat, as in 1948, it may be forced to act as it did then'. However, this time the ethnic cleansing would have to be more thorough: If the first Israeli Prime Minister David Ben-Gurion

> was already engaged in expulsion, maybe he should have done a complete job. I know that this stuns the Arabs and the liberals and the politically correct types. But my feeling is that this place would be quieter and know less suffering if the matter had been resolved once and for all. If Ben-Gurion had carried out a large expulsion and cleansed the whole country – the whole Land of Israel, as far as the Jordan River. It may yet turn out that this was his fatal mistake. If he had carried out a full expulsion – rather than a partial one – he would have stabilised the State of Israel for generations . . . If the end of the story turns out to be a gloomy one for the Jews, it will be because Ben-Gurion did not complete the transfer in 1948. Because he left a large and volatile demographic reserve in the West Bank and Gaza and within Israel itself.[58]

Morris has been vehemently criticized by Israel's new historians since he gave that interview. Along with Ilan Pappe and Avi Shlaim, Jaqueline Rose and Shlomo Sand have also expressed critical reservations about the founding myths of the Israeli state and the theories of segregation and militarism that are central to mainstream discourse in the country.[59] For Rose, Zionism 'had to be staged'[60] by 'playwrights' such as Theodor Herzl and for Sand the 'burdens of memory did not appear spontaneously but rather were piled layer upon layer by gifted reconstructions of the past, beginning in the second half of the nineteenth century'.[61] Critical approaches like these have delivered a very effective antidote to the official history of Israel held up by the protagonists of the state. They also reveal an understanding that the Israeli politics of segregation overshadows the reality of a conjoined Israeli–Palestinian narrative. As I have argued throughout this book: where there is power, there is resistance. It has been inevitable that the militaristic power politics of the Israeli state, heralded by successive Israeli leaders, has given way to a dialectic that has lent itself to the resistance of Israel's foremost enemies today: HAMAS and Hezbollah.[62] To be more precise, Israel's invasion of Lebanon in 1982 gave impetus to the formation of Hezbollah and the Islamic resistance that it spearheaded (*al-Muqawama al-Islamiyya*) under the guidance of the Iranian revolutionaries. The massive Israeli suppression of the first intifadah in 1987, on the other side, accelerated the creation of the Palestinian-Islamic resistance movement HAMAS (*al-Harakat al-Muqawama al-Islamiyya*). Both movements are never exterior in relation to Israeli power. They cannot function politically or mobilize their constituents ideologically without the dialectic with Israel in which they are embedded. Their very raison d'être is tied to the Israeli state. In short: The self-declared 'Muqawama' or resistance axis spanning from Gaza (HAMAS) and southern Lebanon (Hezbollah) to Syria and Iran is exactly non-existent without Israeli power acting upon it.

The two most recent conflicts involving Israel demonstrate the logic of that power-resistance dialectic. In June 2006, when a HAMAS-led commando assault along the Israeli-Gazan border led to the death of two Israeli soldiers and the abduction of Corporal Gilad Shalit, Israel launched a simultaneous invasion of south and north Gaza that made approximately 25,000 Palestinians homeless, destroyed roads, bridges and electrical power plants, and bombed civilian ministries and the offices of the HAMAS leader Ismail Haniya who was elected as prime minister by the Palestinians in 2006 in the first free and fair elections in an Arab country. The commando assault was launched in retaliation over the bombing of Gaza which persisted throughout 2006 (and escalated again in 2008), itself a response to Qassam missiles that were launched towards the Israeli town of Sderot. In turn, HAMAS argued that the missile attacks were meant to retaliate for Israel's aerial and rocket attacks in Gaza ↔ Israeli power, Palestinian resistance, ad infinitum.

A similar action–action dynamic can be discerned from the dialectics of violence that ensued amid a raid of a Hezbollah commando into northern Israel on 12 July 2006 which resulted in the abduction of two additional Israeli soldiers. Israel responded with a sustained air bombardment of southern Beirut, which led to the deaths of hundreds of civilians and the bombardment of Beirut international airport, the main highway linking Lebanon to Syria, Al-Manar TV station, the headquarter of Hezbollah in Beirut, in an apparent effort to assassinate Seyyed Hassan Nasrallah, and four bridges that link Bint-Jbeil, Tyre, and Marjayoun to Sidon and Nabatieh.[63] In both examples, violence appears exactly as dialectical; power and resistance, resistance and power, are entirely constitutive of each other. Ultimately, the two invasions are near-perfect examples of the dialectical effect of violence that Fanon described and that I discussed in depth in the conceptual chapters of this study:

> The violence which has ruled over the ordering of the colonial world, which has ceaselessly drummed the rhythm for the destruction of native social forms and broken up without reserve the systems of reference of the economy, the customs of dress and external life, that same violence will be claimed and taken over by the native at the moment when, deciding to embody history in his own person, he surges into the forbidden quarters.[64]

The violent colonization of the native's territory is reflected in the way in which the colonized enacts that violence in order to reclaim his subjectivity and freedom. The idea of Israel begins and sustains itself through an iron wall strategy and calls forth an active violence from the colonized. In this dialectic, there is no safe haven to which Israel, HAMAS and Hezbollah can escape; their fate is entirely intertwined. It must follow quite logically that the Zionist dream of detachment is a myth and that the policies of spatialization have failed. If Zionism imagined the successful detachment of Eretz Israel, it has effected the opposite: the immanence of several 'others' into the Israeli narrative: HAMAS, Hezbollah, FATAH, the PLO, Arafat, Ayatollah Khomeini, Khaled Mesha'al, Saddam Hussein, Mahmoud Ahmadinejad, the Quds elite force of Iran's Islamic Revolutionary Guards and so on. In fact, today's range of Hezbollah's

Katyusha rockets and the Qassam rockets launched by HAMAS are indicative of the transnational forces behind them: the more Israeli power displays its military prowess, the farther they are assembled to range; the more Israel fortifies the blockade of Gaza, the more intricate the tunnel and smuggling network that links Gaza to the outside world; the more the Israeli narrative is artificially detached from the region in which it is embedded, the more it will be encroached upon by competing narratives.

It was with this understanding of overlapping spaces and interdependent power/resistance dynamics that Edward Said leapt out of a cloistered Palestinian habitat. 'Neither Palestine nor Israeli history at this point is a thing in itself without the other', he wrote with great conviction in his later years. To his mind, Israel and Palestine engaged themselves within a 'composite' ideational field where detachment was increasingly impossible. Consequently, a conjoined Israeli-Palestinian narrative was needed in order to appreciate the interdependencies that the violent (and peaceful) interaction between the two ideas necessitates:[65]

> Ideally of course the goal is to achieve consensus by scholars and activist intellectuals that a new, synthetic paradigm might slowly emerge which would re-orient the combative and divisive energies we've all had to contend with into more productive and collaborative channels. This cannot occur, I believe, without some basic agreement, a compact or entente whose outlines would have to include regarding the Other's history as valid but incomplete as usually presented [invented?], and second, admitting that despite the antinomy these histories can only continue to flow together, not apart, within a broader framework based on the notion of equality for all.[66]

Ilan Pappe has recently written that efforts in this direction have been made by critical Israeli and Palestinian historians who came together as the Palestine Israel Academic Dialogue (PALISAD) in the 1990s. Honouring the work of Said, the 'group studied Israeli and Palestine history in a dialectical manner, looking at national narratives and their power and varied topics such as collective memory and oral evidence'. Such movements away from the cloistered territory of modern 'isms' are a necessary component to shake off the perils of identity politics and the deceptive certainty of national 'origins'. As a way of summarizing the conclusion of the interregnums in this book: In today's ideational tapestry of West Asia there is quite literally no intellectual and geographic space that Jews, Turks, Iranians, Palestinians, Arabs, Christians, Muslims, Copts, Kurds might claim for themselves in total independence from the neighbour. In the nomadic spaces of West Asia and North Africa, the neighbour is immanent to the self; waging war against her is always also an act of self-mutilation. The twenty-first-century reality is that peace cannot be safeguarded on a national or civilizational' basis, and that the rational option is to make a viable neighbour policy a priority. The security threats emanating from the global system require a strategy that moves beyond notions of territoriality and ideological cohesion and embraces as far as possible a non-militaristic approach to international affairs. To these ends, emphasizing and then moving beyond the linkages between us and them, rather than perpetuating any supposed opposition, is vital. Both a new generation with a global mindset and members of minorities expressing ideas from outside the mainstream are well placed to contribute to this process. In many ways they are proof that, for a long time, and without realizing it, we have been living in the end times of the west and the east, the Orient and the Occident, or the myths of national origin. It is time to cast geo-politics aside, all the better to live at peace with ourselves *and* our global neighbours.

Notes

Introduction

1 The term is conceptualized in Arshin Adib-Moghaddam, *A Metahistory of the Clash of Civilisations: Us and Them beyond Orientalism* (London: Hurst, 2011), 155.
2 See further Reem Abou-El-Fadl, 'The Road to Jerusalem through Tahrir Square: Anti-Zionism and Palestine in the 2011 Egyptian Revolution', *Journal of Palestine Studies*, Vol. 41, No. 1 (Winter 2012), 6–26.
3 Harriet Sherwood, 'Egypt Cancels Israeli Gas Contract', *The Guardian*, 23 April 2012. Available at www.guardian.co.uk/world/2012/apr/23/egypt-cancels-israeli-gas-contract, accessed 12 December 2012.
4 See further Jack Goody, *Renaissances: The One or the Many?* (Cambridge: Cambridge University Press, 2010).
5 Roger Owen, *State, Power and Politics in the Making of the Modern Middle East*, second edition (London: Routledge, 2000), 35–36.
6 I have expressed this for the first time in Arshin Adib-Moghaddam, 'The Arab Revolts, Islam and Postmodernity', *Middle East Journal of Culture and Communication*, Vol. 5, No. 1 (2012), 15–25.
7 Owen, *State, Power and Politics*, 13.
8 Ibid., 15.
9 Ibid., 16.
10 Ibid.
11 See further Shadi Mokhtari, 'The New Politics of Human Rights in the Middle East', *Foreign Policy*, 30 October 2012. Available at http://mideast.foreignpolicy.com/posts/2012/10/30/the_new_politics_of_human_rights_in_the_middle_East. accessed 12 November 2012.
12 *The Guardian Weekend*, 31 March 2012, 24.

Interregnum 1

1 George Orwell, 'Politics and the English Language' (1946), in W.F. Bolton and D. Chrystal, *The English Language, Vol. 2, Essays of Linguists and Men of Letters* (Cambridge: Cambridge University Press, 1969), 228.

2   See further Arshin Adib-Moghaddam, *A Metahistory of the Clash of Civilisations* (London: Hurst, 2011), xiii, 5–6.

3   Ibid., 20–25.

4   Dominic Sachsenmaier, *Global Perspectives on Global History: Theories and Approaches in a Connected World* (Cambridge: Cambridge University Press, 2011), 45.

5   John M. Hobson, *The Eurocentric Conception of World Politics: Western international theory, 1760–2010* (Cambridge: Cambridge University Press, 2012), 1.

6   'Blair admits regret over deaths in Iraq', *Channel 4 News*, 21 January 2011. Available at www.channel4.com/news/blair-says-force-may-be-needed-against-iran, accessed 2 January 2012.

7   Ibid.

8   See further John L. Esposito and Ibrahim Kalin (eds), *Islamophobia: The Challenge of Pluralism in the 21st Century* (Oxford: Oxford University Press, 2011); Peter Morey and Amina Yaqin, *Framing Muslims: Stereotyping and Representation After 9/11* (Cambridge, MA: Harvard University Press, 2011); and Salman Sayyid and Abdoolkarim Vakil (eds), *Thinking Through Islamophobia: Global Perspectives* (London: Hurst, 2011).

9   Quoted in *The Independent* (Extra Section), 29 January 2008, 3.

10 Christopher Hitchens, 'Don't Mince Words: The London Car Bomb Plot Was Designed to Kill Women', *Slate*, 2 July 2007. Available at www.slate.com/articles/news_and_politics/fighting_words/2007/07/dont_mince_words.html, accessed 6 January 2012.

11 Nathan Lean, *The Islamophobia Industry: How the Right Manufactures Fear of Muslims* (London: Pluto Press, 2012), 13.

12 See further Steven Salaita, *Anti-Arab Racism in the USA: Where It Comes from and What It Means for Politics Today* (London: Pluto Press, 2006) and Tim Jon Semmerling, *Evil Arabs in American Popular Film: Orientalist Fear* (Austin: University of Texas Press, 2006).

13 See further Richard W. Bulliet, *The Case for Islamo-Christian Civilisation* (New York: Columbia University Press, 2004).

14 Max Horkheimer, *Critical Theory: Selected Essays*, trans. Matthew J. O'Connell (New York: Continuum, 2002), 231.

15 Ibid., 232.

16 Theodor W. Adorno, *Critical Models: Interventions and Catchwords*, trans. Henry W. Pickford (New York: Columbia University Press, 2005), 282.

17 Ibid., 282–283.

18 Horkheimer, *Critical Theory*, p. 244.

19 Teodor Shanin, *The Roots of Otherness: Russia's Turn of the Century*, volume II: *Russia, 1905–1907: Revolution as a Moment of Truth* (New Haven: Yale University Press, 1986), 30–31.

20 Gilles Deleuze and Claire Parnet, *Dialogues II*, trans. Hugh Tomlinson and Barbara Habberjam (London: Continuum, 2002), 72.

21 See further Asef Bayat, *Life as Politics: How Ordinary People Change the Middle East* (Stanford: Stanford University Press, 2010), 77 ff. On Iran see Asef Bayat, *Street Politics: Poor People's Movements in Iran* (New York: Columbia University Press, 1997).

22 See further Ali Harb, *Soft Power Revolutions in the Arab World: The Deconstruction of Dictatorships and Fundamentalisms* (Beirut: Al Dar Al Arabiya Liloloum Publishers, 2011).

23 Who would doubt that a weakened Saddam Hussein would have been swept away by the Arab revolt without the death of hundreds of thousands of Iraqis and the displacement of millions?

24 Rashid Khalidi, 'Preliminary Historical Observations on the Arab Revolutions of 2011', *Jadaliyya*, 21 March 2011. Available at www.jadaliyya.com/pages/ index/970/preliminary-historical-observations-on-the-arab-re, accessed 2 December 2011. See further Bassam Haddad, Rosie Bsheer, and Ziad Abu-Rish (eds), *The Dawn of the Arab Uprisings: End of an Old Order?* (London: Pluto, 2012).

25 U.S. State Department, 'Background Note: Tunisia', 13 October, 2010.

26 'In the Name of Security: Routine Abuses in Tunisia', *Amnesty International*, 23 June 2008. Available at www.amnesty.org/en/library/asset/MDE30/007/2008/ en/b8527bf4–3ebc-11dd-9656–05931d46f27f/mde300072008eng.html, accessed 22 November 2012.

27 Matthew Cole and Sarah O Wali, 'New Egyptian VP Ran Mubarak's Security Team, Oversaw Torture', *ABC News*, 1 February 2011. Available at http://abcnews. go.com/Blotter/egypt-crisis-omar-suleiman-cia-rendition/story?id=12812445#. T9DAKbCvKSo, accessed 21 December 2011.

28 'EU Socialists, Conservatives, Play 'Dictator Badminton' over Tunisia', *EUobserver. com*, 18 January 2011. Available at http://euobserver.com/political/31663, accessed 23 January 2012.

29 Country data for Tunisia according to *The World Bank*. Available at http://data. worldbank.org/country/tunisia, accessed 23 October 2012.

30 *International Monetary Fund*, 'Tunisia: 2010 Article IV Consultation', IMF Country Report No. 10/282, Washington, September 2010. Available at www.imf.org/ external/pubs/ft/scr/2010/cr10282.pdf, accessed 12 January 2011.

31 *International Monetary Fund*, 'Arab Republic of Egypt: 2010 Article IV Consultation', IMF Country Report No. 10/94, Washington, April 2010. Available at www.imf.org/external/pubs/ft/scr/2010/cr1094.pdf, accessed 12 June 2012.

32 Hdeel Abdelhady, 'Egypt Needs a Mindset Revolution', *Al-Ahram Weekly*, Issue no. 1067, 6–12 October 2011. Available at http://weekly.ahram.org.eg/2011/1067/ op2.htm, accessed 12 June 2012.

33 'US Embassy Cables: Egypt's Strategic Importance to the US', *The Guardian*, 28 January 2011. Available at www.guardian.co.uk/world/us-embassy-cables-documents/199866, accessed 8 December 2011.

34 Adam Schatz, 'Mubarak's Last Breath', *London Review of Books*, Vol. 32, No. 10, 27 May 2010. Available at www.lrb.co.uk/v32/n10/adam-shatz/mubaraks-last-breath, accessed 10 January 2011.

35 Tony Karon, 'What the US Loses if Mubarak Goes', *Time*, 31 January 2011. Available at www.time.com/time/world/article/0,8599,2045248,00.html, accessed 1 March 2011.

36 Steven Cook, 'Contingency Planning Memorandum No. 4: Political Instability in Egypt', *Council on Foreign Relations: Centre for Preventive Action*, August 2009, 7.

37 Ibid., 1.

38 See further Arshin Adib-Moghaddam (ed.), *A Critical Introduction to Ayatollah Khomeini* (Cambridge: Cambridge University Press, forthcoming 2013).

Interregnum 2

1 Telephone Interview, 22 January 2010.

2 Telephone Interview, 11 January 2010.

3 Telephone Interview, 1 November 2009.

4 Muhammad Sahimi, 'Ali Motahari's Extraordinary Interview', *Tehran Bureau*, 17 August 2011. Available at www.pbs.org/wgbh/pages/frontline/tehranbureau/2011/08/ali-motaharis-extraordinary-interview.html#ixzz1VNGani2X, accessed 18 November 2011.

5 I have elaborated on such media misrepresentations in Arshin Adib-Moghaddam, *Iran in World Politics: The Question of the Islamic Republic* (London: Hurst, 2008), Introduction.

6 See further Hamid Dabashi, *Post-Orientalism: Knowledge and Power in Time of Terror* (London: Transaction Publishers, 2008).

7 On the constitutional system in Iran see further Asghar Schirazi, *The Constitution of Iran: Politics and the State in the Islamic Republic* (London: I.B. Tauris, 1998).

8 Damien McElroy and Ahmad Vahdat, 'Iran's Ayatollah Khamenei Loves Caviar and Vulgar Jokes, Defector Claims', *The Telegraph*, 31 December 2009. Available at www.telegraph.co.uk/news/worldnews/middleeast/iran/6913069/Irans-Ayatollah-Khamenei-loves-caviar-and-vulgar-jokes-defector-claims.html, accessed 1 January 2010.

9 'Ayatollah Khamenei's Jet Put on Standby', *Radio Netherlands Worldwide*, 29 December 2009. Available at www.rnw.nl/english/article/iran-has-plane-ready-take-leader-safety, accessed 12 January 2010.

10 Fareed Zakaria, 'The Fantasy of an Iranian Revolution', *The Washington Post*, 21 June 2010. Available at www.washingtonpost.com/wp-dyn/content/article/2010/06/20/AR2010062002366.html, accessed 11 January 2011.

11 On the concept of a pluralistic momentum in Iranian politics see Adib-Moghaddam, *Iran in World Politics*, Part 4.

12 For an excellent account of these campaigns see Neil MacMaster, *Burning the Veil: The Algerian War and the 'Emancipation' of Muslim Women, 1954–62* (Manchester: Manchester University Press, 2009).

13 'US Embassy Cables: Egypt Succeeding in Blocking Iran (30 April 2009)', *The Guardian*, 6 December 2010. Available at www.guardian.co.uk/world/us-embassy-cables-documents/204990, accessed 1 January 2011.

14 'Codel McConnell's Meeting with Mindef Tantawi', *Wikileaks*, 16 April 2009. Available at http://wikileaks.org/cable/2009/04/09CAIRO666.html, accessed 12 June 2012.

15 'US Embassy Cables: Mubarak: Egypt's President-for-Life (19 May 2009)', *The Guardian*, 9 December 2010. Available at www.guardian.co.uk/world/us-embassy-cables-documents/207723, accessed 1 March 2011.

16 Ibid.

17 The string of intelligence failures with regard to Iran is brought out succinctly in Robert Jervis, *Why Intelligence Fails: Lessons from the Iranian Revolution and the Iraq War* (Ithaca: Cornell University Press, 2010).

18 Sandhya Somashekhar, 'Clinton Calls for Democracy in Egypt, but not Mubarak's Ouster', *The Washington Post*, 30 January 2011. Available at www.washingtonpost.com/wp-dyn/content/article/2011/01/30/AR2011013002239.html, accessed 3 February 2011.

19 E-mail Interview, 15 April 2012.

20 'Greek Protests Leave Dozens Injured: Turmoil in Athens Follows Vote to Approve Austerity Program', *CBC News*, 29 June 2011. Available at www.cbc.ca/news/world/story/2011/06/29/greece-austerity-parliament.html, accessed 12 July 2011.

21 See Barbara Hardinghaus and Julia Arnalia Heyer, 'Wave of Suicide Shocks Greece', *Spiegel Online*, 15 August 2012. Available at www.spiegel.de/international/europe/economic-crisis-triggers-wave-of-suicides-in-greece-a-850129-druck.html, accessed 12 September 2012.

22 See Siobhan Kennedy, 'Topshop Protests over Sir Philip Green's Taxes', *Channel 4 News*, 4 December 2010. Available at www.channel4.com/news/topshop-protest-over-sir-philip-greens-taxes, accessed 1 January 2011.

23 For a personal account see Charles Jones, 'The Dangers of Austerity', *Al-Jazeera*, 15 December 2010. Available at www.aljazeera.com/indepth/opinion/2010/12/2010121418547100351.html, accessed 12 October 2011.

24 'Interview with Jody McIntyre', *BBC*, 14 December 2010. Available at www.bbc.
    co.uk/blogs/theeditors/2010/12/interview_with_jody_mcintyre.html, accessed
    23 December 2010.

25 'Access Agreement Submissions for 2012–13', *Office For Fair Access*, 20 April 2011.
    Available at www.offa.org.uk/press-releases/access-agreement-submissions-for-
    2012–13/, accessed 12 January 2012 and 'Tuition Fees: All Universities to Charge at
    least £6,000', *Channel 4 News*, 20 April 2011. Available at www.channel4.com/news/
    tuition-fees-all-universities-to-charge-at-least-6–000, accessed 2 May 2011.

26 'RBS Chief Stephen Hester's £7,7m Package Agreed', *BBC*, 19 April 2011. Available
    www.bbc.co.uk/news/uk-scotland-edinburgh-east-fife-13132635, accessed 21 April
    2011.

27 Mark Niquette, 'Public Worker Protests Spread from Wisconsin to Ohio',
    Bloomberg, 18 February 2011. Available at www.bloomberg.com/news/2011–02–
    17/public-employee-union-protests-spread-from-wisconsin-to-ohio.html, accessed
    21 January 2011.

28 Stephanie Armour, 'Wisconsin Vote on Unions Corrupts Democracy, Trumka
    Says', *Bloomberg*, 10 March 2011. Available at www.bloomberg.com/news/2011–
    03–10/wisconsin-vote-on-worker-rights-corrupts-democracy-afl-cio-s-trumka-
    says.html, accessed 12 June 2011. For a comprehensive analysis see Michael
    Leachman, Erica Williams and Nicholas Johnson, 'New Fiscal Year Brings further
    Budget Cuts to most States, Slowing Economic Recovery', *Center on Budget and
    Policy Priorities*, 28 June 2011 www.cbpp.org/cms/index.cfm?fa=view&id=3526,
    accessed 23 July 2011.

29 'World Development Indicators' (Syria and Libya 2009), *The World Bank*.
    Available from http://data.worldbank.org/data-catalog/world-development-
    indicators?cid=GPD_WDI, accessed 11 January 2012.

30 Amy Gardner and Michael A. Fletcher, 'Ohio Senate Panel Approves Union-Rights
    Bill, Sending It to Full Senate', *The Washington Post*, 4 March 2011. Available at
    www.washingtonpost.com/wp-dyn/content/article/2011/03/01/AR2011030106108.
    html, accessed 12 June 2011.

31 'New Fiscal Year Brings further Budget Cuts to most States', 2.

32 Al Goodman, 'Thousands of Spaniards Call for Economic Reform in New
    Protest', *CNN*, 20 June 2011. Available at http://edition.cnn.com/2011/WORLD/
    europe/06/19/spain.protests/index.html, accessed 3 July 2011.

33 Al Goodman, 'Spain's Jobless Rate Tops 21% as all Major Sectors Lose Jobs', *CNN*,
    29 April 2011. Available at http://edition.cnn.com/2011/WORLD/europe/04/29/
    spain.unemployment/index.html, accessed 21 May 2011.

34 Naomi Wolf, 'The Shocking Truth about the Crackdown on Occupy', *The
    Guardian*, 25 November 2011. Available at www.guardian.co.uk/commentisfree/
    cifamerica/2011/nov/25/shocking-truth-about-crackdown-occupy, accessed
    10 December 2011.

35 See further Lin Noueihed and Alex Warren, *The Battle for the Arab Spring: Revolution, Counter-Revolution and the Making of a New Era* (London: Yale University Press, 2012), 45–50.

36 See further among others Rashid Khalidi, Lisa Anderson, Muhammad Muslih and Reeva Simon (eds), *The Origins of Arab Nationalism* (New York: Columbia University Press, 1993).

37 See further Saeb Eigner, *Art of the Middle East: Modern and Contemporary Art of the Arab World and Iran* (London: Merrell, 2010), 20–23.

38 Ibid., 141.

39 Jonathan Harris (ed.), *Identity Theft: The Cultural Colonization of Contemporary Art* (Liverpool: Liverpool University Press, 2008), 37.

40 James Ron, *Frontiers and Ghettos: State Violence in Serbia and Israel* (Berkeley: University of California Press, 2003), 133.

41 Ibid., 133.

42 Frantz Fanon, *Black Skin, White Masks* (London: Pluto, 1986), 218.

43 See further Atef Alshaer, 'Humanism, Nationalism and Violence in Mahmoud Darwish's Poetry', *Warfare and Poetry in the Middle East*, ed. Hugh Kennedy (London: I.B. Tauris, 2013, forthcoming).

44 Steven Best and Douglas Kellner, *The Postmodern Turn* (London: The Guildford Press, 1997), 133.

45 Pablo Picasso, 'Why I Joined the Communist Party', in Charles Harrison and Paul Wood (eds), *Art in Theory 1900–2000: An Anthology of Changing Ideas* (Oxford: Blackwell Publishing, 2003), 648.

46 Harris, *Identity Theft*, 11.

47 'Fallen Faces of the Uprising', *Egypt Independent*, 7 February 2011. Available at www.egyptindependent.com/news/fallen-faces-uprising-ahmed-basiony, accessed 11 January 2012.

48 'Poetry as Protest', *The Atlantic*, 31 January 2011. Available at www.theatlantic.com/daily-dish/archive/2011/01/poetry-as-protest/176488/, accessed 13 March 2013.

49 See further Adib-Moghaddam, *A Metahistory of the Clash of Civilisations: Us and Them Beyond Orientalism* (London: Hurst, 2011), 155.

50 See Arlene B. Tickner and David L. Blaney (eds), *Thinking International Relations Differently* (Abingdon: Routledge, 2012) and Meghana Nayak and Eric Selbin, *Decentring International Relations* (London: Zed Books, 2010).

51 Adib-Moghaddam (ed.), *A Critical Introduction to Ayatollah Khomeini* (Cambridge: Cambridge University Press, forthcoming 2013).

52 Sayyid Qutb, 'Prologue, from *In the Shade of the Qu'ran*, Volume 7: *Surah 8, Al-Anfal* (The Spoils of War)', Albert J. Bergesen (ed.), *The Sayyid Qutb Reader: Selected Writings on Politics, Religion, and Society* (Abingdon: Routledge, 2008), 59.

53 Ibid.

54 Ibid.

55 'Gamal Banna: Criticism of Al-Ikhwan not Acceptable,' *Asharq al-Awsat*, 28 June 2012, trans. Mideaswire.com.

56 'Interview Transcript: Rachid Ghannouchi', *The Financial Times*, 18 January 2011. Available at www.ft.com/cms/s/0/24d710a6–22ee-11e0-ad0b-00144feab49a. html#axzz2HrUt64VC, accessed 12 March 2011.

57 See further, Adib-Moghaddam, *Ayatollah Khomeini*.

58 "Persian Perspective: A Chat with Ali Akbar Salehi: Foreign Minister of Iran', *World Policy Blog*, 22 October 2012. Available at www.worldpolicy.org/blog/2012/10/22/ persian-perspective-chat-ali-akbar-salehi-foreign-minister-iran, accessed 11 January 2012.

59 Muhammad Salim Al-Awa, 'Political Pluralism from an Islamic Perspective,' in John J. Donohue and John L. Esposito (eds), *Islam in Transition: Muslim Perspectives*, 2nd ed. (Oxford: Oxford University Press, 2007), 283.

60 Ibid.

61 Ibid.

62 Ibid.

63 Ibid., 284.

64 Ibid.

65 See further Raymond William Baker, *Islam without Fear: Egypt and the New Islamists* (Harvard: Harvard University Press, 2006), 176–178.

Interregnum 3

1 Felix Guattari, *Psychoanalyse et transversalité* (Paris: Maspero/La Découverte, 1972/2003), my translation, 80.

2 Maximilien de Robespiere, 'Report on the Principles of Political Morality (5 February 1794)', in Keith Michael Baker, John W. Boyer and Julius Kirshner (eds), *University of Chicago Readings in Western Civilisation, Vol. 7: The Old Regime and the French Revolution* (Chicago: The University of Chicago Press, 1987), 374.

3 Quoted in Fred Halliday, *Revolution and World Politics: The Rise and Fall of the Sixth Great Power* (Durham, NC: Duke University Press, 1999), 244, emphasis in original.

4 Maurice Merleau-Ponty, *Humanism and Terror: The Communist Problem*, trans. John O'Oneill (New Brunswick, NJ: Transaction Publishers, 2000), 91.

5 This is further elaborated in Alain Badiou, *Le Siècle* (Paris: Seuil, 2005).

6 Halliday, *Revolution and World Politics*, 249.

7 Frantz Fanon, *The Wretched of the Earth*, trans. Constance Farrington (New York: Grove, 1968), 88.

8 Edward Said, *Culture and Imperialism* (London: Vintage, 1993), 324.

9   Che Guevara, *Guerrilla Warfare* (London: Penguin, 1969), 15.

10   Fanon, *The Wretched of the Earth*, 73.

11   See further, Jean-Paul Sartre, *Critique of Dialectical Reason, Vol. 1*, new edition, trans. Alan Sheridan-Smith (London: Verso, 2004), 79.

12   Ibid., 438, emphasis in original.

13   Ibid.

14   Ibid.

15   Ibid., 439, emphasis in original.

16   Ibid., 718.

17   Ibid.

18   Robert J. C. Young, 'Sartre the "African Philosopher"', in Jean Paul Sartre, *Colonialism and Neocolonialism*, trans. Azzedine Haddour, Steve Brewer and Terry Mc Williams (Abingdon: Routledge, 2006), 6.

19   For an annotated overview of the scholarly literature on non-violent action see April Carter, Howard Clark and Michael Randle (eds), *People, Power and Protest since 1945: A Bibliography of Nonviolent Action* (London: Housmans, 2006). For a more recent survey and empirical case studies see Adam Roberts and Timothy Garton-Ash (eds), *Civil Resistance and Power Politics: The Experience of Non-Violent Action from Ghandi to the Present* (Oxford: Oxford University Press, 2011).

20   Kurt Schock, *Unarmed Insurrections: People Power Movements in Nondemocracies* (Minneapolis: University of Minnesota Press, 2005). See also Stephen Zunes, 'Unarmed Insurrections against Authoritarian Governments in the Third World: A New Kind of Revolution?', *Third World Quarterly*, Vol. 15, No. 3 (1994), 403–426.

21   Schock, *Unarmed Insurrections*, xvii.

22   Peter Ackerman and Jack Duvall, *A Force more Powerful: A Century of Nonviolent Conflict* (London: Palgrave, 2000), 7.

23   Gene Sharp, *The Politics of Nonviolent Action* (Boston: Porter Sargent Publishers, 1973), 16.

24   Max Weber, *Economy and Society* (Berkeley: University of California Press, 1978), 53.

25   Gene Sharp, 'The Politics of Nonviolent Action and the Spread of Ideas about Civil Resistance', Paper prepared for the Conference on 'Civil Resistance and Power Politics', St. Anthony's College, Oxford University, Oxford, March 2007, 4. Available at www.aeinstein.org/lectures_papers/OXFORD_PNVA.pdf, accessed 3 March 2010.

26   Gene Sharp, *Social Power and Political Freedom* (Boston: Porter Sargent, 1980), xi.

27   Schock, *Unarmed Insurrections*, 38.

28   Ackerman and Duvall, *A Force more Powerful*, 504.

29   Ibid., 458.

30 Schock, *Unarmed Insurrections*, 45. See also Roland Bleiker, *Popular Dissent, Human Agency, and Global Politics* (Cambridge: Cambridge University Press, 2000) and Robert J. Burrowes, *The Strategy of Nonviolent Defense: A Gandhian Approach* (Albany: State University of New York Press, 1996).

31 Schock, *Unarmed Insurrections*, 44–45.

32 Slavoj Žižek, *Violence: Six Sideways Reflections* (London: Profile Books, 2008), 9.

33 Ibid., 9–10.

34 Edward Said, *Reflections on Exile and other Essays* (Cambridge, MA: Harvard University Press, 2000), 433.

35 Neil Macmaster, *Burning the Veil: The Algerian War and the Emancipation of Muslim Women, 1954–62* (Manchester: Manchester University Press, 2009), 222–223.

36 Žižek, *Violence*, 13.

37 Ibid., 91.

38 Ibid., 96.

39 Said, *Culture and Imperialism*, 253.

40 Slavoj Žižek, 'Europe must Move beyond Mere Tolerance', *The Guardian*, 25 January 2011. Available at www.guardian.co.uk/commentisfree/2011/jan/25/european-union-slovenia, accessed 12 March 2011.

41 Ibid.

42 Ernesto Laclau and Chantal Mouffe, *Hegemony and Socialist Strategy: Towards a Radical Democratic Politics*, 2nd ed. (London: Verso, 2001), 167, emphasis in original.

43 Ibid.

44 Ibid.

45 Chantal Mouffe, 'The Radical Centre: A Politics without Adversary', *Soundings*, No. 9 (Summer 1998), 16.

46 Laclau and Mouffe, *Hegemony and Socialist Strategy*, 67.

47 Quoted in ibid., 67–68.

48 Fanon, *Wretched of the Earth*, 93.

49 Michael Hardt and Antonio Negri, *Multitude: War and Democracy in the Age of Empire* (London: Hamish Hamilton, 2004), 99.

50 Ibid., 101, emphasis added.

51 Ibid., 226.

52 Ibid., emphasis in original.

53 Ibid., 227.

54 Michael Hardt and Antonio Negri, *Empire* (Cambridge: Harvard University Press, 2000), 138–139, emphasis in original.

55 Ibid., 143.

56 Ibid., 146.

57 Ibid., 147 and 149.
58 Hardt and Negri, *Multitude*, 317.

Interregnum 4

1 Edward Said, *Orientalism: Western Conceptions of the Orient* (London: Penguin, 1995), 3.

2 See further on this issue Robert J.C. Young, *White Mythologies: Writing, History and the West* (London: Routledge, 1991) or Zachary Lockman, *Contending Visions of the Middle East: The History and Politics of Orientalism* (Cambridge: Cambridge University Press, 2004).

3 See further Adib-Moghaddam, *A Metahistory of the Clash of Civilisations: Us and Them Beyond Orientalism* (London: Hurst, 2011).

4 Said, *Reflections on Exile and Other Essays* (Cambridge, MA: Harvard University Press, 2000), 241.

5 See more recently the contributions in Ian Netton (ed.), *Orientalism Revisited: Art, Land, Voyage* (Abingdon: Routledge, 2012).

6 Michel Foucault, *Society must Be Defended: Lectures at the Collège de France*, ed. Mauro Bertani and Alessandro Fontana, trans. David Macey (London: Penguin, 2004), 29.

7 Michel Foucault, 'Truth and Power', *Power: Essential Works of Foucault, vol. 3*, ed. James D. Faubion, trans. Rober Hurley et al. (London: Penguin, 2002), 131.

8 In that sense Orientalism is a 'regime of truth' rather than merely a 'discourse'.

9 Foucault, 'Truth and Power', 132–133.

10 Ibid., 133.

11 See further Brent L. Pickett, 'Foucault and the Politics of Resistance', *Polity*, Vol. 28, No. 4 (Summer 1996), especially 450ff.

12 Michel Foucault, 'Nietzsche, Genealogy, History', in Paul Rabinow (ed.), *The Foucault Reader* (London: Penguin, 1984), 93.

13 Ibid., 36.

14 See further Pickett, 'Foucault and the Politics of Resistance', especially 450ff.

15 James Miller, *The Passion of Michel Foucault* (New York: Simon & Schuster, 1993), 178–179.

16 David Gary Shaw, 'Happy in Our Chains? Agency and Language in the Postmodern Age', *History and Theory*, Vol. 40, No. 4 (December 2001), 5. For comparable views see Peter Dews, *Logics of Disintegration: Post-Structuralist Thought and the Claims of Critical Theory* (London: Verso, 2007); and Thomas McCarthy, 'The Critique of Impure Reason: Foucault and the Frankfurt School', *Political Theory*, Vol. 18, No. 3 (August 1990), 437–469.

17 'By this word 'governmentality' I mean three things', Foucault writes. 'First, by
    'governmentality' I understand the ensemble formed by institutions, procedures,
    analyses and reflections, calculations, and tactics that allow the exercise of this very
    specific, albeit very complex, power that has the population as its target, political
    economy as its major form of knowledge, and apparatuses of security as its essential
    technical instrument. Second, by 'governmentality' I understand the tendency,
    the line of force, that for a long time, and throughout the West, has constantly led
    towards the pre-eminence over all other types of power – sovereignty, discipline,
    and so on – of the type of power that we can call "government" … Finally by
    "governmentality" I think we should understand the process, or rather, the
    result of the process by which the state of justice of the Middle Ages became the
    administrative state in the fifteenth and sixteenth centuries and was gradually
    "governmentalised". Michel Foucault, *Security, Territory, Population: Lectures at
    the College de France 1977–1978*, ed. Michel Senellart, trans. Graham Burchell
    (London: Palgrave Macmillan, 2009), 108–109.

18 For a persuasive depiction of Foucault as a 'dialectician' see John Grant, 'Foucault
    and the Logic of Dialectics', *Contemporary Political Theory*, Vol. 9, No. 2 (Summer
    2010), 220–238.

19 Michel Foucault, *The Order of Things: An Archaeology of the Human Sciences*, trans.
    A.M. Sheridan Smith (London: Routledge, 1989), 354.

20 Said, *Reflections on Exile*, 241.

21 Sandra Bartky, 'Foucault, Femininity and the Modernisation of Patriarchal
    Power', in Irene Diamond and Lee Quinby (eds), *Feminism and Foucault: Paths of
    Resistance* (Boston: Northeastern University Press, 1988), 79.

22 Thomas McCarthy, 'The Critique of Impure Reason: Foucault and the Frankfurt
    School', *Political Theory*, Vol. 18, No. 3 (August 1990), 443.

23 Michael L. Fitzhugh and William H. Leckie, Jr, 'Agency, Postmodernism and the
    Causes of Change', *History and Theory*, Vol. 40, No.4 (December 2001), 60.

24 Said, *Reflections on Exile*, 242.

25 Gilles Deleuze, 'Michel Foucault's Main Concepts', in idem. *Two Regimes of
    Madness: Texts and Interviews 1975–1995*, ed. David Lapoujade, trans. Ames
    Hodges and Mike Taormina (New York: Semiotext(e), 2007), 261.

26 Ibid.

27 Ibid., 262, emphasis in original.

28 Ibid.

29 Quoted in ibid., 264. Deleuze added the emphasis.

30 Ibid., 262.

31 Ibid., 265.

32 Ibid., 264.

33 For a similar article see Nathan Widder, 'Foucault and Power Revisited', *European
    Journal of Political Theory*, Vol. 3, No. 4 (2004), 411–432.

34 Jeffrey T. Nealon, *Foucault beyond Foucault: Power and Its Intensifications since 1984* (Stanford: Stanford University Press, 2008), 108.

35 Michel Foucault, *The Will to Knowledge: The History of Sexuality, Volume 1*, trans. Robert Hurley (London: Penguin, 1998), 93.

36 See among others Anthony Giddens, *The Transformation of Intimacy: Sexuality, Love & Eroticism in Modern Societies* (Stanford: Stanford University Press, 1992), 24ff; Jürgen Habermas, *The Philosophical Discourse of Modernity* (Cambridge: MIT Press, 1987), part 10; and Michael Walzer, 'The Politics of Michel Foucault', in David Couzens Hoy (ed.), *Foucault: A Critical Reader* (Oxford: Blackwell, 1986), 51–68.

37 Foucault, 'The Subject and Power', 341–342.

38 Deleuze, 'Michel Foucault's Main Concepts', 260, emphasis in original.

39 Foucault, 'The Subject and Power', 342.

40 Kevin Jon Heller, 'Subjectification and Resistance in Foucault', *Substance*, Vol. 25, No. 1, Issue 79 (1996), 78–110.

41 Ibid., 84.

42 Gayatri Chakravorty Spivak, *Outside in the Teaching Machine* (London: Routledge, 1993), 34–35.

43 Foucault, 'Truth and Power', 120.

44 Nealon, *Foucault beyond Foucault*, 104, emphasis in original.

45 Mark G.E. Kelly, *The Political Philosophy of Michel Foucault* (London: Routledge, 2008), 108.

46 Michel Foucault, *Society must Be Defended*, 29.

47 Peter Berger and Stanley Pullberg, 'Reification and the Sociological Critique of Consciousness', *History and Theory*, Vol. 4, No. 2 (1965), 196–197.

48 Ibid., 200.

49 Peter L. Berger, *The Sacred Canopy: Elements of a Sociological Theory of Religion* (New York: Anchor, 1969), 8.

50 Ibid., 11.

51 Ibid.

52 Michel Foucault, 'Revolutionary Action: "Until Now"', in idem., *Language, Countermemory, Practice: Selected Essays and Interviews by Michel Foucault*, ed. Donald F. Bouchard (Ithaca: Cornell University Press, 1977), 233.

53 Said, *Reflections on Exile*, 242.

54 Barry Smart, *Michel Foucault*, rev. ed. (London: Routledge, 2002), 134.

55 Foucault, 'Revolutionary Action', 230.

56 See further Jonathan Arac, 'Foucault and Central Europe: A Polemical Speculation', *boundary 2*, Vol. 21, No. 3 (Autumn 1994), 197–210.

57 Foucault, *Security, Territory, Population*, 201–202.

58 Ibid., 202.

59 Foucault, *Power*, 341.

60   Foucault, *Security, Territory, Population*, 201–202.

61   Paul Veyne, *Foucault: His Thought, His Character*, trans. Janet Lloyd (Cambridge: Polity, 2010), 126 and 128.

62   James Miller, *The Passion of Michel Foucault* (New York: Simon & Schuster, 1993), 309.

63   Quoted in Didier Eribon, *Michel Foucault*, trans. Betsy Wing (Cambridge, MA: Harvard University Press, 1991), 282.

64   Quoted in ibid., 287.

65   Craig Keating, 'Reflections on the Revolution in Iran: Foucault on Resistance', *Journal of European Studies*, Vol. 27, No. 2 (1997), 194. For a comparable point see also Georg Stauth, 'Revolution in Spiritless Times: An Essay on Michel Foucault's Enquiries into the Iranian Revolution', *International Sociology*, Vol. 6, No. 3 (1991), 259.

66   See Janet Afary and Kevin B. Anderson, *Foucault and the Iranian Revolution: Gender and the Seductions of Islamism* (Chicago: The University of Chicago Press, 2005), 136–137.

67   Michel Foucault, 'The Mythical Leader of the Iranian Revolt', *Corriere della sera*, 26 November 1978, in Afary and Anderson, *Foucault and the Iranian Revolution*, 220.

68   Michel Foucault, 'A Revolt with Bare Hands', *Corriere della sera*, 5 November 1978, in Afary and Anderson, *Foucault and the Iranian Revolution*, 213.

69   Michel Foucault, 'Response to Atoussa H.', *Le Nouvel Observateur*, 13 November 1978, in Afary and Anderson, *Foucault and the Iranian Revolution*, 210. See also 'Dialogue between Michel Foucault and Baqir Parham', *Nameh-ye Kanun-e Nevisandegan* (Publication of the Center of Iranian Writers), No. 1 (Spring 1979), 9–17, in Afary and Anderson, *Foucault and the Iranian Revolution*, 183–189.

70   Afary and Anderson, *Foucault and the Iranian Revolution*, 30–31. See also Ian Almond, *The New Orientalists: Postmodern Representations of Islam from Foucault to Baudrillard* (London: IB Tauris, 2007).

71   'Dialogue between Michel Foucault and Baqir Parham', 186. Foucault was very impressed with the writings of Ali Shariati, one of the pre-eminent intellectuals in 1970s Iran. Foucault was correct to point out the centrality of Shariati to the events in Iran, to see him as 'a shadow that haunt(ed) all political and religious life' and to observe that his 'name was the only one that was called out, besides that of Khomeini'. Michel Foucault, 'What Are the Iranians Dreaming [Rêvent] About', *Le Nouvel Observateur*, 16–22 October 1978, in Afary and Anderson, *Foucault and the Iranian Revolution*, 207–208. But the Shi'ism that Foucault thought particular to Iran was a hybrid construct, not an ahistorically coded 'political spirituality'. This is particularly apparent in Shariati, where the 'West' is in the 'East', where the Shia myths and imagery were re-enacted within the frame of 'Sartrean third worldism' and a new form of Islamo-feminist militancy that positioned the daughter of the Prophet Muhammad next to Che Guevara, Abraham, Jesus and Frantz Fanon.

On the hybridity of contemporary discourses of Islam see Adib-Moghaddam, *A Metahistory of the Clash of Civilisations.*

72   Michiel Leezenberg, 'Power and Political Spirituality: Michel Foucault and the Islamic Revolution in Iran', *Arcadia*, Vol. 33 No. 1 (1998), 76.

73   Said, *Reflections on Exile*, 196.

74   These have been recently published in English. See Michel Foucault, *Manet and the Object of Painting*, trans. Matthew Barr (London: Tate, 2009).

75   Michel Foucault, 'The Army—When the Earth Quakes', *Corriere della sera*, 28 September 1978, in Afary and Anderson, *Foucault and the Iranian Revolution*, 190.

76   Foucault, 'A Revolt with Bare Hands', 211.

77   Michel Foucault, 'The Challenge to the Opposition', *Corriere della sera*, 7 November 1978, in Afary and Anderson, *Foucault and the Iranian Revolution*, 213.

78   Ibid., 218.

79   Michel Foucault, 'The Mythical Leader of the Iranian Revolt', *Corriere della sera*, 26 November 1978, in Afary and Anderson, *Foucault and the Iranian Revolution*, 221. It is not so much that Foucault must be criticized for identifying a 'perfectly unified collective will' in the revolution, as Afary and Anderson suggest, or for emphasizing Khomeini's role as a point of fixation of the masses. Few scholars of the revolution would disagree that in the build-up to the mass demonstrations that brought down the Shah, Khomeini was a unifying symbol for the protesters. See further Adib-Moghaddam, *Iran in World Politics: The Question of the Islamic Republic* (London: Hurst, 2008), especially part 1.

80   Foucault, 'What Are the Iranians Dreaming [Rêvent] About', 207.

81   Foucault, 'The Mythical Leader of the Iranian Revolt', 221.

82   Foucault, *The Will to Knowledge*, 96.

83   It is striking that Foucault refers to Max Horkheimer, one of the standard bearers of the critical theory of the Frankfurt School in Germany, in his last writings on Iran. See Michel Foucault, 'Is It Useless to Revolt?', *Le Monde*, 11–12 May 1979, in Afary and Anderson, *Foucault and the Iranian Revolution*, 264.

84   A reference to a Mullah 'manufacturing the Iranian truth' is emblematic for the scattered instances of critique that were slowly emerging the closer the revolutionary ideals were turned into a new 'regime of truth'. See Foucault 'The Challenge to the Opposition', 219.

85   Foucault, 'Response to Atoussa H', 210.

86   Foucault, 'The Mythical Leader of the Iranian Revolt', 220.

87   Michel Foucault, 'A Powder Keg Called Islam', *Corriera della sera*, 13 February 1979, in Afary and Anderson, *Foucault and the Iranian Revolution*, 241.

88   'Iran: The Spirit of a World without Spirit', originally published in March 1979, in Afary and Anderson, *Foucault and the Iranian Revolution*, 256.

89   Ibid., 260.

90 Ibid., 255.

91 Foucault, 'Is It Useless to Revolt?', 263–264.

92 Quoted in James Schmidt and Thomas E. Wartenberg, 'Foucault's Enlightenment: Critique, Revolution and the Fashioning of the Self', in Michael Kelly (ed.), *Critique and Power: Recasting the Foucault/Habermas Debate* (Chicago: MIT Press, 1994), 296.

93 'Iran: The Spirit of a World without Spirit', 260.

94 Foucault, 'Is it Useless to Revolt?', 265.

95 Olivier Roy, 'L'enigme du soulèvement (Enigma of the Uprising)', *Vacarme*, No. 29 (Autumn 2004). English version available at www.vacarme.org/article1799.html, accessed 12 November 2010].

96 Foucault, 'Is It Useless to Revolt?', 265.

97 Afary and Anderson, *Foucault and the Iranian Revolution*, 129.

98 Michel Foucault, 'Tehran: Faith against the Shah', *Corriere della sera*, 8 October 1978, in Afary and Anderson, *Foucault and the Iranian Revolution*, 202.

99 Ibid.

100 Veyne, *Foucault*, 1, emphasis in original.

101 More work has to be done on the confluence between the negative dialectics of Adorno and Horkheimer and Foucault's' power-resistance dialectic and Said's concept of 'contrapuntality'.

102 Foucault, 'Is It Useless to Revolt?', 266.

103 Ibid., 267.

104 See further Foucault, *Society must Be Defended*, 7–10.

105 See further Michel Foucault, 'Michel Foucault and Zen: A Stay in a Zen Temple (1978)', in Jeremy R. Carrette (ed.), *Religion and Culture* (Manchester: Manchester University Press, 1999), 110–114.

106 Said, *Reflections on Exile*, 243–244.

Interregnum 5

1 Anthony Giddens, *Beyond Left and Right: The Future of Radical Politics* (Cambridge: Polity, 1994), 1.

2 Fred Halliday, *Revolution and World Politics: The Rise and Fall of the Sixth Great Power* (Durham, NC: Duke University Press, 1999), 36.

3 Giddens, *Beyond Left and Right*, 1.

4 See Antonio Gramsci, *Selections from the Prison Notebooks*, ed. and trans. Quinton Hoare and Geoffrey Nowell Smith (London: Lawrence and Wishart, 1971), 58ff. The concept of 'passive revolution' is revisited persuasively in Adam David Morton, *Unravelling Gramsci: Hegemony and Passive Revolution in the Global Economy* (London: Pluto Press, 2007).

5 Isaac Kraminick, 'Reflections on Revolution: Definition and Explanation in Recent Scholarship', *History and Theory*, Vol. 11, No. 1 (1972), 30–31.

6 Similarly, Hannah Arendt emphasizes the element of a complete transformation, a temporal break with the prevalent order, with regard to the revolutions in France and America: 'These two things together – a new experience which revealed man's capacity for novelty' she writes, 'are at the root of the enormous pathos which we find in both the American and the French Revolutions, this ever-repeated insistence that nothing comparable in grandeur and significance had ever happened in the whole recorded history of mankind': Hannah Arendt, *On Revolution* (London: Penguin, 1990), 34.

7 Fred Halliday, *Revolution and World Politics,* 38. Halliday further argues that Theda Skocpol's theory of revolution – in *States and Social Revolutions: A Comparative Analysis of France, Russia and China* (Cambridge: Cambridge University Press, 1979) – unnecessarily prioritizes war, and external factors in general, in the making and success of revolutionary movements, 46–47. A similar argument against Skocpol's top–down approach is presented by Nikki Keddie (ed.), *Debating Revolutions* (New York: New York University Press, 1996), viii and in Said Amir Arjomand, *The Turban for the Crown: The Islamic Revolution in Iran* (Oxford: Oxford University Press, 1988), 191–192.

8 A comprehensive re-treatment of subjectivity and agency is offered by Elías Palti, 'The "Return of the Subject" as a Historical-Intellectual Problem', *History and Theory*, Vol. 43, No. 1 (February 2004), 57–82.

9 See further Abd-al-Rafie Haghighat, *Tarikh-e Honar-haye Meli va Honarmandane Irani* [The History of National Arts And Iranian Artists], Vol. 1 of the Complete Works of Abd-al-Rafie Haghighat (Tehran: Moalefan va Motarjeman-e Iran, 1990), 662. During the same period there emerged also a photography movement in Iran. See Yahya Zoka, *Tarikh-e Akasi va Akasaan-e Pishgam dar Iran* [The History of Photography and Pioneer Photographers in Iran] (Tehran: Elmi & Farhangi Press, 1997), 178–180.

10 Ruhollah Khomeini, 'Declaration on the Occasion of Id' al-Fitr, 6 September, 1978, in Hamd Algar (ed. and trans.), *Islam and Revolution: Writings and Declarations of Imam Khomeini* (1941–1980) (London: Mizan Press, 1981), 234.

11 See Adib-Moghaddam (ed.), *A Critical Introduction to Ayatollah Khomeini* (Cambridge: Cambridge University Press, forthcoming 2013).

12 See Ervand Abrahamian, *A History of Iran* (Cambridge: Cambridge University Press, 2008), 39; Homa Katouzian, *State and Society in Iran: The Eclipse of the Qajars and the Emergence of the Pahlavis* (London: I.B. Tauris, 2006), 33ff.; and Nikki Keddie, *Religion and Rebellion in Iran: The Iranian Tobacco Protest of 1891–1892* (Abingdon: Frank Cass, 1966), 131.

13 See further Abrahamian, *A History of Iran*, 45–49.

14 Fakhreddin Azimi, *The Quest for Democracy in Iran: A Century of Struggle against Authoritarian Rule* (Cambridge, MA: Harvard University Press, 2008), 3.

15 See Abrahamian, *A History of Iran*, 6.

16 Hamid Enayat, *Modern Islamic Political Thought: The Response of the Shi'i and the Sunni Muslims to the Twentieth Century* (London: Macmillan, 1982), 174.

17 Ibid., 167.

18 See further Hamid Algar, *Religion and State in Iran, 1785–1906: The Role of the Ulema in the Qajar Period* (Berkeley, CA: University of California Press, 1980) and Abdul-Hadi Hairi, *Shi'ism and Constitutionalism in Iran: A Study of the Role Played by the Persian Residents of Iraq in Iranian Politics* (Leiden: E.J. Brill, 1977).

19 I have engaged with this political economy in *Iran in World Politics: The Question of the Islamic Republic* (New York: Columbia University Press, 2008).

20 See Ahmad Kasravi, *Tarikh-e mashrute-yeh Iran* [History of the Iranian Constitution] (Tehran: Negah Publications, 2008) and Mohammad Hussein Naini, *Tanbih al-ummah wa tanzih al-millah* [Advising the Muslim community and Purifying the Religion] (Qom: Bustan-e Ketabe Qom Press, 2003).

21 For an elaborate account see further Mahmoud Khoshchereh, *The Structure of Authoring in Nima Yushij's Poetry: A Bakhtinian Reading*, Open access dissertation and theses, paper 6400 (2011). Available at http://digitalcommons.mcmaster.ca/cgi/viewcontent.cgi?article=7443&context=opendissertations, accessed 23 October 2012. For a useful overview see Ahmad Karimi-Hakkak and Kamran Talattof (eds), *Essays on Nima Yushij: Animating Modernism in Persian Poetry* (Leiden: Brill, 2004).

22 Cited in Khoshchereh, *The Structure of Authoring in Nima Yushij's Poetry*, 254–259.

23 On the mechanism of political introjection see *Iran in World Politics: The Question of the Islamic Republic* (New York: Columbia University Press, 2008), part 1.

24 On the history and politics of the Iranian Left see Stephanie Cronin (ed.), *Reformers and Revolutionaries in Modern Iran: New Perspectives on the Iranian Left* (Abingdon: Routledge, 2004).

25 Michael Hardt and Antonio Negri, *Labour of Dionysus: A Critique of the State-Form* (Minneapolis: University of Minnesota Press, 1994), 287.

26 Charles Kurzman, *The Unthinkable Revolution in Iran* (Cambridge, MA: Harvard University Press, 2004).

27 Quoted in Anja Pistor-Hatam, 'Writing Back? Jalal Al-e Ahmad's (1923–69): Reflections on Selected Periods of Iranian History', *Iranian Studies*, Vol. 40, No. 5 (December 2007), 565.

28 Quoted in Ali Rahnema, *An Islamic Utopian: A Political Biography of Ali Shariati* (London: I.B. Tauris, 2000), 305.

29 There is an emphasis on nativism in Mehrzad Boroujerdi, *Iranian Intellectuals and the West: The Tormented Triumph of Nativism* (Syracuse: Syracuse University Press, 1996).

30 Bobby Sands Street is located near the UK embassy in Tehran. In 1981, the Iranian government was officially represented at Bobby Sands' funeral and presented to Mrs. Sands a plaque honouring his activism. The Tehran city council also renamed a street in Tehran after Khaled Eslambouli who assassinated the former Egyptian president Anwar Sadat, although the Iranian foreign ministry has repeatedly tried to amend the name. In 2011, the city council decided to rename a street in central Tehran Rachel Aliene Corrie Street, after the American pro-Palestinian activist who was killed while protesting against the demolition of Palestinian homes in the Gaza strip eight years ago. It is the first time since Iran's Islamic revolution in 1979 that an Iranian street had been named after a citizen of the United States.

31 Che Guevara, *Guerrilla Warfare* (Harmondsworth: Penguin, 1969), 21, emphasis in original.

32 CIA, Directorate of Intelligence, 1972. *Intelligence Report: Centres of Power in Iran*. Available from: www.state.gov/documents/organization/70712.pdf, accessed 24 December 2009, 11.

33 Mohammad Reza Shah Pahlavi, 'A Future to Outshine Ancient Glories', *Life*, 31 May 1963, 66.

34 Stockholm International Peace Research Institute, *World Armaments and Disarmament Year book for 1977* (Cambridge, MA: MIT Press, 1977), 228–229.

35 See further Ervand Abrahamian, *Iran between Two Revolutions* (Princeton: Princeton University Press, 1982), 435–436.

36 The first census in Iran was undertaken in 1956, but it was largely considered to be unreliable or 'unscientific'. See further Ferydoon Firoozi, 'Iranian Censuses 1956 and 1966: A Comparative Analysis', *Middle East Journal*, Vol. 24, No. 2 (Spring 1970), 220–228.

37 Michel Foucault, *Discipline and Punish: The Birth of the Prison*, trans. Alan Sheridan (London: Penguin, 1991), 11.

38 Subsequently, Karl-Heinz Kurras who shot Ohnesorg in the courtyard of Krumme Strasse 66 in Berlin was cleared of all charges in two trials.

39 See further my *A Metahistory of the Clash of Civilisations: Us and Them Beyond Orientalism* (London/New York: Hurst/Columbia University Press, 2011), Chapter 3.

40 Susan Buck-Morss, *Dreamworld and Catastrophe: The Passing of Mass Utopia in East and West* (Cambridge, MA: MIT Press, 2002), 2–3.

41 Michel Foucault, *The Will to Knowledge: The History of Sexuality, Volume 1*, trans. Robert Hurley (London: Penguin, 1998), 96.

42 See further Ali Rahnema, *An Islamic Utopian*, 228ff.

43 Khomeini quoted in Baqer Moin, *Khomeini: Life of the Ayatollah* (London: I.B. Tauris, 1999), 104. On Israel, Khomeini was particularly uncompromising, declaring elsewhere that Iranians, Muslims and the oppressed of the world never would accept the state of Israel and that Iranians always would support

'their Palestinian and Arab brothers': Ruhollah Khomeini, *Ain-e enghelab-e Islami: Gozidehai az andisheh va ara-ye Imam Khomeini* (Tehran: Moasses-ye tanzim va nashr-e assar-e Imam Khomeini, 1373/1994), 200. For a sophisticated expose of Khomeini's resistance discourse see Latife Reda Ali, *Khomeini's Discourse of Resistance: The Discourse of Power of the Islamic Revolution,* PhD thesis, School of Oriental and African Studies (SOAS), University of London, July 2012.

44 Michel Foucault, *Power: Essential works of Foucault 1954–1984, Vol. 3,* trans. Robert Hurley et al., ed. James D. Faubion (London: Penguin, 2002), 451.

45 On this 'lapse' in Foucault's theory see Michael L. Fitzhugh and William H. Leckie, Jr, 'Postmodernism, and the Causes of Change', *History and Theory,* Vol. 40, No. 4 (December 2001), especially 63ff.

46 See further Adib-Moghaddam, *Iran in World Politics: The Question of the Islamic Republic* (London: Hurst, 2008), especially 43–67.

47 See further Ervand Abrahamian, *Tortured Confessions: Prisons and Public Recantations in Modern Iran* (Berkeley: University of California Press, 1999), 106 and Fred Halliday, *Iran: Dictatorship and Development* (Harmondsworth: Penguin, 1979), 75ff.

48 Mir-Hossein Mousavi, 'I stand by my firm belief of this election being null and void', *Information Clearing House,* 20 June 2009. Available at www.informationclearinghouse.info/article22904.htm, accessed January 2013.

49 See www.vaja.ir/Public/Home/, accessed 12 December 2012.

50 See further Adib-Moghaddam, *Iran in World Politics,* especially 164ff.

51 See further: 'Iran and Global Scientific Collaboration in the 21st Century', *Association of Professors and Scholars of Iranian Heritage,* 3 September 2011. Available at www.apsih.org/index.php/news/english-news/275-iran-and-global-scientific-collaboration-in-the-21st-century, accessed 12 January 2012. On the growth of the science sectors see also The Royal Society, *Knowledge, Networks and Nations: Global Scientific Collaboration in the 21st Century,* London, March 2011. Available at http://royalsociety.org/uploadedFiles/Royal_Society_Content/policy/publications/2011/4294976134.pdf, accessed 12 June 2011, 21.

52 The Royal Society, *Knowledge, Networks,* 21.

53 Ibid., 65.

54 See further Adib-Moghaddam, *Iran in World Politics,* especially 159–164.

55 Ibid., 160–162.

56 Mohammad-Hossein Jamshidi (ed.), *Andishey-e siasiy-e imam Khomeini* (Tehran: Pajoheshkade-ye imam Khomeini va enghelabe islami, 1384 [2005]), 245, 246.

57 See further Elaheh Rostami-Povey, *Women, Work and Islamism: Ideology and Resistance in Iran,* new ed. (London: Zed Books, 2010).

Interregnum 6

1 Edward W. Said, *On Late Style* (London: Bloomsbury, 2006), 13.

2 Ibid., 12–13.

3 'Transcript of Interview with Iranian President Mohammad Khatami', *CNN*, 7 January 1998. Available at http://edition.cnn.com/WORLD/9801/07/iran/interview. html, accessed 12 January 2006.

4 'Obama's Video Message to Iranians: "Let's Start Again"', *The Guardian*, 21 March 2009. Available at www.guardian.co.uk/world/2009/mar/21/barack-obama-iran-video-message, accessed 12 March 2010.

5 See among others David Campbell, *Writing Security: United States Foreign Policy and the Politics of Identity* (Manchester: Manchester University Press, 1993); David Campbell, *Politics without Principle: Sovereignty, Ethics, and the Narratives of the Gulf War* (London: Lynne Rienner, 1992); and Richard Jackson, *Writing the War on Terrorism: Language, Politics and Counterterrorism* (Manchester: Manchester University Press, 2005).

6 Arshin Adib-Moghaddam, *Iran in World Politics: The Question of the Islamic Republic* (London: Hurst, 2008) and Arshin Adib-Moghaddam, *The International Politics of the Persian Gulf: A Cultural Genealogy* (London: Routledge, 2006).

7 Karl Marx, *Survey from Exile* (Harmondsworth: Penguin, 1973), 146.

8 Max Horkheimer, *Critical Theory: Selected Essays* (London: Continuum, 1997), 200.

9 Ibid., 200–201.

10 Michel Foucault, *The Archaeology of Knowledge* (Abingdon: Routledge, 2002), 41.

11 Walter, Benjamin, *Reflections: Essays, Aphorism, Autobiographical Writings*, ed., P. Demetz (New York: Schocken Books, 1986), 289.

12 Ibid.

13 Craig Calhoun, *Critical Social Theory: Culture, History, and the Challenge of Difference* (Oxford: Blackwell, 1995), 51.

14 Seyla Benhabib, *Critique, Norm and Utopia: A Study of the Foundations of Critical Theory* (New York: Columbia University Press, 1986), 241.

15 Thomas T. Risse, ''Let's Argue!' Communicative Action in World Politics', *International Organization*, Vol. 54, No. 1 (2000), 7, emphasis added.

16 Foucault, *Power*, 131.

17 Edward W. Said, *Covering Islam: How the Media and the Experts Determine How We See the Rest of the World* (London: Vintage, 1997), 6.

18 Ibid., 7.

19 See further William O. Beeman, *The Great Satan vs. the Mad Mullahs: How the United States and Iran Demonize Each Other* (London: Greenwood, 2005).

20 CIA, Directorate of Intelligence, *Intelligence Report: Centres of Power in Iran*, 1972. Available at www.state.gov/documents/organization/70712.pdf, accessed 21 July 2009, 7.

21 Ibid.

22 'Conversation among President Nixon, Ambassador Douglas MacArthur II, and General Alexander Haig', Washington, 8 April 1971, 3:56–4:21 pm. Available at www.state.gov/r/pa/ho/frus/nixon/e4/71804.htm, accessed 12 June 2009.

23 Roger M. Savory, 'The Principle of Homeostasis Considered in Relation to Political Events in Iran in the 1960's', *International Journal of Middle East Studies (IJMES)*, Vol. 3, No. 3 (1972), 286.

24 Ibid., 293.

25 Ibid., 294.

26 Edward W. Said, *Orientalism: Western Conceptions of the Orient* (London: Penguin, 1995), 3.

27 Ibid., 122.

28 'Conversation among President Nixon, Ambassador Douglas MacArthur II, and General Alexander Haig'.

29 Ervand Abrahamian, *A History of Modern Iran* (Cambridge: Cambridge University Press, 2008), 86.

30 Ibid., 87.

31 *Tārīkh-e Sāl-e Sevvum-e Dabiristan* (Tehran, no publisher 1319 [1941], 2.

32 See further Arshin Adib-Moghaddam, *The International Politics of the Persian Gulf: A Cultural Genealogy* (London: Routledge, 2006), 16ff. and Firoozeh Kashani-Sabet 'Cultures of Iranianness: The Evolving Polemic of Iranian Nationalism', in Nikki R. Keddie and Rudi Matthee (eds), *Iran and the Surrounding World: Interactions in Culture and Cultural Politics* (Seattle: University of Washington Press, 2002), 166ff.

33 Mohammad Reza Pahlavi, *Mission for My Country* (New York: McGraw-Hill, 1961), 18.

34 Quoted in Mangol Bayat-Philipp, 'A Phoenix too Frequent: Historical Continuity in Modern Iranian Thought', *Asian and African Studies*, Vol. 12 (1978), 211.

35 Oriana Fallaci, *Interview with History* (New York: Houghton-Mifflin, 1977), 264.

36 'US Embassy Cables: US Hits Out at Iranian Negotiators in 1979', *The Guardian*, 28 November 2010. Available at www.guardian.co.uk/world/us-embassy-cables-documents/13, accessed 12 January 2012.

37 Mark Bowden, *Guests of the Ayatollah: The First Battle in the West's War with Militant Islam* (London: Atlantic, 2006), 4–5.

38 Ibid., 5.

39 Jalal Al-e Ahmad, *Plagued by the West (Gharbzadegi)*, trans. Paul Sprachman (New York: Caravan, 1982), 19.

40 Ali Shariati, 'On Martyrdom (*Shahadat*)', in John J. Donohue and John L. Esposito (eds), *Islam in Transition: Muslim Perspectives*, 2nd ed. (Oxford: Oxford University Press, 2007), 364.

41 Ruhollah Khomeini, *Islam and Revolution: Writings and Declarations of Imam Khomeini*, trans. and anno. Hamid Algar (Berkeley: Mizan Press, 1981), 48–49.

42 Masoumeh Ebtekar, *Takeover in Tehran: The Inside Story of the 1979 U.S. Embassy Capture* (Vancouver: Talon, 2000), 80.

43 Ibid., 241.

44 White House Memorandum, 5 October 1972, 'Progress Report on the Kurdish Support Operations'. Available at www.state.gov/documents/organization/72019. pdf, accessed 20 July 2009.

45 Ibid., 1.

46 I have outlined this in detail in Adib-Moghaddam, *Iran in World Politics*, 102–115.

47 US Department of State, August 1972, 'Continuing Terrorist Activities in Iran'. Available at www.state.gov/documents/organization/70763.pdf, accessed 20 May 2009), 1.

48 Ibid.

49 White House Memorandum, 17 January 1986, 'Covert Action Finding Regarding Iran (with attached Presidential finding)'. Available at www.gwu.edu/~nsarchiv/NSAEBB/NSAEBB210/15-Reagan%20Finding%201–17–86%20(IC%2002181).pdf, accessed 20 July 2009, 1.

50 Ibid., 4.

51 See also Ken Booth and Nicholas J. Wheeler, *The Security Dilemma: Fear, Cooperation and Trust in World Politics* (London: Palgrave, 2008).

52 Sun Tzu, *The Art of War*, trans. Samuel B. Griffith (Oxford: Oxford University Press, 1963), 84.

53 Scott Peterson, 'Iran's Cyber Prowess: Could It really Have Cracked Drone', *The Christian Science Monitor*, 24 April 2012. Available at www.csmonitor.com/World/Middle-East/2012/0424/Iran-s-cyber-prowess-Could-it-really-have-cracked-drone-codes, accessed 12 June 2012.

54 See R. Scott Kemp, 'Bold Steps in the Digital Darkness?', *Bulletin of the Atomic Scientists*, 7 June 2012. Available at http://thebulletin.org/web-edition/op-eds/cyberweapons-bold-steps-digital-darkness, accessed 12 July 2012.

55 'Iran Set to Build First Cyber Army', *Press TV*, 20 February 2012. Available at www.presstv.ir/detail/227739.html, accessed 12 March 2012.

56 See Nicole Perlroth, 'Cyber Attacks from Iran and Gaza on Israel more Threatening than Anonymous Efforts', *The New York Times*, 20 November 2012. Available at http://bits.blogs.nytimes.com/2012/11/20/cyber-attacks-from-iran-and-gaza-on-israel-more-threatening-than-anonymouss-efforts/, accessed 1 December 2012.

57 See Rachael King, 'Virus Aimed at Iran Infected Chevron Network', *The Wall Street Journal*, 9 November 2012. Available at http://online.wsj.com/article/SB10001424127887324894104578107223667421796.html, accessed 12 December 2012 and Ellen Nakashima, 'Iran Blamed for Cyber Attacks on US Banks and Companies', *The Washington Post*, 21 September 2012. Available at http://articles.washingtonpost.com/2012–09–21/world/35497878_1_web-sites-quds-force-cyberattacks, accessed 1 November 2012.

58   Gilles Deleuze, *The Logic of Sense* (London: Continuum, 2004), 55.

59   Former Iranian President Mohammad Khatami unveiled a bust of Baskerville in
     the Constitution House of the north-western Iranian town of Tabriz. It bears the
     inscription 'Howard C. Baskerville – – Patriot and Maker of History'. See further
     Firouzeh Mirrazavi, 'Constitution House of Tabriz', *Iran Review*, 2 November 2010.
     Available at www.iranreview.org/content/Documents/Constitution_House_of_
     Tabriz.htm, accessed 12 December 2011.

Interregnum 7

1   In the word formation 'Israeli–Palestinian conundrum' all elements are entirely
    interlinked, representing yet another disjunctive synthesis that this study focuses
    on in order to bring out overlapping spaces.

2   On a recent conceptualization of the neighbour with reference to Freud and
    Levinas see Slavoj Žižek, Eric L. Santner and Kenneth Reinhard, *The Neighbour:
    Three Inquiries in Political Theology* (Chicago: The University of Chicago Press,
    2005).

3   Slavoj Žižek, *How to Read Lacan* (London: Granta 2006), 43.

4   Emmanuel Levinas, *The Levinas Reader*, ed. Sean Hand (Oxford: Blackwell, 1989),
    294, emphasis added.

5   Ibid.

6   Ibid.

7   Jack Goody, *The Theft of History* (Cambridge: Cambridge University Press, 2006).

8   See further Adib-Moghaddam, *A Metahistory of the Clash of Civilisations: Us and
    Them beyond Orientalism* (London: Hurst, 2011).

9   Ibid., especially 265ff.

10 Levinas, *The Levinas Reader*, 282.

11 Emmanuel Levinas, *Difficult Freedom: Essays on Judaism*, trans. Sean Hand
    (Baltimore: Johns Hopkins University Press, 1990), 17.

12 Michael L. Morgan, *Discovering Levinas* (Cambridge: Cambridge University Press,
    2007), 407.

13 Emmanuel Levinas, 'Politics After!', in Emmanuel Levinas, *Beyond the Verse:
    Talmudic Readings and Lectures* (Bloomington: Indiana University Press, 1994), 188.

14 See Gil Anidjar, *The Jew, the Arab: A History of the Enemy* (Stanford: Stanford
    University Press, 2003).

15 Quoted in C. Fred Alford, *Levinas, the Frankfurt School and Psychoanalysis*
    (London: Continuum, 2002), 96.

16 On the functionality of the other for the invention of European identity see
    Iver B. Neumann, *Uses of the Other: 'The East' in European Identity Formation*
    (Manchester: Manchester University Press, 1999).

17   See further Howard Caygill, *Levinas and the Political* (London: Routledge, 2002), 45–46.

18   Emmanuel Levinas, 'La pensée juive aujourd'hui', in *Difficile liberté* (Paris: Albin Michel, 2006), 210. Translated as 'Jewish thought today' in Levinas, *Difficult Freedom: Essays on Judaism*, 160.

19   Raoul Mortley, *French Philosophers in Conversation: Derrida, Irigaray, Levinas, Le Doeuff, Schneider, Seres* (London: Routledge, 1991), 18.

20   Recent research has delved into this issue more deeply see Jason Caro, 'Levinas and the Palestinians', *Philosophy and Social Criticism*, Vol. 35, No. 6 (July 2009), 671–684.

21   Levinas, *The Levinas Reader*, 283.

22   Jaqueline Rose, *The Question of Zion* (Princeton: Princeton University Press, 2005), 24.

23   Eyal Weizman, *Hollow Land: Israel's Architecture of Occupation* (London: Verso, 2012).

24   Vladimir Jabotinsky, 'The Iron Wall (We and the Arabs)', first published in Russian under the title 'O Zheleznoi Stene' in *Rassvyet*, 4 November 1923. Published in English in the *Jewish Herald* (South Africa), 26 November 1937. Available at www.marxists.de/middleast/ironwall/ironwall.htm, accessed 23 May 2008.

25   Ibid.

26   Ibid.

27   Ibid.

28   See further Talmiz Ahmad, *Children of Abraham at War: The Clash of Messianic Militarisms* (Delhi: Aakar Books, 2010), 80.

29   Ibid.

30   See further Lenni Brenner, *The Iron Wall: Zionist Revisionism from Jabotinsky to Shamir* (London: Zed, 1984).

31   See Brian Urquhart, *Ralph Bunche: An American Odyssey* (London: W.W. Norton, 1998), 179.

32   Quoted in Noam Chomsky, *Pirates and Emperors, Old and New: International Terrorism in the Real World* (Cambridge, MA: South End Press, 2003), 136.

33   Menachem Begin, *The Revolt*, rev. ed. (New York: Nash Publishing, 1977), 59.

34   Ibid., 48, 49. So strong was the contempt of the 'Orient' that the Oriental Jews as well were considered to be backward. See further Ella Shohat, 'Sephardim in Israel: Zionism from the Standpoint of Its Jewish victims', in Anne McClintock, Aamir Mufti and Ella Shohat (eds), *Dangerous Liaisons: Gender, Nation and Postcolonial Perspectives* (Minneapolis: University of Minnesotta Press, 1997), 39–68.

35   Quoted in Naim Stifan Ateek and Michael P. Prior (eds), *Holy Land, Hollow Jubilee: God, Justice and the Palestinians* (London: Melisende, 1999), 27. See further Aviezer Ravitzky, 'Religious Radicalism and Political Messianism in Israel', in Emmanuel Sivan and Menachem Friedman (eds), *Religious Radicalism and Politics in the Middle East* (Albany: State University of New York Press, 1990).

36   Quoted in Alain Dieckhoff, *The Invention of a Nation: Zionist Thought and the Making of Modern Israel*, trans. Jonathan Derrick (New York: Columbia University Press, 2002), 202.

37   See further Zeev Sternhell, *The Founding Myths of Israel*, trans. David Maisel (Princeton: Princeton University Press, 1998).

38   See further Shlomo Sand, *The Invention of the Jewish People*, trans. Yael Lotan (London: Verso, 2009), 264–265.

39   Ibid., 257.

40   Hannah Arendt, *The Jews as Pariah: Jewish Identity and Politics in the Modern Age* (London: Grove Press, 1978), 187.

41   'Military Expenditure as a Share of GDP (2005–2010)', *Stockholm International Peace Research Institute*. Available at www.sipri.org/research/armaments/milex/resultoutput/milex_gdp, accessed 12 December 2012.

42   See further Ilan Pappe, *Out of the Frame: The Struggle for Academic Freedom in Israel* (London: Pluto Press, 2010).

43   *Dangerous Liaisons: Israel and America*, dir. Nick Read, prod. George Carey and Eamon Matthews, written and presented by Jacqueline Rose (Channel 4, UK, 24 August 2002), transcript of interview with Benjamin Netanyahu, 11.

44   This is expressed in a typically macho and authoritarian style in Benjamin Netanyahu, *A Place among the Nations* (London: Bantham, 1993).

45   See further Wendy Brown, *Walled States, Waning Souvereignty* (Brookly, NY: Zone Books, 2010).

46   Levinas, *The Levinas Reader*, 282.

47   Rose, *The Question of Zion*, 127.

48   Shohat, 'Sephardim in Israel', 57.

49   Ilan Pappe, *The Ethnic Cleansing of Palestine* (Oxford: One World, 2006), 258.

50   Ibid., 253.

51   'Survival of the Fittest: When Ethnic Cleansing Is Justified', *Haaretz*, 8 January 2004. Available at www.haaretz.com/survival-of-the-fittest-cont-1.61341, accessed 12 June 2005.

52   Ibid.

53   I have shown that al-Qaeda type movements operate on the basis of a similar logic. See Adib-Moghaddam, *A Metahistory of the Clash of Civilisations*, 251–253.

54   'Survival of the fittest'.

55   Ibid.

56   Ibid.

57   Ibid.

58   Ibid.

59   See beyond the works already cited Avi Shlaim, *The Iron Wall: Israel and the Arab World* (New York: Norton, 2000).

60 Rose, *The Question of Zion*, 67.

61 Sand, *The Invention of the Jewish People*, 17.

62 For a history of resistance to Israel see Ilan Pappe, *A History of Modern Palestine: One Land, Two Peoples*, 2nd ed. (Cambridge: Cambridge University Press, 2006), especially 127ff. and 163ff. See also Rashid Khalidi, *Palestinian Identity: The Construction of Modern National Consciousness* (New York: Columbia University Press, 1997), in particular 192–209.

63 See Hassan M. Fattah and Steven Erlanger, 'Israel Attacks Beirut Airport and Sets up Naval Blockade', *The New York Times*, 13 July 2006. Available at www.nytimes. com/2006/07/13/world/middleeast/13cnd-mideast.html?_r=2&ex=131044320 0&en=481a59f41c258e72&ei=5088&partner=rssnyt&emc=rss, accessed 14 July 2006; 'Min. Sheetrit: Hezbollah Chief Nasrallah Is a Doomed Man', *Haaretz*, 14 July 2006. Available at www.haaretz.com/news/min-sheetrit-hezbollah-chief-nasrallah-is-a-doomed-man-1.193105, accessed 12 February 2007; or Robert Fisk, 'From My Home I Saw What the War on Terror Meant', *The Independent*, 14 July 2006. Available at www.informationclearinghouse.info/article13978.htm, accessed 15 August 2006.

64 Frantz Fanon, *The Wretched of the Earth,* trans. Constance Farrington (New York: Grove, 1968), 40.

65 Edward W. Said, 'Afterword: The Consequences of 1948', in Eugene L. Rogan and Avi Shlaim (eds), *The War for Palestine*, 2nd ed. (Cambridge: Cambridge University Press, 2007), 259.

66 Ibid., 260.

Bibliography

Abou-El-Fadl, Reem. 'The Road to Jerusalem through Tahrir Square: Anti-Zionism and Palestine in the 2011 Egyptian Revolution', *Journal of Palestine Studies*, Vol. 41, No. 1 (Winter 2012), 6–26.

Abrahamian, Ervand. *A History of Modern Iran*. Cambridge: Cambridge University Press, 2008.

—. *Tortured Confessions: Prisons and Public Recantations in Modern Iran*. Berkeley, CA: University of California Press, 1999.

—. *Iran Between Two Revolutions*. Princeton: Princeton University Press, 1982.

Ackerman, Peter and Jack Duvall. *A Force More Powerful: A Century of Nonviolent Conflict*. London: Palgrave, 2000.

Adib-Moghaddam, Arshin (ed.). *A Critical Introduction to Ayatollah Khomeini*. Cambridge: Cambridge University Press, forthcoming 2013.

—. 'The Arab Revolts, Islam and Postmodernity', *Middle East Journal of Culture and Communication*, Vol. 5, No. 1 (2012), 15–25.

—. *A Metahistory of the Clash of Civilisations: Us and Them Beyond Orientalism*. London: Hurst, 2011.

—. *Iran in World Politics: The Question of the Islamic Republic*. London: Hurst, 2008.

—. *The International Politics of the Persian Gulf: A Cultural Genealogy*. London: Routledge, 2006.

Adorno, Theodor W. *Critical Models: Interventions and Catchwords*. Trans. Henry W. Pickford. New York: Columbia University Press, 2005.

Afary, Janet and Kevin B. Anderson. *Foucault and the Iranian Revolution: Gender and the Seductions of Islamism*. Chicago: The University of Chicago Press, 2005.

Ahmad, Talmiz. *Children of Abraham at War: The Clash of Messianic Militarisms*. Delhi: Aakar Books, 2010.

Al-e Ahmad, Jalal. *Plagued by the West (Gharbzadegi)*. Trans. Paul Sprachman. New York: Caravan, 1982.

Alford, Fred. *Levinas, the Frankfurt School and Psychoanalysis*. London: Continuum, 2002.

Algar, Hamid. *Religion and State in Iran, 1785–1906: The Role of the Ulema in the Qajar Period*. Berkeley: University of California Press, 1980.

Ali, Latife Reda. *Khomeini's Discourse of Resistance: The Discourse of Power of the Islamic Revolution*. PhD thesis, School of Oriental and African Studies (SOAS), University of London, July 2012.

Almond, Ian. *The New Orientalists: Postmodern Representations of Islam from Foucault to Baudrillard*. London: I.B. Tauris, 2007.

Anidjar, Gil. *The Jew, the Arab: A History of the Enemy*. Stanford: Stanford University Press, 2003.

Alshaer, Atef. 'Humanism, Nationalism and Violence in Mahmoud Darwish's Poetry', in Hugh Kennedy (ed.), *Warfare and Poetry in the Middle East*. London: I.B. Tauris, forthcoming 2013.

Arac, Jonathan. 'Foucault and Central Europe: A Polemical Speculation', *boundary 2*, Vol. 21, No. 3 (Autumn 1994), 197–210.

Arendt, Hannah. *On Revolution*. London: Penguin, 1990.

—. *The Jews as Pariah: Jewish Identity and Politics in the Modern Age*. London: Grove Press, 1978.

Arjomand, Said Amir. *The Turban for the Crown: The Islamic Revolution in Iran*. Oxford: Oxford University Press, 1988.

Al-Awa, Muhammad Salim. 'Political Pluralism from an Islamic Perspective', in John J. Donohue and John L. Esposito (eds), *Islam in Transition: Muslim Perspectives*, second edition. Oxford: Oxford University Press, 2007.

Azimi, Fakhreddin. *The Quest for Democracy in Iran: A Century of Struggle against Authoritarian Rule*. Cambridge, MA: Harvard University Press, 2008.

Badiou, Alain. *Le Siècle*. Paris: Seuil, 2005.

Baker, Raymond William. *Islam without Fear: Egypt and the New Islamists*. Harvard: Harvard University Press, 2006.

Bartky, Sandra. 'Foucault, Femininity and the Modernisation of Patriarchal Power', in Irene Diamond and Lee Quinby (eds), *Feminism and Foucault: Paths of Resistance*. Boston: Northeastern University Press, 1988, 61–86.

Bayat, Asef. *Life as Politics: How Ordinary People Change the Middle East*. Stanford: Stanford University Press, 2010.

—. *Street Politics: Poor People's Movements in Iran*. New York: Columbia University Press, 1997.

Bayat-Philipp, Mangol. 'A Phoenix too Frequent: Historical Continuity in Modern Iranian Thought', *Asian and African Studies*, Vol. 12 (1978), 44–52.

Beeman, William O. *The Great Satan vs. the Mad Mullahs: How the United States and Iran Demonize Each Other*. London: Greenwood, 2005.

Begin, Menachem. *The Revolt*, revised edition. New York: Nash Publishing, 1977.

Benjamin, Walter. *Reflections: Essays, Aphorism, Autobiographical Writings*. Ed. P. Demetz. New York: Schocken Books, 1986.

Benhabib, Seyla. *Critique, Norm and Utopia: A Study of the Foundations of Critical Theory*. New York: Columbia University Press, 1986.

Berger, Peter L. *The Sacred Canopy: Elements of a Sociological Theory of Religion*. New York: Anchor, 1969.

Berger, Peter and Stanley Pullberg. 'Reification and the Sociological Critique of Consciousness', *History and Theory*, Vol. 4, No. 2 (1965), 196–211.

Bergesen, Albert J. (ed.). *The Sayyid Qutb Reader: Selected Writings on Politics, Religion, and Society*. Abingdon: Routledge, 2008.

Best, Steven and Douglas Kellner. *The Postmodern Turn*. London: The Guildford Press, 1997.

Bleiker, Roland. *Popular Dissent, Human Agency, and Global Politics*. Cambridge: Cambridge University Press, 2000.

Booth, Kenneth and Nicholas J. Wheeler. *The Security Dilemma: Fear, Cooperation and Trust in World Politics*. London: Palgrave, 2008.

Boroujerdi, Mehrzad. *Iranian Intellectuals and the West: The Tormented Triumph of Nativism*. Syracuse: Syracuse University Press, 1996.

Bowden, Mark. *Guests of the Ayatollah: The First Battle in the West's War with Militant Islam*. London: Atlantic, 2006.

Brenner, Lenni. *The Iron Wall: Zionist Revisionism from Jabotinsky to Shamir*. London: Zed, 1984.

Brown, Wendy. *Walled States, Waning Sovereignty*. Brooklyn, NY: Zone Books, 2010.

Buck-Morss, Susan. *Dreamworld and Catastrophe: The Passing of Mass Utopia in East and West*. Cambridge, MA: MIT Press, 2002.

Bulliet, Richard W. *The Case for Islamo-Christian Civilisation*. New York: Columbia University Press, 2004.

Burrowes, Robert J. *The Struggle for Nonviolent Defense: A Gandhian Approach*. Albany: State University of New York Press, 1996.

Calhoun, Craig. *Critical Social Theory: Culture, History, and the Challenge of Difference*. Oxford: Blackwell, 1995.

Campbell, David. *Writing Security: United States Foreign Policy and the Politics of Identity*. Manchester: Manchester University Press, 1993.

Campbell, David. *Politics without Principle: Sovereignty, Ethics, and the Narratives of the Gulf War*. London: Lynne Rienner, 1992.

Caro, Jason. 'Levinas and the Palestinians', *Philosophy and Social Criticism*, Vol. 35, No. 6 (July 2009), 671–684.

Carrette, Jeremy R. (ed.). *Religion and Culture*. Manchester: Manchester University Press, 1999.

Carter, April, Howard Clark and Michael Randle (eds). *People, Power and Protest since 1945: A Bibliography of Nonviolent Action*. London: Housmans, 2006.

Caygill, Howard. *Levinas and the Political*. London: Routledge, 2002.

Chomsky, Noam. *Pirates and Emperors, Old and New: International Terrorism in the Real World*. Cambridge, MA: South End Press, 2003.

Cook, Steven. 'Contingency Planning Memorandum No. 4: Political Instability in Egypt', *Council on Foreign Relations: Centre for Preventive Action*, August 2009.

Cronin, Stephanie (ed.). *Reformers and Revolutionaries in Modern Iran: New Perspectives on the Iranian Left*. Abingdon: Routledge, 2004.

Dabashi, Hamid. *Post-Orientalism: Knowledge and Power in Time of Terror*. London: Transaction Publishers, 2008.

Deleuze, Gilles. *Two Regimes of Madness: Texts and Interviews 1975–1995*. Ed. David Lapoujade. Trans. Ames Hodges and Mike Taormina. New York: Semiotext(e), 2007.

—. *The Logic of Sense*. London: Continuum, 2004.

Deleuze, Gilles and Claire Parnet. *Dialogues II*. Trans. Hugh Tomlinson and Barbara Habberjam. London: Continuum, 2002.

Dews, Peter. *Logics of Disintegration: Post-Structuralist Thought and the Claims of Critical Theory*. London: Verso, 2007.

Dieckhoff, Alain. *The Invention of a Nation: Zionist Thought and the Making of Modern Israel*. Trans. Jonathan Derrick. New York: Columbia University Press, 2002.

Ebtekar, Massoumeh. *Takeover in Tehran: The Inside Story of the 1979 U.S. Embassy Capture*. Vancouver: Talon, 2000.

Eigner, Saeb. *Art of the Middle East: Modern and Contemporary Art of the Arab World and Iran*. London: Merrell, 2010.

Enayat, Hamid. *Modern Islamic Political Thought: The Response of the Shi'i and the Sunni Muslims to the Twentieth Century*. London: Macmillan, 1982.

Eribon, Didier. *Michel Foucault*. Trans. Betsy Wing. Cambridge, MA: Harvard University Press, 1991.

Esposito, John L. and Ibrahim Kalin (eds). *Islamophobia: The Challenge of Pluralism in the 21st Century*. Oxford: Oxford University Press, 2011.

Fallaci, Oriana. *Interview with History*. New York: Houghton-Mifflin, 1977.

Fanon, Frantz. *Black Skin, White Masks*. London: Pluto, 1986.

—. *The Wretched of the Earth*. Trans. Constance Farrington. New York: Grove, 1968.

Firoozi, Ferydoon. 'Iranian Censuses 1956 and 1966: A Comparative Analysis', *Middle East Journal*, Vol. 24, No. 2 (Spring 1970), 220–228.

Fitzhugh, Michael L. and William H. Leckie, Jr. 'Agency, Postmodernism and the Causes of Change', *History and Theory*, Vol. 40, No.4 (December 2001), 59–81.

Foucault, Michel. *Manet and the Object of Painting*. Trans. Matthew Barr. London: Tate, 2009.

—. *Security, Territory, Population: Lectures at the College de France 1977–1978*. Ed. Michel Senellart. Trans. Graham Burchell. London: Palgrave Macmillan, 2009.

—. *Society must Be Defended: Lectures at the Collège de France*. Ed. Mauro Bertani and Alessandro Fontana. Trans. David Macey. London: Penguin, 2004.

—. *The Archaeology of Knowledge*. London: Routledge, 2002.

—. *Power: Essential Works of Foucault, vol. 3*. Ed. James D. Faubion. Trans. Rober Hurley et. al. London: Penguin, 2002.

—. 'Michel Foucault and Zen: A Stay in a Zen Temple (1978)', in Jeremy R. Carrette (ed.), *Religion and Culture*. Manchester: Manchester University Press, 1999.

—. *The Will to Knowledge: The History of Sexuality, Volume 1*. Trans. Robert Hurley. London: Penguin, 1998.

—. *Discipline and Punish: The Birth of the Prison*. Trans. Alan Sheridan. London: Penguin, 1991.

—. *The Order of Things: An Archaeology of the Human Sciences*. Trans. A.M. Sheridan Smith. London: Routledge, 1989.

—. *Language, Countermemory, Practice: Selected Essays and Interviews by Michel Foucault*. Ed. Donald F. Bouchard. Ithaca: Cornell University Press, 1977.

Giddens, Antony. *Beyond Left and Right: The Future of Radical Politics*. Cambridge: Polity, 1994.

—. *The Transformation of Intimacy: Sexuality, Love & Eroticism in Modern Societies*. Stanford: Stanford University Press, 1992.

Goody, Jack. *Renaissances: The One or the Many?* Cambridge: Cambridge University Press, 2010.

—. *The Theft of History*. Cambridge: Cambridge University Press, 2006.

Gramsci, Antonio. *Selections from the Prison Notebooks*. Ed. and trans. Quinton Hoare and Geoffrey Nowell Smith. London: Lawrence and Wishart, 1971.

Grant, John. 'Foucault and the Logic of Dialectics', *Contemporary Political Theory*, Vol. 9, No. 2 (Summer 2010), 220–238.

Guattari, Felix. *Psychoanalyse et transversalité*. Paris: Maspero/La Découverte, 1972/2003.

Guevara, Ernest Che. *Guerrilla Warfare*. London: Penguin, 1969.

Habermas, Jürgen. *The Philosophic Discourse of Modernity*. Cambridge: MIT Press, 1987.

—. *Theory of Communicative Action, vol. 1: Reason and the Rationalisation of Society*. Boston, MA: Beacon Press, 1984.

Haddad, Bassam, Rosie Bsheer, and Ziad Abu-Rish (eds). *The Dawn of the Arab Uprisings: End of an Old Order?* London: Pluto, 2012.

Haghighat, Abd-al-Rafie. *Tarikh-e Honar-haye Meli va Honarmandane Irani* [The History of National Arts And Iranian Artists], Vol. 1 of the *Complete Works of Abd-al-Rafie Haghighat*. Tehran: Moalefan va Motarjeman-e Iran, 1990.

Halliday, Fred. *Revolution and World Politics: The Rise and Fall of the Sixth Great Power*. Durham, NC: Duke University Press, 1999.

—. *Iran: Dictatorship and Development*. Harmondsworth: Penguin, 1979.

Harb, Ali. *Soft Power Revolutions in the Arab World: The Deconstruction of Dictatorships and Fundamentalisms*. Beirut: Al Dar Al Arabiya Liloloum Publishers, 2011.

Hairi, Abdul-Hadi. *Shi'ism and Constitutionalism in Iran: A Study of the Role Played by the Persian Residents of Iraq in Iranian Politics*. Leiden: E.J. Brill, 1977.

Harris, Jonathan (ed.). *Identity Theft: The Cultural Colonization of Contemporary Art*. Liverpool: Liverpool University Press, 2008.

Hardt, Michael and Antonio Negri. *Multitude: War and Democracy in the Age of Empire*. London: Hamish Hamilton, 2004.

—. *Empire*. Cambridge, MA: Harvard University Press, 2000.

—. *Labour of Dionysus: A Critique of the State-Form*. Minneapolis: University of Minnesota Press, 1994.

Heller, Kevin Jon. 'Subjectification and Resistance in Foucault', *Substance*, Vol. 25, No. 1, Issue 79 (1996), 78–110.

Hobson, John M. *The Eurocentric Conception of World Politics: Western International Theory, 1760–2010*. Cambridge: Cambridge University Press, 2012.

Horkheimer, Max. *Critical Theory: Selected Essays*. London: Continuum, 1997.

Jabotinsky, Vladimir. 'The Iron Wall (We and the Arabs)', first published in Russian under the title 'O Zheleznoi Stene' in *Rassvyet*, 4 November 1923. Published in English in the *Jewish Herald* (South Africa), 26 November 1937. Available at www.marxists.de/middleast/ironwall/ironwall.htm, accessed 23 May 2008.

Jackson, Richard. *Writing the War on Terrorism: Language, Politics and Counterterrorism*. Manchester: Manchester University Press, 2005.

Jamshidi, Mohammad-Hossein (ed.). *Andishey-e siasiy-e imam Khomeini*. Tehran: Pajoheshkade-ye imam Khomeini va enghelabe islami, 1384/2005.

Jervis, Robert. *Why Intelligence Fails: Lessons from the Iranian Revolution and the Iraq War*. Ithaca: Cornell University Press, 2010.

Karimi-Hakkak, Ahmad and Kamran Talattof (eds). *Essays on Nima Yushij: Animating Modernism in Persian Poetry*. Leiden: Brill, 2004.

Kashani-Sabet, Firoozeh. 'Cultures of Iranianness: The Evolving Polemic of Iranian Nationalism', in Nikki R. Keddie and Rudi Matthee (eds), *Iran and the Surrounding World: Interactions in Culture and Cultural Politics* (Seattle: University of Washington Press, 2002), 162–181.

Kasravi, Ahmad. *Tarikh-e mashrute-yeh Iran* [History of the Iranian Constitution]. Tehran: Negah Publications, 2008.

Katouzian, Homa. *State and Society in Iran: The Eclipse of the Qajars and the Emergence of the Pahlavis*. London: I.B. Tauris, 2006.

Keating, Craig. 'Reflections on the Revolution in Iran: Foucault on Resistance', *Journal of European Studies*, Vol. 27, No. 2 (1997), 181–197.

Keddie, Nikki (ed.). *Debating Revolutions*. New York: New York University Press, 1996.

Keddie, Nikki. *Religion and Rebellion in Iran: The Iranian Tobacco Protest of 1891–1892*. Abingdon: Frank Cass, 1966.

Kelly, Mark G. E. *The Political Philosophy of Michel Foucault*. London: Routledge, 2008.

Khalidi, Rashid. 'Preliminary Historical Observations on the Arab Revolutions of 2011', *Jadaliyya*, 21 March 2011. Available at www.jadaliyya.com/pages/index/970/preliminary-historical-observations-on-the-arab-re, accessed 2 December 2011.

Khalidi, Rashid. *Palestinian Identity: The Construction of Modern National Consciousness*. New York: Columbia University Press, 1997.

Khalidi, Rashid, Lisa Anderson, Muhammad Muslih and Reeva Simon (eds). *The Origins of Arab Nationalism*. New York: Columbia University Press, 1993.

Khomeini, Ruhollah. *Ain-e enghelab-e Islami: Gozidehai az andisheh va ara-ye Imam Khomeini*. Tehran: Moasses-ye tanzim va nashr-e assar-e Imam Khomeini, 1373/1994.

—. *Islam and Revolution: Writings and Declarations of Imam Khomeini*, Trans. and annotated by Hamid Algar. Berkeley: Mizan Press, 1981.

Khoshchereh, Mahmoud. *The Structure of Authoring in Nima Yushij's Poetry: A Bakhtinian Reading*. Open access dissertation and theses, paper 6400 (2011). Available at http://digitalcommons.mcmaster.ca/cgi/viewcontent.cgi?article=7443 &context=opendissertations, accessed 23 October 2012.

Kissinger, Henry A. *Years of Upheaval*. London: Weidenfeld and Nicolson, 1982.

Kraminick, Isaac. 'Reflections on Revolution: Definition and Explanation in Recent Scholarship', *History and Theory*, Vol. 11, No. 1 (1972), 26–63.

Kurzman, Charles. *The Unthinkable Revolution in Iran*. Cambridge, MA: Harvard University Press, 2004.

Laclau, Ernesto and Chantal Mouffe. *Hegemony and Socialist Strategy: Towards a Radical Democratic Politics*, second edition. London: Verso, 2001.

Lean, Nathan. *The Islamophobia Industry: How the Right Manufactures Fear of Muslims*. London: Pluto Press, 2012.

Leezenberg, Michiel. 'Power and Political Spirituality: Michel Foucault and the Islamic Revolution in Iran', *Arcadia*, Vol. 33 No. 1 (1998), 72–89.

Levinas, Emmanuel. *Difficult Freedom: Essays on Judaism*. Trans. Sean Hand. Baltimore: Johns Hopkins University Press, 1997.

—. *Beyond the Verse: Talmudic Readings and Lectures*. Bloomington: Indiana University Press, 1994.

—. *Difficult Freedom: Essays on Judaism*. Trans. Sean Hand. Baltimore: Johns Hopkins University Press, 1990.

—. *The Levinas Reader*. Ed. Sean Hand. Oxford: Blackwell, 1989.

Lockman, Zachary. *Contending Visions of the Middle East: The History and Politics of Orientalism*. Cambridge: Cambridge University Press, 2004.

MacMaster, Neil. *Burning the Veil: The Algerian War and the 'Emancipation' of Muslim women, 1954–62*. Manchester: Manchester University Press, 2009.

Marx, Karl. *Survey from Exile*. Ed. D. Fernbach. Harmondsworth: Penguin, 1973.

McCarthy, Thomas. 'The Critique of Impure Reason: Foucault and the Frankfurt School', *Political Theory*, Vol. 18, No. 3 (August 1990), 437–469.

McClintock, Anne, Aamir Mufti and Ella Shohat (eds). *Dangerous Liaisons: Gender, Nation and Postcolonial Perspectives*. Minneapolis: University of Minnesotta Press, 1997.

Merleau-Ponty, Maurice. *Humanism and Terror: The Communist Problem*. Trans. John O'Oneill. New Brunswick, NJ: Transaction Publishers, 2000.

Miller, James. *The Passion of Michel Foucault*. New York: Simon & Schuster, 1993.

Moin, Baqer. *Khomeini: Life of the Ayataollah*. London: I.B. Tauris, 1999.

Morgan, Michael L. *Discovering Levinas*. Cambridge: Cambridge University Press, 2007.

Mokhtari, Shadi. 'The New Politics of Human Rights in the Middle East', *Foreign Policy*, 30 October 2012. Available at http://mideast.foreignpolicy.com/ posts/2012/10/30/the_new_politics_of_human_rights_in_the_middle_East, accessed 12 November 2012.

Morey, Peter and Amina Yaqin. *Framing Muslims: Stereotyping and Representation After 9/11*. Cambridge, MA: Harvard University Press, 2011.

Mortley, Raoul. *French Philosophers in Conversation: Derrida, Irigaray, Levinas, Le Doeuff, Schneider, Serres*. London: Routledge, 1991.

Morton, Adam David. *Unravelling Gramsci: Hegemony and Passive Revolution in the Global Economy*. London: Pluto Press, 2007.

Mouffe, Chantal. 'The Radical Centre: A Politics without Adversary', *Soundings*, No. 9 (Summer 1998), 11–23.

Naini, Mohammad Hussein. *Tanbih al-ummah wa tanzih al-millah* (Advising the Muslim Community and Purifying the Religion). Qom: Bustan-e Ketabe Qom Press, 2003.

Nayak, Meghana and Eric Selbin. *Decentring International Relations*. London: Zed Books, 2010.

Nealon, Jeffrey T. *Foucault beyond Foucault: Power and Its Intensifications since 1984*. Stanford: Stanford University Press, 2008.

Netanyahu, Benjamin. *A Place among the Nations*. London: Bantham, 1993.

Netton, Ian (ed.). *Orientalism Revisited: Art, Land, Voyage*. Abingdon: Routledge, 2012.

Neumann, Iver B. *Uses of the Other: 'The East' in European Identity Formation*. Manchester: Manchester University Press, 1999.

Noueihed, Lin and Alex Warren. *The Battle for the Arab Spring: Revolution, Counter-Revolution and the Making of a New Era*. London: Yale University Press, 2012.

Orwell, George. 'Politics and the English Language (1946)', in W.F. Bolton and D. Chrystal (eds), *The English Language, Vol. 2, Essays of Linguists and Men of Letters* (Cambridge: Cambridge University Press, 1969), 217–228.

Owen, Roger. *State, Power and Politics in the Making of the Modern Middle East*, second edition. London: Routledge, 2000.

Pahlavi, Mohammad Reza. *Mission for My Country*. New York: McGraw-Hill, 1961.

Palti, Elías. 'The 'Return of the Subject' as a Historical-Intellectual Problem', *History and Theory*, Vol. 43, No. 1 (February 2004), 57–82.

Pappe, Ilan. *Out of the Frame: The Struggle for Academic Freedom in Israel*. London: Pluto Press, 2010.

—. *The Ethnic Cleansing of Palestine*. Oxford: One World, 2006.

—. *A History of Modern Palestine: One Land, Two Peoples*, second edition. Cambridge: Cambridge University Press, 2006.

Picasso, Pablo. 'Why I Joined the Communist Party', in Charles Harrison and Paul Wood (eds), *Art in Theory 1900–2000: An Anthology of Changing Ideas*. Oxford: Blackwell Publishing, 2003.

Pickett, Brent L. 'Foucault and the Politics of Resistance', *Polity*, Vol. 28, No. 4 (Summer 1996), pp, 445–466.

Pistor-Hatam, Anja. 'Writing Back? Jalal Al-e Ahmad's (1923–69): Reflections on Selected Periods of Iranian History', *Iranian Studies*, Vol. 40, No. 5 (December 2007), 559–578.

Rabinow, Paul (ed.). *The Foucault Reader*. London: Penguin, 1984.

Rahnema, Ali. *An Islamic Utopian: A Political Biography of Ali Shariati*. London: I.B. Tauris, 2000.

Ravitzky, Aviezer. 'Religious Radicalism and Political Messianism in Israel', in Emmanuel Sivan and Menachem Friedman (eds), *Religious Radicalism and Politics in the Middle East* (Albany: State University of New York Press, 1990), 11–37.

Risse, Thomas. "Let's Argue!' Communicative Action in World Politics', *International Organization*, Vol. 54, No. 1 (2000), 1–39.

Roberts, Adam and Timothy Garton-Ash (eds). *Civil Resistance and Power Politics: The Experience of Non-Violent Action from Gandhi to the Present*. Oxford: Oxford University Press, 2011.

Robespiere, Maximilien de. 'Report on the Principles of Political Morality (5 February 1794)', in Keith Michael Baker, John W. Boyer, and Julius Kirshner (eds), *University of Chicago Readings in Western Civilisation, vol. 7: The Old Regime and the French Revolution*. Chicago: The University of Chicago Press, 1987, 368–384.

Ron, James. *Frontiers and Ghettos: State Violence in Serbia and Israel.* Berkeley: University of California Press, 2003.

Rose, Jacqueline. *The Question of Zion.* Princeton: Princeton University Press, 2005.

Rostami-Povey, Elaheh. *Women, Work and Islamism: Ideology and Resistance in Iran,* new edition. London: Zed Books, 2010.

Roy, Olivier. 'L'enigme du soulèvement (Enigma of the Uprising)', *Vacarme,* No. 29 (Autumn 2004). English version available at www.vacarme.org/article1799.html, accessed 12 November 2010.

Sachsenmaier, Dominic. *Global Perspectives on Global History: Theories and Approaches in a Connected World.* Cambridge: Cambridge University Press, 2011.

Said, Edward W. 'Afterword: The Consequences of 1948', in Eugene L. Rogan and Avi Shlaim (eds), *The War for Palestine,* second edition. Cambridge: Cambridge University Press, 2007, 248–261.

—. *On Late Style.* London: Bloomsbury, 2006.

—. *Reflections on Exile and Other Essays.* Cambridge, MA: Harvard University Press, 2000.

—. *Covering Islam: How the Media and the Experts Determine How We See the Rest of the World.* London: Vintage, 1997.

—. *Orientalism: Western Conceptions of the Orient.* London: Penguin, 1995.

—. *Culture and Imperialism.* London: Vintage, 1993.

Salaita, Steven. *Anti-Arab Racism in the USA: Where It Comes From and What It Means for Politics Today.* London: Pluto Press, 2006.

Sand, Shlomo. *The Invention of the Jewish People.* Trans. Yael Lotan. London: Verso, 2009.

Sartre, Jean Paul. *Colonialism and Neocolonialism.* Trans. Azzedine Haddour, Steve Brewer and Terry Mc Williams. Abingdon: Routledge, 2006.

—. *Critique of Dialectical Reason, Vol. 1,* new edition. Trans. Alan Sheridan-Smith. London: Verso, 2004.

Savory, Roger M. 'The Principle of Homeostasis Considered in Relation to Political Events in Iran in the 1960's,' *International Journal of Middle East Studies (IJMES),* Vol. 3, No. 3 (1972), 282–302.

Sayyid, Salman and Abdoolkarim Vakil (eds). *Thinking through Islamophobia: Global Perspectives.* London: Hurst, 2011.

Schatz, Adam. 'Mubarak's Last Breath', *London Review of Books,* Vol. 32, No. 10 and 27 (May 2010), 6–10.

Schirazi, Asghar. *The Constitution of Iran: Politics and the State in the Islamic Republic.* London: I.B. Tauris, 1998.

Schmidt, James and Thomas E. Wartenberg. 'Foucault's Enlightenment: Critique, Revolution and the Fashioning of the Self', in Michael Kelly (ed.), *Critique and Power: Recasting the Foucault/Habermas Debate.* Chicago: MIT Press, 1994.

Schock, Kurt. *Unarmed Insurrections: People Power Movements in Nondemocracies.* Minneapolis: University of Minnesota Press, 2005.

Semmerling, Tim Jon. *Evil Arabs in American Popular Film: Orientalist Fear.* Austin: University of Texas Press, 2006.

Shanin, Teodor. *The Roots of Otherness: Russia's Turn of the Century, volume II: Russia, 1905–1907: Revolution as a Moment of Truth.* New Haven: Yale University Press, 1986.

Shariati, Ali. 'On Martyrdom (*Shahadat*)', in, John J. Donohue and John L. Esposito (eds), *Islam in Transition: Muslim Perspectives*, second edition. Oxford: Oxford University Press, 2007, 361–365.

Sharp, Gene. 'The Politics of Nonviolent Action and the Spread of Ideas about Civil Resistance.' Paper prepared for the Conference on 'Civil Resistance and Power Politics', St. Anthony's College, Oxford University, Oxford, March 2007, p. 4. Available at www.aeinstein.org/lectures_papers/OXFORD_PNVA.pdf, accessed 3 March 2010.

—. *Social Power and Political Freedom.* Boston: Porter Sargent, 1980.

—. *The Politics of Nonviolent Action.* Boston: Porter Sargent Publishers, 1973.

Shaw, David Gary. 'Happy in Our Chains? Agency and Language in the Postmodern Age', *History and Theory*, Vol. 40, No. 4 (December 2001), 1–9.

Shlaim, Avi. *The Iron Wall: Israel and the Arab World.* New York: Norton, 2000.

Shohat, Ella. 'Sephardim in Israel: Zionism from the Standpoint of Its Jewish Victims', in Anne McClintock, Aamir Mufti and Ella Shohat (eds), *Dangerous Liaisons: Gender, Nation and Postcolonial Perspectives.* Minneapolis: University of Minnesotta Press, 1997, 39–68.

Skocpol, Theda. *States and Social Revolutions: A Comparative Analysis of France, Russia and China.* Cambridge: Cambridge University Press, 1979.

Smart, Barry. *Michel Foucault*, revised edition. London: Routledge, 2002.

Spivak, Gayatri Chakravorty. *Outside in the Teaching Machine.* London: Routledge, 1993.

Stauth, Georg. 'Revolution in Spiritless Times: An Essay on Michel Foucault's Enquiries into the Iranian Revolution', *International Sociology*, Vol. 6, No. 3 (1991), 259–280.

Sternhell, Zeev. *The Founding Myths of Israel.* Trans. David Maisel. Princeton: Princeton University Press, 1998.

Stifan, Naim Ateek and Michael P. Prior (eds). *Holy Land, Hollow Jubilee: God, Justice and the Palestinians.* London: Melisende, 1999.

Sun Tzu. *The Art of War.* Trans. Samuel B. Griffith. Oxford: Oxford University Press, 1963.

Tārīkh-e Sāl-e Sevvum-e Dabiristan. Tehran, no publisher 1319/1941.

Tickner, Arlene B. and David L. Blaney (eds). *Thinking International Relations Differently.* Abingdon: Routledge, 2012.

Urquhart, Brian. *Ralph Bunche: An American Odyssey*. London: W.W. Norton, 1998.

Veyne, Paul. *Foucault: His Thought, His Character*. Trans. Janet Lloyd. Cambridge: Polity, 2010.

Walzer, Michael. 'The Politics of Michel Foucault', in David Couzens Hoy (ed.), *Foucault: A Critical Reader*. Oxford: Blackwell, 1986.

Weber, Max. *Economy and Society*. Berkeley: University of California Press, 1978.

Weizman, Eyal. *Hollow Land: Israel's Architecture of Occupation*. London: Verso, 2007.

Widder, Nathan. 'Foucault and Power Revisited', *European Journal of Political Theory*, Vol. 3, No. 4 (2004), 411–432.

Young, Robert J. C. 'Sartre the "'African Philosopher"', in Jean Paul Sartre, *Colonialism and Neocolonialism*. Trans. Azzedine Haddour, Steve Brewer and Terry Mc Williams. Abingdon: Routledge, 2006, ix–xxviii.

—. *White Mythologies: Writing, History and the West*. London: Routledge, 1991.

Žižek, Slavoj. 'Europe Must Move beyond Mere Tolerance', *The Guardian*, 25 January 2011. Available at www.guardian.co.uk/commentisfree/2011/jan/25/european-union-slovenia, accessed 12 March 2011.

—. *Violence: Six Sideways Reflections*. London: Profile Books, 2008.

—. *How to Read Lacan*. London: Granta 2006.

Žižek, Slavoj, Eric L. Santner and Kenneth Reinhard. *The Neighbour: Three Inquiries in Political Theology*. Chicago: The University of Chicago Press, 2005.

Zoka, Yahya. *Tarikh-e Akasi va Akasaan-e Pishgam dar Iran* [The History of Photography and Pioneer Photographers in Iran]. Tehran: Elmi & Farhangi Press, 1997.

Zunes, Stephen. 'Unarmed Insurrections against Authoritarian Governments in the Third World: A New Kind of Revolution?' *Third World Quarterly*, Vol. 15, No. 3 (1994), 403–426.

Select Internet/Empirical Sources

Abdelhady, Hdeel. 'Egypt Needs a Mindset Revolution', *Al-Ahram Weekly*, No. 1067, 6–12 October 2011. Available at weekly.ahram.org.eg/2011/1067/op2.htm, accessed 12 June 2012.

'Access Agreement Submissions for 2012–13', *Office For Fair Access*, 20 April 2011. Available at www.offa.org.uk/press-releases/access-agreement-submissions-for-2012–13/, accessed 12 January 2012.

Armour, Stephanie. 'Wisconsin Vote on Unions Corrupts Democracy, Trumka Says', *Bloomberg*, 10 March 2011. Available at www.bloomberg.com/news/2011–03–10/wisconsin-vote-on-worker-rights-corrupts-democracy-afl-cio-s-trumka-says.html, accessed 12 June 2011.

'Ayatollah Khamenei's Jet Put on Standby', *Radio Netherlands Worldwide*, 29 December 2009. Available at www.rnw.nl/english/article/iran-has-plane-ready-take-leader-safety, accessed 12 January 2010.

'Blair Admits Regret Over Deaths in Iraq', *Channel 4 News*, 21 January 2011. Available at www.channel4.com/news/blair-says-force-may-be-needed-against-iran, accessed 2 January 2012.

CIA, Directorate of Intelligence, 1972. *Intelligence Report: Centres of Power in Iran*. Available from www.state.gov/documents/organization/70712.pdf, accessed 24 December 2009.

Country data for Tunisia according to *The World Bank*. Available at http://data.worldbank.org/country/tunisia, accessed 23 October 2012.

Cole, Matthew and Sarah O Wali. 'New Egyptian VP Ran Mubarak's Security Team, Oversaw Torture', *ABC News*, 1 February 2011. Available at http://abcnews.go.com/Blotter/egypt-crisis-omar-suleiman-cia-rendition/story?id=12812445#.T9DAKbCvKSo, accessed 21 December 2011.

'Conversation among President Nixon, Ambassador Douglas MacArthur II, and General Alexander Haig.' Washington, 8 April 1971, 3:56–4:21 p.m. Available from www.state.gov/r/pa/ho/frus/nixon/e4/71804.htm, accessed 12 June 2009.

'EU Socialists, Conservatives, Play 'Dictator Badminton' over Tunisia', *EUobserver.com*, 18 January 2011. Available at http://euobserver.com/political/31663, accessed 23 January 2012.

'Fallen Faces of the Uprising', *Egypt Independent*, 7 February 2011. Available at www.egyptindependent.com/news/fallen-faces-uprising-ahmed-basiony, accessed 11 January 2012.

Fattah, Hassan M. and Steven Erlanger. 'Israel Attacks Beirut Airport and Sets Up Naval Blockade', *The New York Times*, 13 July 2006. Available at http://www.nytimes.com/2006/07/13/world/middleeast/13cnd-mideast.html?_r=2&ex=1310443200&en=481a59f41c258e72&ei=5088&partner=rssnyt&emc=rss, accessed 14 July 2006.

Fisk, Robert. 'From My Home I Saw What the War on Terror Meant', *The Independent*, 14 July 2006. Available at www.informationclearinghouse.info/article13978.htm, accessed 15 August 2006.

'Gamal Banna: Criticism of Al-Ikhwan Not Acceptable', *Asharq al-Awsat*, 28 June 2012. Trans. Mideaswire.com.

Gardner, Amy and Michael A. Fletcher. 'Ohio Senate Panel Approves Union-Rights Bill, Sending It to Full Senate', *The Washington Post*, 4 March 2011. Available at www.washingtonpost.com/wp-dyn/content/article/2011/03/01/AR2011030106108.html, accessed 12 June 2011.

Goodman, Al. 'Thousands of Spaniards Call for Economic Reform in New Protest', *CNN*, 20 June 2011. Available at http://edition.cnn.com/2011/WORLD/europe/06/19/spain.protests/index.html, accessed 3 July 2011.

—. 'Spain's Jobless Rate Tops 21% as All Major Sectors Lose Jobs', *CNN*, 29 April 2011. Available at http://edition.cnn.com/2011/WORLD/europe/04/29/spain.unemployment/index.html, accessed 21 May 2011.

'Greek Protests Leave Dozens Injured: Turmoil in Athens Follows Vote to Approve Austerity Program', *CBC News*, 29 June 2011. Available at www.cbc.ca/news/world/story/2011/06/29/greece-austerity-parliament.html, accessed 12 July 2011.

Hardinghaus, Barbara and Julia Arnalia Heyer. 'Wave of Suicide Shocks Greece', *Spiegel Online*, 15 August 2012. Available at www.spiegel.de/international/europe/economic-crisis-triggers-wave-of-suicides-in-greece-a-850129-druck.html, accessed 12 September 2012.

Hitchens, Christopher. 'Don't Mince Words: The London Car Bomb Plot was Designed to Kill Women', *Slate*, 2 July 2007. Available at www.slate.com/articles/news_and_politics/fighting_words/2007/07/dont_mince_words.html, accessed 6 January 2012.

'In the Name of Security: Routine Abuses in Tunisia', *Amnesty International*, 23 June 2008. Available at www.amnesty.org/en/library/asset/MDE30/007/2008/en/b8527bf4–3ebc–11dd–9656–05931d46f27f/mde300072008eng.html, accessed 22 November 2012.

International Monetary Fund. 'Tunisia: 2010 Article IV Consultation', IMF Country Report No. 10/282, Washington, September 2010. Available at www.imf.org/external/pubs/ft/scr/2010/cr10282.pdf, accessed 12 January 2011.

International Monetary Fund. 'Arab Republic of Egypt: 2010 Article IV Consultation', IMF Country Report No. 10/94, Washington, April 2010. Available at www.imf.org/external/pubs/ft/scr/2010/cr1094.pdf, accessed 12 June 2012.

'Interview Transcript: Rachid Ghannouchi', *The Financial Times*, 18 January 2011. Available at www.ft.com/cms/s/0/24d710a6–22ee-11e0-ad0b-00144feab49a.html#axzz2HrUt64VC, accessed 12 March 2011.

'Interview with Jody McIntyre', *BBC*, 14 December 2010. Available at www.bbc.co.uk/blogs/theeditors/2010/12/interview_with_jody_mcintyre.html, accessed 23 December 2010.

'Iran and Global Scientific Collaboration in the 21st Century', *Association of Professors and Scholars of Iranian Heritage*, 3 September 2011. Available at www.apsih.org/

index.php/news/english-news/275-iran-and-global-scientific-collaboration-in-the-21st-century, accessed 12 January 2012.

'Iran Set to Build First Cyber Army', *Press TV*, 20 February 2012. Available at www.presstv.ir/detail/227739.html, accessed 12 March 2012.

Jones, Charles. 'The Dangers of Austerity', *Al-Jazeera*, 15 December 2010. Available at www.aljazeera.com/indepth/opinion/2010/12/2010121418547100351.html, accessed 12 October 2011.

Karon, Tony. 'What the US Loses if Mubarak Goes', *Time*, 31 January 2011. Available at www.time.com/time/world/article/0,8599,2045248,00.html, accessed 1 March 2011.

Kemp, R. Scott. 'Bold Steps in the Digital Darkness?' *Bulletin of the Atomic Scientists*, 7 June 2012. Available at http://thebulletin.org/web-edition/op-eds/cyberweapons-bold-steps-digital-darkness, accessed 12 July 2012.

Kennedy, Siobhan. 'Topshop Protests over Sir Philip Green's Taxes', *Channel 4 News*, 4 December 2010. Available at www.channel4.com/news/topshop-protest-over-sir-philip-greens-taxes, accessed 1 January 2011.

King, Rachael. 'Virus Aimed at Iran Infected Chevron Network', *The Wall Street Journal*, 9 November 2012. Available at http://online.wsj.com/article/SB100014241 2788732489410457810722366742179.html, accessed 12 December 2012.

Leachman, Michael, Erica Williams and Nicholas Johnson. 'New Fiscal Year Brings Further Budget Cuts to Most States, Slowing Economic Recovery', *Center on Budget and Policy Priorities*, 28 June 2011. Available at www.cbpp.org/cms/index.cfm?fa=view&id=3526, accessed 23 July 2011.

McElroy, Damien and Ahmad Vahdat. 'Iran's Ayatollah Khamenei Loves Caviar and Vulgar Jokes, Defector Claims', *The Telegraph*, 31 December 2009. Available at www.telegraph.co.uk/news/worldnews/middleeast/iran/6913069/Irans-Ayatollah-Khamenei-loves-caviar-and-vulgar-jokes-defector-claims.html, accessed 1 January 2010.

Mirrazavi, Firouzeh. 'Constitution House of Tabriz', *Iran Review*, 2 November 2010. Available at www.iranreview.org/content/Documents/Constitution_House_of_Tabriz.htm, accessed 12 December 2011.

'Military Expenditure as a Share of GDP (2005–2010)', *Stockholm International Peace Research Institute*. Available at www.sipri.org/research/armaments/milex/resultoutput/milex_gdp, accessed 12 December 2012.

'Min. Sheetrit: Hezbollah Chief Nasrallah Is a Doomed Man', *Haaretz*, 14 July 2006. Available at www.haaretz.com/news/min-sheetrit-hezbollah-chief-nasrallah-is-a-doomed-man-1.193105, accessed 12 February 2007.

Nakashima, Ellen. 'Iran Blamed for Cyber Attacks on US Banks and Companies', *The Washington Post*, 21 September 2012. Available at http://articles.washingtonpost.

com/2012–09–21/world/35497878_1_web-sites-quds-force-cyberattacks, accessed 1 November 2012.

Niquette, Mark. 'Public Worker Protests Spread from Wisconsin to Ohio', *Bloomberg*, 18 February 2011. Available at www.bloomberg.com/news/2011–02–17/ public-employee-union-protests-spread-from-wisconsin-to-ohio.html, accessed 21 January 2011.

'Obama's Video Message to Iranians: 'Let's Start Again'', *The Guardian*, 21 March 2009. Available at www.guardian.co.uk/world/2009/mar/21/barack-obama-iran-video-message, accessed 12 March 2010.

'Persian Perspective: A Chat with Ali Akbar Salehi: Foreign Minister of Iran', *World Policy Blog*, 22 October 2012. Available at www.worldpolicy.org/blog/2012/10/22/ persian-perspective-chat-ali-akbar-salehi-foreign-minister-iran, accessed 11 January 2012.

Perlroth, Nicole. 'Cyber Attacks from Iran and Gaza on Israel More Threatening than Anonymous Efforts', *The New York Times*, 20 November 2012. Available at http:// bits.blogs.nytimes.com/2012/11/20/cyber-attacks-from-iran-and-gaza-on-israel-more-threatening-than-anonymouss-efforts, accessed 1 December 2012.

Peterson, Scott. 'Iran's Cyber Prowess: Could It Really Have Cracked Drone', *The Christian Science Monitor*, 24 April 2012. Available at www.csmonitor.com/World/ Middle-East/2012/0424/Iran-s-cyber-prowess-Could-it-really-have-cracked-drone-codes, accessed 12 June 2012.

'RBS Chief Stephen Hester's £7,7m Package Agreed', *BBC*, 19 April 2011. Available www.bbc.co.uk/news/uk-scotland-edinburgh-east-fife-13132635, accessed 21 April 2011.

Sahimi, Muhammad. 'Ali Motahari's Extraordinary Interview', *Tehran Bureau*, 17 August 2011. Available at www.pbs.org/wgbh/pages/ frontline/tehranbureau/2011/08/ali-motaharis-extraordinary-interview. html#ixzz1VNGani2X, accessed 18 November 2011.

Somashekhar, Sandhya. 'Clinton Calls for Democracy in Egypt, but not Mubarak's Ouster', *The Washington Post*, 30 January 2011. Available at www.washingtonpost. com/wp-dyn/content/article/2011/01/30/AR2011013002239.html, accessed 3 February 2011.

'Survival of the Fittest: When Ethnic Cleansing Is Justified', *Haaretz*, 8 January 2004. Available at www.haaretz.com/survival-of-the-fittest-cont-1.61341, accessed 12 June 2005.

Stockholm International Peace Research Institute. *World Armaments and Disarmament Year book for 1977*. Cambridge, MA: MIT Press, 1977.

The Royal Society. *Knowledge, Networks and Nations: Global Scientific Collaboration in the 21st Century*, London, March 2011. Available at http://royalsociety.org/

uploadedFiles/Royal_Society_Content/policy/publications/2011/4294976134.pdf, accessed 12 June 2011.

'Transcript of Interview with Iranian President Mohammad Khatami', *CNN*, 7 January 1998. Available at http://edition.cnn.com/WORLD/9801/07/iran/interview.html, accessed 12 January 2006.

'Tuition Fees: All Universities to Charge at Least £6,000', *Channel 4 News*, 20 April 2011. Available at www.channel4.com/news/tuition-fees-all-universities-to-charge-at-least-6-000, accessed 2 May 2011.

U.S. Department of State. 'Background Note: Tunisia', 13 October 2010.

U.S. Department of State. 'Continuing Terrorist Activities in Iran', August 1972. Available from www.state.gov/documents/organization/70763.pdf, accessed 20 May 2009.

'US Embassy Cables: Egypt Succeeding in Blocking Iran (30 April 2009)', *The Guardian*, 6 December 2010. Available at www.guardian.co.uk/world/us-embassy-cables-documents/204990, accessed 1 January 2011.

'US Embassy Cables: Egypt's Strategic Importance to the US', *The Guardian*, 28 January 2011. Available at www.guardian.co.uk/world/us-embassy-cables-documents/199866, accessed 8 December 2011.

US Embassy Cables: US Hits Out at Iranian negotiators in 1979', *The Guardian*, 28 November 2010. Available at www.guardian.co.uk/world/us-embassy-cables-documents/13, accessed 12 January 2012.

White House Memorandum, 17 January 1986. 'Covert Action Finding Regarding Iran (with attached Presidential finding)'. Available from www.gwu.edu/~nsarchiv/NSAEBB/NSAEBB210/15-Reagan%20Finding%201–17–86%20(IC%2002181).pdf, accessed 20 July 2009.

White House Memorandum, 5 October 1972. 'Progress Report on the Kurdish Support Operations'. Available from www.state.gov/documents/organization/72019.pdf, accessed 20 July 2009.

Wolf, Naomi. 'The Shocking Truth about the Crackdown on Occupy', *The Guardian*, 25 November 2011. Available at www.guardian.co.uk/commentisfree/cifamerica/2011/nov/25/shocking-truth-about-crackdown-occupy, accessed 10 December 2011.

'World Development Indicators' (Syria and Libya 2009). *The World Bank*. Available from http://data.worldbank.org/data-catalog/world-development-indicators?cid=GPD_WDI, accessed 11 January 2012.

Zakaria, Fareed. 'The Fantasy of an Iranian Revolution', *The Washington Post*, 21 June 2010. Available at www.washingtonpost.com/wp-dyn/content/article/2010/06/20/AR2010062002366.html, accessed 11 January 2011.

Index